Rags to Rabbi

Carmen Welker

Rags to Rabbi

Printed in the United States of America

ISBN 978-1-934916-03-2

All rights reserved, including the right to reproduce this book or any part thereof in any form, except for inclusion of brief quotations in a review, without the written permission of the author and Netzari Press.

August 2009 errata/update edition

Copyright 2008, 2009
Carmen Welker
Carmen@BeTorahObservant.com

www.netzaripress.com

Dedication

This book is dedicated to my very supportive husband, Bill, without whom this project would not have been possible; and to my beloved foster parents Max and Elfriede Neumann who were chosen by God to take care of me for the first eight and a half years of my life. It is also dedicated to Goldie Sellner, the woman I called "Mom" throughout most of my adulthood, who played a more important role in my life than she will ever know!

About the cover

I chose for the cover of this book an old photograph of myself at age four, mainly to show the sheer poverty of the foster home in which I grew up in post-War Germany. The old house, which had no running water or electricity, was basically a three-room shack that used to serve as an old Army barracks at the edge of town during WWII. Shown with me in this picture from 1955 is my dog, Tyras.

Although my foster parents, Max and Elfriede Neumann, were destitute, they gave me the one thing a child needs most besides the basics of food, shelter and water, and that is love. Their love is what made me "normal" and sustained me through the tough times that followed when my natural mother took me back into her own dysfunctional world

Since animals have always played a big part in my life, I've chosen a photograph for the back cover that includes our dog "Dallas."

Table of Contents

Dedication iii
About the cover iv
Prologue vii
Chapter 1 1
Chapter 2 9
Chapter 3 23
Chapter 4 35
Chapter 5 47
Chapter 6 57
Chapter 7 71
Chapter 8 79
Chapter 9 91
Chapter 10 97
Chapter 11 105
Chapter 12 117
Chapter 13 133
Chapter 14 149
Chapter 15 181
Chapter 16 189
Chapter 17 197
Chapter 18 207
Chapter 19 221

Chapter 20 237
Chapter 21 247
Chapter 22 269
Chapter 23 277
Chapter 24 289
Chapter 25 303
Chapter 26 315
Chapter 27 321
Chapter 28 325
Chapter 29 345
Chapter 30 351
Chapter 31 357
Chapter 32 371
Epilogue 379

Prologue

It is a fact of life that everyone experiences hard times. Our lives are full of and high and low points; and, more often than not, the low points seem to outweigh the high – as was the case in my life, which consisted of one unfortunate event after the next, with no end in sight.

My story is one of turmoil and intrigue, which contains some amazing twists and turns that ultimately culminated in a wonderfully positive outcome that rivals any fairy tale. While there were a few good times to offset the bad, this book concentrates on those events that needed to be told to paint the complete picture – and it is for this reason I included some excruciatingly graphic details.

I'm middle-aged now, but by the time I graduated from high school in 1969, I had already seen more sorrow than most people experience in a lifetime. My saga began in post-war Germany when I was given away at birth to live with a poor but loving foster family who took good care of me for almost nine years. Suddenly and without warning, my life was ripped out from under me when my natural mother and her new American husband appeared on the scene to take me away with them to live in America.

Nobody would have guessed that the well-respected Army First Sergeant who adopted me was a raving pedophile who ended up sexually abusing me from the age of nine through almost fifteen, when my mother, thankfully, divorced him. In the meantime, because my mother never wanted me in the first place, we never bonded, and so I felt totally alone in the world, "burying" my secret sorrows until the day I became old enough to run away from home.

Over the course of the years I lived in countless places and attended a total of fourteen different schools while, among other things, dealing with the endless chaos of my mother's life as she flitted from relationship to relationship, which included eight marriages.

I thought my problems would be over once I joined the Army and got away from home, but little did I know that it isn't easy to escape the demons of our childhood, which tend to follow us around to keep us imprisoned beneath the "baggage" we collected along the way.

I was forty-four before I discovered there was deliverance from the past – and it came from a place I *never* expected….God!

This book is about the healing that only God can bring. If you're an atheist, especially one who has been sexually abused, I would urge you to put aside your feelings long enough to finish this book. I promise you, you won't look at God the same way once you're done!

Chapter 1

Wietze, Germany; late summer, 1959:

I watched in bored detachment as the morning sun made its way across the living room floor of our tiny, three-room hovel. Presently, it was forming elongated, slanted windowpane patterns across my legs and, for lack of anything else to do at the moment, I caught myself staring at the dust motes slowly tumbling toward the ancient, stained sofa on which I reclined. It was a beautiful morning, and I wanted more than anything to go outside and play. But, unfortunately, since I had convinced Mama I was too sick to go to school, I knew that would not be possible.

I hated school, and played "hooky" as often as I could because my teacher was always harassing me about my poor arithmetic skills. Moreover, my fellow third-graders were relentless in their taunts about me, personally. They were forever reminding me that my family was poor and dirty and that I smelled bad. Mama said that wasn't true, though. She told me that, just because we didn't have much and lived on *Sozialhilfe* (welfare), it didn't mean we weren't a clean and decent family. We couldn't help the fact that we didn't have running water or electricity, and so bathing on a regular basis was out of the question. But, that didn't mean we were dirty.

"Mama," I whined, mostly out of boredom. "I'm thirsty. Bring me some water."

"Just a minute," she called from the kitchen. "I'm buttering your bread right now."

My thoughts drifted to my best friends, Reni, Annette and Wera, and I found myself wishing it was a Sunday and we were all playing outside in the garden having "pretend" tea or coffee. Or better yet, at Wera's house, watching television. Wera's family were the only ones I knew of who had a television, and they occasionally invited me whenever a special children's show came on. It was always a lot more fun than having Mama read to me – although I did enjoy the romance novels she read to Papa and me every evening after supper, by the anemic light of the old kerosene lamp hanging on the kitchen wall.

Emitting a melodramatic sigh designed to show Mama how bored I was, I tossed my blanket aside and loudly roused myself to sit on my haunches. Truly, I would have to figure out a way to get Mama to let me go outside and play. If Papa were here this morning, I could go mushroom hunting with him in the nearby woods, or climb on the *Salzberg* behind our house, or something. The salt hill, which was the spoils of the excavated salt mines dumped at the edge of town where we lived, had been there all my life, and I had spent many wonderful hours climbing and exploring its jagged crooks and crannies.

Outside, our dog Tyras began to bark, which meant that someone was coming up the narrow dirt lane. I figured it was probably just another passer-by, or maybe Frau Link coming to plead with Papa for the newspaper delivery money again. The last time she came by, she actually broke into tears because Papa had once again lied about not having the money. He had told her most of our welfare money went to feed me, but I'm sure Frau Link knew better than that, because it was no secret that Max Neumann was a drunkard who spent most of his time in the bar at Rauschenbach's. Over the last few months, however, Papa had been doing odd jobs here and there, and so he didn't really have the time to hang out in the local bars anymore.

A flicker in my peripheral vision caused me to turn my head in time to see several shadowy figures passing by the window. I sat up and strained my neck to see who it was. "Mama, someone's coming!" I cried excitedly. We didn't have many friends or visitors, and so it was always a major treat when someone showed up uninvited, or otherwise.

Seconds later, three dark silhouettes filed through the door and stood in the scant light of the kitchen. The closest one, I realized with a start, was *Polizist* Neumann, the town's only police officer, who just happened to have the same last name as us. Next to him, a blonde woman was shadowed by an austere, dark-haired man in a tan military uniform. The uniform didn't look like any of those worn by the German or British soldiers stationed in nearby Celle, and I wondered who this stranger might be.

Opting to remain on the sofa because I had to continue pretending to be sick on a school day, I stared anxiously at the policeman because he had NEVER come to our house before. Was he here because I had missed too many school days? I cringed at the thought.

Something in Mama's demeanor didn't seem right as she greeted the trio. I watched her nervously wipe her hands on her apron while Herr Neumann, with his hat in hand, addressed her in hushed tones.

The hair at the nape of my neck rose when Mama's hand flew to her chest and she emitted an audible gasp. *"Nein!"* I heard her shout. *"Das kommt nicht in Frage!"* ("That's not going to happen!")

"Elfriede," the policeman said softly. "Please don't make a scene. You knew this was coming."

"But it's too soon! You said you would wait and see if Max could keep a job. He's at work right now...."

Fear knotted in the pit of my stomach as I strained to see and hear. For no real apparent reason, the recurring dream I'd had again last night came to mind – the one where I felt myself swallowing needles that always ended up stuck sideways in my throat. Sometimes, the object in my throat was a large egg that threatened to choke me. But last night, it had been the needles again and, as always, I had awakened in a cold sweat, sitting there for several minutes, trembling, until I realized it was just that silly dream once more....Somehow, this situation with the town policeman felt like needles in my throat, stabbing me, scaring me to the point of hardly being able to breathe. Something was terribly wrong.

Herr Neumann, clearly uncomfortable over whatever was going on, tossed short, nervous glances my way, which suggested – just as I thought – that I was the topic of the conversation. He gently touched Mama's arm and whispered something I couldn't quite make out. In response, Mama shook her head and began to cry.

Suddenly, a paralyzing thought came to me from the archives of my mind: Approximately a year or so ago, we had a visit from a tall, dark stranger whom Mama had said was my real father. His name was Franz Klekawka, and I thought he was the most handsome man I had ever seen. I didn't know who he was until he was heading back down the dirt lane, and Mama whispered, "Carmen, that was your father!" And right after that, she told me that I also had a "real" mother whose name was Lonny, and that I had two brothers named Ingolf and Josef who were in children's homes somewhere. Lonny, Mama said, had given all of us away when we were babies, and I had ended up with Mama and Papa because they wanted a little girl. She said that Franz Klekawka had brought me to them in a shoebox on the back of his bicycle when I was just six weeks old, and then he had divorced Lonny and left her all alone. And then she went on to warn me that Lonny might some day come to take me away….

Although I had been quite upset over this astonishing revelation, I remember attempting to downplay it, and assuring Mama that if that Lonny person ever came around, I would simply hide until she left.

Elfriede was my mother, and my eight-year-old mind was unable to fathom anything beyond that.

Sheer terror slammed up my spine as I realized that the strangers standing at the door *were my real mother and her new husband*...and now it was too late to hide. I was literally trapped in the living room like some caged animal, with no way out.

I recoiled when the man in the tan uniform barked something in a foreign language. Whatever he had said clearly demanded action. *Polizist* Neumann briefly glanced back at them as the blonde woman quietly translated, and then without further ado, he crossed into the small living room where I sat huddled in my warm blanket on the sofa.

"*Herr* Neumann, please," Mama begged as she followed at his heels. Her tear-choked voice sounded terrified, raw and gravelly. "Please, please don't take Carmen from me."

"Elfriede," he said gently, turning on his heel to address her. "We have no choice. Lonny is her mother. She warned you about this months ago."

Time seemed to stand still. I didn't know what to say or do as I glanced helplessly at my foster mother who stood there looking small and defeated, her body wracked with great heaving sobs. Behind her, like a dark looming shadow, the man in the tan uniform appeared, his demeanor exuding a mixture of superiority and impatience. The blonde woman remained stoically in the background, near the living room door, and I found myself hating her very presence because she was directly responsible for this unexpected upheaval in our lives.

Hot tears ran down my cheeks as my eyes darted fearfully around the room. Not knowing what else to do, I reached out for Mama whose cries now bordered on the edge of hysteria. "Mama, I don't want to go with them," I whined weakly. "I'm not going...."

Suddenly and without warning, the American reached around Mama and snatched me up into his arms, and before I had a chance to realize what was happening, I found myself being carried into the kitchen and out the front door. "MAMA!" I shrieked in a voice that transmitted raw terror. "Mama! Mama!" The arms that held me were steel girders, and no amount of struggling could loosen their iron grip on my skinny little torso.

Through my tears, I managed to peer over the man's shoulder to catch a final blurry glimpse of the woman who had been my mother for almost nine years. Like me, she was powerless in this situation; she merely stood there, howling by the side of our old brick house, helplessly watching her little girl being kidnapped.

Moments later, I found myself in the back seat of a huge American car. A small, blond boy cowered against the window on the other side, his large brown eyes glued to mine as we beheld each other with mutual dread and apprehension. Outside, Lonny and the American spoke briefly with Officer Neumann, and then, without further ado, they materialized inside the car. After an awkward pause, my "real mother" broke the silence, and I heard her voice clearly for the first time when she turned to say, "All right, Carmen, that's enough now. Stop your crying!"

Her words were shockingly intense as they blasted through the surrealistic fog in my mind. An innate sense of preservation along with a healthy fear of the unknown instantly stayed my tears and I sat there, lost and helpless, staring at this stranger who had abducted me. My eyes were drawn to her ruby red lips as she spoke. Until then, I had never seen a woman who wore make-up of any kind, and I found myself gawking at her with a morbid fascination. I didn't like her, and there was no doubt the feeling was mutual.

"I'm your mother," she said matter-of-factly. "This man here is my husband. You can call him Daddy. And that little boy next to you is Teddy; he's your brother. We're your family now and we'll all be moving to America soon."

"Daddy" was watching me intently, his squinted green eyes crinkling as he pulled his worm-like lips into a tight smile. Something in his prematurely wrinkled face told me he was not a nice man. He was, easily, the ugliest person I had ever seen!

Seconds later, as the car roared into life and we began to make our way along the dirt path that led to Wietze's main street, the thought occurred to me that I never got to say "goodbye" to my best friends Reni, Annette and Wera….

Chapter 2

It didn't take long for me to figure out that, while it may ultimately have been a good thing to have been removed from the poverty-stricken conditions of the Neumann household, my new, lower-middle income family had problems of their own.

Right from the start, my mother Lonny acted as if nothing at all had transpired; as if the ordeal of my being forcefully and without warning removed from the only family I'd ever known was just another normal event. She never discussed that fateful day with me, and she never inquired about my feelings or told me why she had given me away, in the first place. It was as if I had simply turned a page in my book of life and now there was a new chapter. It didn't matter that this new chapter included a brand new father and mother with a different set of rules for me, or that I suddenly went from being an only child to having to share everything with a younger brother who was clearly my mother's "favorite." There was no attempt to acclimate me to the Forrester household at all; I was simply expected to accept these changes without question or complaint. *My* feelings were irrelevant.

Perhaps I would have felt differently about Lonny if she had made an effort to be a little warmer, more friendly and understanding; or at the very least, come across as if she actually cared about me. As it was, she did none of these things. Her words and body language let me know in no uncertain terms that she was the grown-up and I was a mere child who was to be seen and not heard – which happened to be a favorite mantra in the household.

I felt as if the onus was on me, a little girl whose life, due to no fault of her own, had just been turned upside-down, to make this new arrangement work. It was a complete switch from the way things worked at the Neumanns where I had been the center of attention.

The small apartment in southern Germany that I was forced to call "home" for a year before moving to the United States felt like a prison, and I often fantasized about running away and finding my way back to the Neumanns. Fortunately, I was smart enough to realize that a little run-away girl wouldn't get very far....

The sad part was, not only was there no bonding between Lonny and me, but her husband, Austin William ("Bill") Forrester, turned out to be a total "control freak" who was almost impossible to live with. A U.S. Army First Sergeant, Bill was used to giving orders and expecting them to be carried out immediately and without question. When "Daddy" barked the command, "Go get me my house shoes," it didn't matter whatever else you were doing; you stopped at once and got his house shoes, because he didn't like to repeat himself. If you didn't instantly obey, you risked being thumped on the forehead with his knuckles, or whacked on the rear end with his doubled-up military belt, and then, verbally berated.

Bill taught me English and, later on, the multiplication tables, using some "flash cards" he had designed himself. Whenever he felt I wasn't learning quickly enough, he let me have it with that dreaded belt. For as long as I live, I will never forget that seven times nine is sixty-three because, whenever I got that one wrong, he would humiliate me with a rhyme that I came to loathe after awhile: "Seven times nine is sixty-three, which any fool can easily see. *Say it*, fool!"

Bill taught me many things, and I soon became conditioned to yearn for his approval – which, unfortunately, didn't come easy, as he wasn't one to dish out compliments. He taught me how to speak, read and write English; he taught me the multiplication tables; he taught me proper table manners and how to hold my fork right and how to say, "Yes sir and no ma'am" to grown-ups.

And he taught me about sex – because it just so happened that First Sergeant Bill Forrester was a raving pedophile....

No one knew; not my mother, not his superiors, not his co-workers, not his friends or relatives – no one. Somehow, it was clear to me that if I had even *thought* about telling someone back then, in the early Sixties, nobody would have believed me; I knew that any "tattling" would have instantly backfired, and so, I was trapped with no way out.

The first time this "well-respected Army sergeant" ever did any inappropriate touching was when my younger brother and I had colds, and he seized the opportunity to rub Vick's Vapo Rub onto our chests while my mother was in the living room, smoking cigarettes and watching TV. It took me about three seconds to realize "Daddy's" touches weren't normal; that he was doing some things he could surely get in trouble for. But I was held hostage by a paralyzing fear of this man who didn't hesitate to beat me with his belt, and so the only thing I dared to do was to try to push his hand away – an act that was instantly stopped in its tracks by a stern glance from those hideous squinted green snake eyes.

By the time my "Vick's Vapo rub" ended a few minutes later, I was exhausted and sweaty and filled with a mixture of emotions. What's more, I was extremely ashamed of myself for not having had the guts to go to my mother and tell on him. Instead, I lay there cowering after he left, praying to God that He would never let me catch another cold....

* * * *

Actual sexual contact between "Daddy" and me didn't occur until we moved to Fort Carson, Colorado, in 1960, just before I turned ten. My mother, who felt she had to help subsidize Bill's meager Army income, was hired for the evening shift as a waitress at the Broadmoor Hotel – and that's when my nightmare began, because Bill immediately took advantage of the fact that no one was around at night to take notice of his strange behavior.

The "first time" took place one evening while my kid brother Teddy and I lay on the floor watching "Bonanza" on our old black-and-white TV set in the living room. Five-year-old Teddy normally never made it past eight p.m. and he often started snoring a few minutes after a movie began and ultimately had to be carried upstairs to bed every night.

Anyway, on this particular evening, things ended up radically different because Daddy, quite out of character, invited us to join him on the sleeper sofa that he had opened into a bed. With the Vicks VapoRub incident still looming largely in my frontal lobe, I immediately sensed danger. The thought of being "that close" to Bill again sent a pang of dread down my spine. Yet, whenever Daddy spoke, I instantly obeyed, and so, feeling like I had no other choice, I hesitantly roused myself from the floor to perch at the foot of the bed.

Teddy didn't have to be invited twice; he got up and virtually bounced onto the sofa and was nestled in front of Bill within seconds. "Come on already, Carmen," he cried excitedly. "We're missing Bonanza!"

"Yeah, come on over here, sis," Bill crooned gently. His voice sounded unnatural, like an ancient castle door that had been oiled with honey. "Here, lay down between Teddy and me and watch TV."

Bill's unique odor engulfed me as he pressed close; it was pungent – a mixture of sweat and rodent and stale cigarette smoke – and I fought to keep from gagging.

The urge to extricate myself and make a mad dash for the front door became overwhelming, but I didn't dare move for fear of making Daddy angry. Where would I have gone and what would I have done once I got outside? I couldn't tell the neighbors. And so I simply lay there like some trapped animal, waiting.

A few minutes later, when Teddy's soft snores filled the room, Bill wasted no time returning him to the floor in front of the television. In the next instant, before I had a chance to realize what was going on, he was on top of me, groping inside my pajamas and rubbing himself against me, sweating and snorting like a pig in a barnyard…

The whole thing was over within seconds, and although I had no clue as to what had actually just happened, I knew that my adoptive father had just committed an unspeakable sin. Too terrified to speak, I simply lay there, waiting for his next move, praying all the while that my mother wouldn't come home unexpectedly, because she would surely be angry with me.

To my relief, he suddenly roused himself and stood beside the sofa, peering down at me through the eerie greenish-gray light emanating from the TV. "Sis," he said, "you know you can't tell anyone, right? Your mother will kill us both."

Choking back some threatening tears, I nodded and hoped he would let me up so I could go upstairs, crawl into my own bed and try to forget that this night ever happened.

"If you ever tell, you'll get us both in trouble," he continued. "I know you don't want that. I love you even more than I love your mother, and that's why I wanted to share this special thing with you. Your mother doesn't care about you, but I do. You know that, right?"

"…Uh-huh…."

"Okay, then, go on upstairs and wash up, and get to bed. Tomorrow's another school day, and it's getting late." Having said that, he turned to gather my sleeping little brother into his arms and headed up the stairs.

I felt completely numb as I rose from the sofa bed, unsure as to what I was supposed to feel. While terror and enormous disgust had dominated my initial reaction, I had also experienced a certain sadistic glee over the fact that I now had something "over" my mother whom I secretly hated – even though down deep, I felt guilty about that particular feeling.

That night I fell asleep pretending I was back in the safety of Mama's arms in the old shack by the *Salzberg*, listening to the sound of her voice as she rocked me to sleep....

* * * *

Without recounting the sordid details, "Daddy" began to abuse me almost nightly, always taking great care to keep from having actual intercourse. As leverage, and to justify his actions, he did everything in his power to turn me against my mother (which really didn't take much convincing), doing his best to persuade me that he just wanted me to "feel good" because he was my loving father and only real friend. His most fervent desire, he told me, was to make up for the love that my mother was constantly depriving me of.

"Lonny gave you and your brothers Ingolf and Josef away because she didn't want you," he reminded me repeatedly. "I'm the one who made her get you back. If it wasn't for me, you'd still be living in that three-room shack with those filthy Neumanns. Or, worse still, if the cops had removed you from the Neumanns since they were unfit parents, you could have ended up back with Lonny and that drunken Jew mother of hers, and then you might have become a whore, just like them."

To prove his love and trust, he began to "confide" all kinds of things about my mother – terrible secrets I wasn't supposed to know, such as the fact that she had a history of prostitution, several abortions, and a total of four children and two previous marriages under her belt before she ever met and married Bill. He said he married Lonny only because she was beautiful and exciting, and he thought he could "make an honest woman out of her."

As much as I hated my mother, these revelations bothered me because, in all honesty, I didn't like being pitted against her, or having to deal with the associated guilt feelings that plagued me night and day. It was the proverbial two-edged sword and both edges were cutting my soul to pieces. Our nonexistent mother-daughter relationship had already suffered enough; but this awful, crushing secret between "Daddy" and me was a death knell for any hopes of possible future bonding because Bill was standing in the way. Despite the fact that I absolutely loathed Lonny, down deep I felt sorry for her and did not want to see her hurt. She was, after all, my mother and a small part of me wanted desperately to please and to be loved by her.

Regardless, the nightly "flings" I endured at once terrified and sickened me. I hated Bill. I hated the smell of him; I hated his breath whenever he came close. I hated the confusion the sexual contact was causing me, and I hated myself for having this awful secret whenever I looked at my mother. School was my only refuge, and even that felt different somehow because I now looked at the boys differently, and found myself wondering if any of my little girlfriends were forced to "do things" with their daddies, too….

Over the next few months, in hopes that Bill would eventually tire of me and my "childish" games and start leaving me alone, I began to hide in the closets at night whenever I heard him coming up the stairs to my bedroom. But, to my surprise – apparently under the erroneous impression that I wanted to play – he went along with it, patiently going from room to room, checking all the closets until he found me.

Little did he know that, while I was sitting in those dark closets waiting for the inevitable, I was silently praying and begging God to *please* not let Daddy find me. But, he always did. And so, naturally, I wondered if my foster grandmother back in Wietze when I was approximately five, might have lied when she held me on her lap once to explain God. I remember feeling as if someone had poured warm water into my soul while she talked, because I was actually able to *sense* His Presence.

But now I was beginning to have my doubts. If He indeed *was* real, then why was He allowing all these terrible things to happen to me? Why had He allowed me to be taken from my happy foster home? Why was He not stopping Daddy from doing these awful things to me?

During those awful days at Fort Carson, my needle and/or egg in throat dreams intensified. They weren't dreams, *per se* but, rather, more like visions received in the seconds after dropping off to sleep. They always began with the feeling that I had swallowed needles (or sometimes, a huge egg) that lodged sideways in my throat, cutting off my windpipe – which startled me out of my sleep and caused me to sit up in bed, gasping for air. Drenched in sweat, I would sit there trembling, trying not to swallow for fear that I would die if the needles (or egg) slid too far down – until I finally realized I was in bed and couldn't possibly have swallowed anything. These episodes had plagued me ever since I could remember, and yet the sheer terror they induced was completely fresh with every occurrence.

* * * *

While Daddy was showing me how to become a "good girl" who knew how to keep from getting pregnant, my mother had aspirations of turning me into her personal maid. At the ripe old age of ten, I discovered it was "high time" I learned how to cook and clean and become a surrogate mother for Teddy. Every morning before school, I had to mop the floors and dust all the furniture, often enduring Lonny's thorough inspections afterwards, which normally revealed I was an inadequate housekeeper. I don't remember any compliments on my work, but I will never forget the disgusted looks on her face whenever she ran her fingers along the banister or the floorboards, making a visible show of letting me know I hadn't done the job to her satisfaction.

Making matters worse was that my fear of *her* ultimately ended up being greater than my fear of "Daddy" because Mother didn't hesitate to scream or slap me upside the head whenever I upset her. Bill's yelling and hitting, on the other hand, pretty much ended once he started "touching" me, and so my fear of him subsided over time....Down deep I had the satisfaction of knowing he was probably afraid of upsetting me lest I decided to tell "our secret"....

The bottom line was, I was a constant disappointment to Lonny in one way or another. Even my appearance irked her; it was clear she wished I were prettier. According to my mother, I was skinny and shapeless; I had buckteeth, no hips, a big nose and kinky-curly, unruly hair that refused to be tamed. Once, while I was standing on a chair in front of the bathroom mirror attempting to try a new hairstyle, she cackled hysterically and made a comment I'll never forget with that German accent I came to detest: "Carmen," she said, "I don't know why you're bothering. With that big nose of yours, you're never gonna be Miss America, anyway!"

Joining my mother in a hollow laugh over her "joke," I tried to pretend her comments hadn't bothered me; but the truth was, I was devastated to realize how much she hated my appearance. And it didn't help that the boys on the school bus were forever taunting me about my nose and unruly hair, too. Between them and my mother, I concluded that I was too ugly for words, and that Daddy had been correct in his declaration about being the *only* one who truly loved me.

The bottom line was, my mother was an enemy to be avoided, and I even went so far as to try to hide the fact that I had shattered my right elbow one afternoon in a roller skating accident. I knew she would be angry if she found out, because it meant *she* would have to do the dishes and the house cleaning. Of course, once I started going into shock, it was impossible to keep my broken arm a secret, and so I ultimately ended up in the Army hospital's emergency room.

At first Lonny seemed to make a genuine effort to try to contain her feelings, but immediately after the eight-hour operation when the doctors informed her that my cast would have to stay on for eight weeks, she didn't hesitate to unleash her wrath about the inconvenience my clumsiness was going to cause her....

Rags to Rabbi

Chapter 3

I changed schools a grand total of four times while in the fifth grade. That was the year Bill retired from the Army and took us to Springfield, Missouri where we moved from house to house in search of that elusive place in which my mother could feel comfortable.

The sexual abuse, of course, followed me everywhere we went. It had become something that was simply a part of my life, something I had to accept, as basic as breathing or eating, or going to school.

The pressure of being my adoptive father's "lover" and my mother's chief cook and bottle washer, house keeper and babysitter was not without consequence, as it culminated in endless night terrors and regular sleep-walking episodes. The first incident occurred in the house on Kearney Street, where I walked into the living room one night and excitedly informed my mother in perfect German that "everything is full of fleas." I woke up feeling dazed and quite silly when she loudly asked "what the hell" I thought I was doing and relating the things I had just said. Unbeknownst to either of us at the time, my strange babblings turned out to be prophetic because, when we moved a few months later to a new house just outside the Springfield city limits, we soon realized that the place was crawling with fleas, and were forced to set off several "bombs" to get rid of them.

By the time I was twelve, we had settled long enough in one place to allow me to finish an entire school year at Ritter School on Radio Lane. Unfortunately, for some reason, Bill's seventy-two year old father, Lloyd, came to live with us for a few months, and I found myself with another problem on my hands, because it seemed the old man – like his son – also had a penchant for little girls. Grandpa hounded me constantly to have sex with him, but because I knew my food source and the roof over my head didn't depend on him, I ignored his advances and bided my time because I knew he was only with us temporarily. I wasn't about to tell on him because Daddy would have probably killed him, while my mother would have demanded to know what I had done to turn the old man on....

That same year held significance for me for several reasons, all of them negative. I remember at some point my mother (although I don't remember why, but it was apparently one of her attempts to be "motherly"), promised Teddy and me that she would give us a dollar for every "A" on our next report card. When I brought home thirteen "A's" that next semester she went ballistic, asking me "what the hell" I was thinking, because she wasn't rich and couldn't afford to dole out "that kind of money." I honestly don't remember exactly what she gave me, if anything, but it wasn't thirteen dollars. And I remember that, that little incident deeply hurt my feelings and drove home the point that absolutely nobody in this world could be trusted. In my world, all the men were sexual deviates and my mother, the person responsible for ruining my entire life, was an emotionally absent person whose every pore oozed superiority and a severe dislike of my presence, which she clearly saw as an imposition.

"Well, don't worry about it," Daddy told me later. "You don't need any allowance, anyway. I provide everything you need. Money is the root of all evil and I want you to learn that you have to work hard in order to earn it. You can't just expect it to be handed to you."

I attended Willard Junior High in the seventh and eighth grades after my parents bought a ten-acre farm. It was the first place my parents had ever purchased, and it was to serve as a brand new start where Teddy and I could finally stay in one school system. Unfortunately, by that time, my parents' marriage was pretty much on the rocks, and the house resonated with the constant fighting and arguments – partly because of my mother's penchant for staying out all night after work to party.

Once when she came home in the wee hours of the morning, Daddy-dearest roused us kids from bed and made us get up to take a look at our "drunken Jewish *Kraut* mother" who was barely able to stand up. Using his bellowing "Army voice," he ordered us to sit at the dining room table while he hurled a barrage of curses and verbal threats at her. That particular scene ended when he grabbed Lonny by the back of the head and slammed her forehead down against the table – and act that sent both Teddy and me scurrying in fear and horror to our respective bedrooms. Our mother survived the attack, but ended up, for several weeks, covering with make-up the hideous black and blue lump on her head. It didn't take a rocket engineer to figure out that a divorce was on the horizon.

Most fights in those days were actually over my little brother, because Bill simply could not leave the poor kid alone. He was forever hacking around on his son about everything and anything. To Bill, Teddy was a lazy, stupid, sissy Mama's boy who was going to amount to nothing in this world. Nightly suppertime became a living nightmare as Bill spent the entire time harassing Teddy for not holding his fork right, or for chewing his food too slowly, or because "the little ingrate" had committed the unforgivable crime of disliking certain foods.

I'll never forget the time Bill smashed my brother's face into his plate. It happened when Teddy was forced to eat something he didn't like (and I'll admit, he didn't like many things), but this time, Teddy actually threw up after being forced to swallow a mouthful of fried potatoes. This act sent Bill, who didn't have a sympathetic bone in his body, into an explosive rage. Before anyone had a chance to react, he reached across the table and thumped his son's forehead with his knuckles and in the next instant, he grabbed the kid's head and smashed his face into the vomit-filled plate. When Teddy began to cry, I thought Bill would have a coronary because, in our house, boys weren't allowed to cry. But before Bill had a chance to do or say anything else, my mother jerked Teddy away from the table and whisked him off to the bathroom.

Bill thankfully just sat there, red-faced and angry, muttering about "Lonny's son" being a blankety-blank little sissy and a pansy who would never become a real man.

I never hated that man more than I did in that moment. I even had visions of shooting him that night with his own .22 rifle and burying his body in the enormous rock pile on the back of our property. (There is an endless supply of rocks in Missouri; they seem to be able to multiply, and so, no matter how many you clean off your property, you cannot ever get rid of them. Bill, who believed kids should learn the value of work, had assigned us to pick up rocks for at least an hour every afternoon, after school, and so over a year's time, the pile had become huge. I decided that, if I buried him way down deep, no one would ever find him – but thank God, my fear of prison was greater than my hatred of Bill!)

It was always something to behold Bill's squinted green eyes as he glared at Teddy and watched every move the child made, while Lonny sat there and weakly attempted to defend her son. Sometimes it would escalate into a verbal altercation that usually ended up with our mother storming out the door in a huff as she headed to her evening waitressing job; other times the forced silence around the table spoke volumes about how Teddy was the center of *all* our problems. Supper time was an awful time in the Forrester household, and to this day, I have a hard time sitting around a table to eat whenever children are present because those old "tapes" just keep on playing and bringing back my childhood....

While Teddy was forced to endure mental and physical abuse at the hands of his father during the daytime, my turn always came with the nightfall. I didn't know which one of us had the "better" deal, but I felt Teddy did because he at least had our mother to stand up for him while I had nobody.

Just before I turned fourteen, it became clear that divorce was just around the corner – partly because I knew my mother was seeing another man. She had, a couple of times, taken Teddy and me along on her dates with a guy named Steve, and so I figured it was time for me to spread my wings and gear up to "divorce" Bill, too. My plan was to get brave and somehow throw a monkey wrench into his regular visits to my bedroom. The idea how to approach this actually dropped into my lap one day when, during lunch at school, my girlfriend and I happened onto the subjects of "incest" and "statutory rape" where I was enlightened to the fact that the perpetrator could go to prison! I had never heard this before and so it was, of course, unbelievably good news for me. So, without any hesitation at all, I decided to use it against Bill as soon as possible – which, as it happened, turned out to be that very night when he crept into my room for another of our "liaisons." Unfortunately, in my happy delirium about a future without anymore sexual abuse, I never took into consideration that my plan could backfire.

"Murphy's Law" kicked in when I saw Bill's silhouette hovering in the doorway because my resolve, for some reason, went out the window, and I completely forgot what I had planned to tell him. Instead of waiting for the right moment to present my "did you know what you're doing is against the law?" spiel, I stupidly blurted: "Daddy, if you rape me tonight, I'm gonna call the cops on you!"

A shudder slammed through my body the instant those words left my lips, but it was too late to retract them. It was crystal clear from the rigid stance and the awful, pregnant silence that Austin William Forrester, my resident terrorist, rapist and jailer, had heard and received my threat, and all hell was about to break loose. My breath caught in the realization that tonight could very well be my last night on Earth....

All I managed to hear over the rushing in my ears and the mad hammering of my heart was, "What did you say, sis?" It was more of a growl than the sound of a human voice, and I clutched my bed covers in fear. **"What did you just say!"**

"Nothing, Daddy," I croaked. In desperation, I attempted to will God to somehow reach down from heaven and erase my words from Bill's mind. But as usual, God was paying no attention to me.

Bill simply stood there, stiff and motionless for several long moments, and I knew he was deciding his next move – which would probably be to beat the tar out of me. In hopes to dispel some of his anger, I emitted a tiny, forced giggle and told him I was just kidding.

What happened next seemed surreal as Bill suddenly materialized beside my bed, snatched me up by the hair and sent me flying out into the hallway like some discarded dirty rag. The breath was literally knocked out of me as I bounced off my brother's bedroom door and landed on my rump on the hardwood floor. Before I had a chance to fully realize what had transpired, he was upon me, kicking me in the gut, pulling me up by my hair and slamming me against the hallway walls.

"You wanna screw with me?" he growled at one point, pressing his nose against mine. "Huh? You wanna take me on, little girl? Come on! Take me on; I *dare* you!"

"Daddy!" I shrieked as my fear escalated. "Daddy – oh God, oh God, no! Please don't hurt me!" A distant part of me wondered why my little brother Teddy wasn't coming to help me....

"Shut up!" Bill hissed. I recoiled as his spittle flew into my face. "*Shut up, you little b---!*"

"God, please help me!"

Grabbing the collar of my pajama top, he pinned me against the wall, and glared at me with murderous eyes. "What did I tell you about using the Lord's Name in vain in this house? *Huh?* You don't use the Lord's Name in vain in this house, do you understand?"

In the back of my mind, I remembered his occasional use of Bible scriptures whenever he thought it would suit his purpose. Among his favorites were, "Honor thy parents" and "Money is the root of all evil." And just days earlier, he had wowed our neighbors, the McGinnises, with his knowledge about how the Book of Revelation supposedly revealed God's actions in the "end times." I remember cringing when he made a point about "the yellow race" – the Chinese army of millions – coming out of the East in attempt to destroy the world before Jesus' return to Earth.

Filled with a paralyzing fear in the terrible clutches of my father, I repressed an overpowering, odd urge to laugh as it dawned on me that this supposed "Christian" was a raving hypocrite.

Suddenly he released his grip on my pajamas and shoved me down the hallway towards the kitchen. A hard, swift kick in the rear end sent a shrieking pain along my backbone just seconds before my head connected with the refrigerator. Realizing this was going to get worse before it got better, I quickly regained my balance and attempted to evade his next punch, but he was too quick. His hideous eyes were on fire as he approached me, and I knew there would be no stopping him now.

"TEDDY, HELP!" I shouted, hoping that the presence of my little nine-year-old brother would shock Bill back to reality. But Teddy never came out of his room, and I remember being very angry with him for that.

In the next instant, I found myself on the floor once more, being repeatedly kicked and punched in the stomach. I endured one kick, two, three, four…With every kick and punch, I backed further into the living room in hopes to reach the front door so I could run out into the night, but I simply could not get away. He must have kicked me at least ten times before I realized I couldn't feel the kicks anymore – and to add to my dilemma, my bladder suddenly gave way and I felt myself sitting in warm liquid. *This is it*, I thought. *I'm going to die now.*

But then, as quickly as it had started, the attack came to an end. For some reason – perhaps he noticed I had wet myself – Bill simply stepped back and just stood there above me, silhouetted against the kitchen light, his chest heaving in exhaustion. I lay there in a great, wounded heap, hardly breathing and too stunned to cry, waiting for his next move.

His voice sounded flat and tired when he said, "Clean up this g--damn floor; you made a mess." And without further ado, he turned and trudged off towards his bedroom.

Back in the sixties, no one ever talked about sexual abuse, and no one discussed "good touches" and "bad touches" and "tell someone if Uncle Joe makes you feel uncomfortable." Therefore, paralyzing fear and shame kept me silent until my internal injuries made me so sick that my mother was finally forced to notice a couple days later when, panicked, she took me to a hospital. The doctor who examined me apparently realized I wasn't going to give him straight answers about the horrible bruises on my abdomen as long as my mother was present, and so he eventually ordered her to leave so I could be properly questioned and admitted for observation.

After my IV had been placed and I had settled into my hospital bed, he came into the room, sat down at the foot of the bed and gently said, "Now, Carmen, what really happened?"

Only God Himself knows how badly I would have loved to spill the beans – and if I could go back in time, I would do things so much differently! But back then, my fear of Bill Forrester overrode my desire for revenge, and so I did everything in my power to continue the lie that I had been thrown from a horse, into a rock pile. If Bill were to go to prison, Lonny's life would be shattered, and there was no doubt she would make my life a living hell because somehow she would devise a way to pin the blame on me...Plus, if Daddy had done *this* to me after just being *threatened*, there's no telling how he would react if I were to actually tell on him.

And so I was ready to testify on a stack of Bibles that I had fallen from a horse. I just wanted to make it to high school graduation in four years so I could finally leave home and make my own way in this awful world....

I'm not sure whether or not the doctor believed me, but my destiny once again turned on a dime when, on the very next day, my mother stormed into the room to announce that she had left Bill and that we were moving to the Lake of the Ozarks region.

Before I had a chance to respond, she unceremoniously yanked the IV out of my arm and turned on her heel to see someone about getting me discharged from the hospital.

Chapter 4

The true reason my mother divorced Bill remains a mystery to this day, but Bill later told me (during my court-ordered two-week summer vacations with him) that she hadn't left him but, rather, he had thrown *her* out because he had caught her with "one of her boyfriends"....

Whatever happened, the bottom line is, life with Lonny was no picnic. After she left Bill, we moved to the Lake of the Ozarks area where she had found a waitressing position at a ski resort called Tan-Tar-A. As her new role of sole provider, she made sure I knew that she was depending on me now "more than ever" to keep an eye Teddy and to do the cooking and cleaning and to help her out in any way I could. And, although she admitted that, at age fourteen, I would probably desire to join my school mates in a "social life" – football games, dances and other school events – the reality was, I would have my hands full with my responsibilities, and my social life would just have to be put on hold for another couple of years.

Of course, this rule wouldn't apply to my *mother's* social life, regardless of *her* responsibilities. Hers was in full swing with parties and barhopping and dragging home one guy after the next, night after night....

All this changed, however, when she met and married her fourth husband, Oliver, whose swarthy good looks, dark hair and large brown eyes made her "fall in love at first sight."

Oliver, a soft-spoken, easy-going accountant at the resort where she worked, was the complete opposite of Bill Forrester, and it was very interesting to note how differently my mother acted toward him. As a matter of fact, once the "new" wore off, she began treating her handsome husband with the same supercilious contempt and disrespect she always displayed toward me!

Like me, it seemed Oliver could do nothing to please Lonny; and, consequently, he was forced to endure an endless barrage of verbal abuse and put-downs during their short, two-and-a-half-year marriage. I specifically remember one time when Lonny was angry about something and ranted from morning until night, to drive home the point that she was the "REAL bread-winner in this house." *She* made more money than he did, and if it weren't for *her*, our family would never be able to make ends meet....Her wrath knew no bounds and her words cut like a knife – and what's more, she seemed driven to impart pain. The less Ollie fought back, the louder she yelled. I couldn't help but wonder why she had never treated Forrester this way....With Bill Forrester she had always been the victim; but now with a meeker husband, she had clearly taken on the role of relentless victimizer!

Anyway, I'll never forget the wounded, embarrassed and emasculated look on Ollie's face, and I promised myself I would never treat a husband of mine that way. Nor would I ever give a child away; nor treat my child like a personal slave; nor would I ever marry a pedophile....

One would think that this situation would have brought Oliver and me close, but I purposely kept him at arm's length because I didn't want him misinterpreting any "friendliness" on my part. And so I just kept my mouth shut and concentrated on getting good grades at school during those dark and dreary days in which we once again moved around every few months before finally settling down in a half-way decent house.

The only thing that kept me sane in those days was that Oliver stood up for me the couple of times I asked permission to attend a football game or a dance. And, of course, there was my writing. I had always, as long as I could remember, had aspirations of being an author, and so, spurred on by my English teacher, Mrs. DuGan, I decided to start my first book entitled, "When I Find Forever." The story was about a young child, given away at birth and then forcefully taken away by her natural mother....

I didn't get much written before Lonny discovered the manuscript in my room one day and, without my consent, read the few completed chapters while I was at school. "Livid" does not accurately describe the way she came across later, when I got home, but suffice it to say, that very day she completely doused my literary aspirations.

Things plugged along fairly well for a while, until my mother decided she simply had to have a child with Ollie. Like some giddy school girl, she happily announced one day that she was pregnant, making sure to let us know that, since she had never had a "planned pregnancy" before, now, at age thirty-six, her time had come because she was "finally truly in love for the first time in my life." The news was bitter-sweet for me because I knew that ultimately, I would end up raising this kid, as well – which meant I would now have *two* kids to take care of, and any dreams of a social life would have to wait until I was old enough to leave home.

To my surprise, my brother Teddy took the news even harder than I did, because he was devastated to discover that he had been an unwanted child. Although he desperately tried to hide it, the disappointment was simply too much to bear. The final straw for him came immediately after our baby brother was born, when our mother callously referred to the tiny pink bundle as "my first love child." With a broken heart and spirit Teddy, at that point, determined life with his abusive father would be the lesser of two evils; and so he boldly told our mother he wanted to go and live with his father, Bill Forrester, in Springfield.

There was an incident approximately a month before Lonny gave birth, wherein Ollie came home alone late one night and, in obvious frustration, he handed me the car keys along with instructions to extricate my mother from the arms of some guy at Webb's Place, a local bar where my mother liked to hang out. Although I only had a learner's permit at the time, I got dressed and drove the twelve miles through the forested darkness, angry that I had been saddled, as Forrester liked to say, with a "drunken Jewish slut of mother" who kept making the same mistakes over and over again. It was one thing to have heard from the evil lips of Bill Forrester that Lonny was a "whore," but it galled me even more to discover he had been right! I had personally witnessed her making a business deal with a man once after we moved to the Lake of the Ozarks area, when she was apparently strapped for cash; and so it really was no surprise that she would, in a drunken state, attempt to play around. But eight months pregnant and in front of her own husband – someone like Ollie who was kind and sweet and true blue? And what about the poor infant inside of her? Every time she got drunk, the baby got drunk….

I felt like choking her – especially when I saw her swollen and inebriated body perched on a barstool at Webb's Place, hanging all over some unshaven guy in a cowboy hat. Luckily for me, she came along without a fight. But, any respect I might have had for her was forever gone after that evening, and I found myself fervently wishing I could get out from under her thumb somehow, because life with Lonny was a living hell.

One night, shortly after the Webb's Place incident (I don't know if it was in retaliation against Lonny or what), Ollie found his way to my bed while my mother was passed out in another of her drunken stupors. I couldn't believe this was happening to me yet again, and so, lying beside him trembling uncontrollably due to a mixture of fear and anger, I knew I had one of two choices: Kick him square in the gonads, or attempt to reason with him.

Since Ollie had always been kind to me, I couldn't bring myself to hurt him. Therefore, I pulled myself together long enough to remind him that he was married to my mother who could come walking in any second to kill us both. And then, for some reason, I broke down and tearfully confided my long-kept secret about Bill Forrester and his years of sexual abuse. "I can't go through this again, Ollie," I cried. "It's nothing personal, but I don't want to do this with my mother's husbands. It's not right. I'm just a kid. Please. I know you're drunk, but in the morning when you've sobered up, you'll probably be very sorry."

Ollie, who had lain quietly by my side, admitted he was stunned at my admission, and when I finished speaking, he apologized for having added to my misery. "Does your mother know?" he asked as he rose to leave.

"No, and I really don't want her knowing."

As far as I know Ollie never said a word to my mother and neither of us ever spoke about this "incident" until I saw him again years later and he broached the subject in order to apologize once more for his actions on that night long ago….

* * * *

When baby brother, Lonnie, came home from the hospital, it was just as I figured – he became *my* full time responsibility. But to make a long story short, my patience with our mother came to an abrupt halt when little Lonnie was about a year old and Mother had just divorced Ollie and moved us into a small apartment. The "straw that broke the camel's back" came when she left me home alone with the baby for *four days* in a row after going on another drunken binge. During that time, she never once bothered to call to see whether or not we were all right; and to make matters worse, her selfish act forced me to miss almost a week of school.

And so I totally lost it when she finally strolled through the door towards noon on the fourth day with her now ex-husband Oliver in tow, acting as though nothing unusual had transpired.

"Kids, I'm home!" she crooned, grinning from ear to ear and swaying a bit as she crossed from the foyer into the tiny kitchen. I bristled at the sight of her while little Lonnie let out a happy screech and toddled up to his mother to collect some whiskey-laden kisses.

"Where the hell have you been for the last four days?" I blurted out before I had a chance to stop myself. My voice quivered on the edge of hysteria. I had never before dared to challenge my mother this way, but I couldn't help myself; my chained rage simply had to be released.

Lonny stiffened in obvious surprise at my insolence. "None of your business," she snapped. "I was out and now I'm back. That's all you need to know. And you'd better watch your mouth!"

"It certainly *is* my business!" I snapped. "You just left me alone for four days with *your* kid, without any food in the house! I didn't know where you were and I didn't know how to find you. And I had to miss school *again* because of you!"

"So what are you trying to tell me?" Her clenched teeth and raised voice made me realize she wasn't going to take much more of my mouth. "What's wrong with you? I thought you said you didn't mind helping me out!"

Bitter tears began to flow as I glared at the woman I loathed with every fiber of my being. Right then I detested the very sight of her; I hated her voice, her dyed blond hair, her hideous and grating German accent, and most of all, her superior, excruciatingly egotistical attitude.

Ollie stepped forward and weakly mumbled something about calming down, but I was on a roll, ready to get into a fistfight, if need be.

"Don't mind helping you out?" I said with a sarcastic snort. "I don't have a choice, Mother! I'm your little slave girl. I do everything around here. When I'm not in school, I'm at home cooking, cleaning and babysitting, while *you're* out partying and running around! I feel like Lonnie is *my* child because you're never here! *I'm* his mother, not you!"

The tension in the air was electric, but surprisingly, my mother just stood there for a moment, the look on her face reflecting genuine astonishment. Finally, she glanced over at Ollie and then back at me, her gaze very calm and even. "Well, Carmen," she said slowly, "if you're so g__d__ unhappy with your life, then get the hell out of my house."

Her words shocked me into momentary silence, but I didn't have to be told twice! She had just given me an excuse to exit her life and I wasn't about to turn it down! So, without hesitation, I ran to my bedroom to fetch my purse and then dashed out the front door before she had a chance to change her mind. I had no clue where I was going, but I intended to get as far away from my crazy mother as I could possibly get!

Within a few minutes, I reached Highway 54. My mind raced as I automatically began walking down the side of the road towards Camdenton, where I attended high school. The other direction would lead me to Lake Ozark and Eldon, hick-towns and tourist traps where I knew no one, and so that wasn't an option.

Myriad thoughts crashed into each other as I walked along, desperately groping for an answer as to what my next move should be. At first I thought about asking my girlfriend, Connie Shelton, if I could live with her for a while until I figured out what to do. But then I realized if my mother discovered I was still in the area, she would force me to move back home. After all, I was just sixteen and still underage. So then I thought about hitchhiking to California and trying to find a girlfriend who had run away from home a few months before and gone to live with some relatives there. But the logical side of me figured this would be too dangerous and so I quickly discarded the idea.

The bottom line was, no matter where I ended up, I simply *had* to finish high school because I couldn't live with the stigma of being a dropout. Unfortunately, I had just started my junior year, and so I had a ways to go yet. Who would rent an apartment to a sixteen year old, and where would I get that kind of money, anyway?

And so I walked on until I found myself at the bowling alley Tan-Tar-A, the resort where my mother worked. I sat there for hours, slowly sipping a Coke and thinking, afraid to leave the safety of this place as nightfall began to approach. Finally, I came to the conclusion that my only reasonable option – as much as I hated the idea - would be to move back in with Bill Forrester until I finished high school. There was no other viable alternative because I knew my mother would track me down and make me come back home.

At least, if I lived with Forrester, I would – like Teddy – be safe in the womb of the lesser of two evils. And to his credit, he had been behaving differently, ever since Lonny divorced him.

And so, bone weary and with a heavy heart, I called him from a pay phone to inform him I had just run away from home and needed a place to stay.

To my surprise, he sounded overjoyed over the news that he would have "both of his kids back."

"Of course, you can come home, sweetheart," he cried excitedly. "Give me your exact location and I'll be there in about an hour."

While my heart palpitated over this decision, my soul silently rejoiced in the knowledge that I would be rid of Lonny forever. But there was still one thing that needed to be discussed before I would agree to move back in with him; I had nothing to lose by being upfront about it. My throat tightened as I formed the words with all the determination I could muster: "Daddy," I said, "there's just one stipulation and that is, I'm not moving back there to be your sex slave. I'll cook and clean and take care of Teddy, but I don't want to have sex with you anymore. I'm your daughter, not your wife."

I held my breath as I waited for his response, and to my utter relief, he immediately agreed without argument. "Teddy and I are on our way, sis!" he said, without skipping a beat.

My stomach was in knots by the time I hung up the phone, but I felt better knowing I had a safe place to sleep that night.

* * * *

Just as I suspected, Lonny found me a couple of days later. She, of course, played the victim and did her level best to convince me to come back home. Little Lonnie, she said, missed his "sissy" and they just wanted me to "come home" (translation: she needed her cook, cleaner and baby sitter).

She cried, she threatened, she attempted to cajole me back into her life, but I stood my ground and told her I would rather die than to ever see her face again.

So, then she began working on Teddy to "come home," and he ultimately did – and from that point on, he became her new babysitter and all-around helper.

Chapter 5

By the time I graduated from high school in 1969, I had already lived through more situations than most people in the Western world experience in a lifetime. I had been given away at birth and then literally been ripped from the hands of my loving foster parents; was taken to a foreign country against my will; attended fourteen different schools; endured sexual abuse at the hands of my adoptive father, and had been forced to stand by my alcoholic mother as she went from one relationship to the next in search of that ever-elusive happiness.

Teddy and I did our best to keep in contact, but our connection seemed to be pretty much over. My mother had knocked herself out to turn him against me, and there was an obvious wedge between us now. The closeness we shared in years past was gone and, for some reason, he blamed me for everything – especially the fact that, with me out of the picture, Mother had made him her fulltime baby sitter. I invited him to move back to Springfield to live with his dad and me, but he said he couldn't do that to our mother as she depended on him. He said she had to have someone to take care of her whenever she got drunk....

Feeling helpless and not really knowing what to do or say, I only hoped that one day Teddy would be able to break the spell Lonny had on him.

We did share a good laugh at one point, though, when he called to tell me that Lonny had married some cook in the Osage Beach region named John Bybee. When I asked Teddy to pass on my congratulations, he laughed and said, "Well, I would, but they're already divorced. It lasted all of two weeks because John refused to put up with her shenanigans...."

Life for me went fairly smooth during my final year in high school. Bill kept his bargain and refrained from touching me for the next year and a half, and I kept my end of the deal by keeping his house, doing the cooking and helping him take care of the farm. In the meantime, he had fallen in love with a waitress named Goldie who came out to see him every day after work. Goldie liked to call Bill "Sarge" – a nickname that caused him to break into a silly grin because it reminded him of his old Army days, which he sorely missed.

I fell in love with Goldie from the moment I met her. She and I spent hours picking blackberries and making cobblers and participating in endless "girl talk." I was glad she was in my life for several reasons, the main one being that if Daddy had her, he wouldn't bother me....

Everything went well until I fell in love with a boy when I was a senior in high school – an act which, not surprisingly, sent Bill into a jealous rage.

The guy's name was David, and he had been a "blind date" set up by my neighbor. David had just graduated from high school and was working on some farm outside the Springfield city limits while deciding on a future career. Although Bill basically knew nothing about David, he let me know in no uncertain terms that David was "destined to shovel horse manure" for the rest of his life because he was literally "from the wrong side of the track" – someone who lived in Springfield's low rent district, and who would probably never amount to anything because his parents hadn't amounted to anything. In other words, I could "do better."

But I was simply too much in love to care what Daddy thought. As far as I was concerned, falling in love with David was the best thing that had ever happened to me; it was my saving grace, my shelter from all the storms of my life. David was my chestnut-haired, blue-eyed knight in shining armor, and as far as I was concerned, the sun rose and set on him. David was my reason for existing; I lived and breathed David and would have done whatever he asked of me, even if it had meant my own death. He was my life, my very soul. He took me on fun dates and made me feel beautiful; and the happiest day of my life was when he gave me an engagement ring. We dreamed, we lived and loved and talked endlessly about our future together as husband and wife. His love sustained me, and nothing else mattered – not even Bill's constant harassment and jealous outbursts after every date. I even developed a sort of mother-daughter relationship with David's mother, who reminded me so much of my beloved foster mother in Germany.

The one drawback in my romance with David was that, together we discovered that I had a major problem with intimacy. And so when David pressed me about my various "hang-ups," I eventually broke down one evening and told him that Bill had sexually abused me for years, and that certain touches "felt like Daddy." Naturally, David wanted to murder Bill Forrester, but managed to pull himself together when I tearfully begged him to keep my secret, as I was positive that Bill would kill me if he knew I had told anyone. Ultimately, we concluded that he would confront my father after we were married, when I was safely out of the house.

Of course, I loved David all the more for his sympathy and understanding, and this awful secret we now shared brought us ever closer. I trusted David with all my heart and felt that he truly understood the pain of my sexual abuse, and I lived for the day when he would steal me away on that legendary white horse and ride with me into the sunset where I would eventually be able to overcome all my "hang-ups" and we would live happily ever after!

In the meantime, life was at least bearable on the Forrester farm. During that time, I even renewed my effort to re-establish contact with my foster mother in Germany (I had been previously prevented from attempting to contact her, among other reasons, because "postage to Germany costs too much money"). Mama was thrilled to hear from me and made me promise to come for a visit one day soon. Through our correspondence, I discovered that my foster father had accidentally killed himself in a drunken fall down a flight of stairs back in the early seventies, and that Mama was now living on the opposite end of Wietze with someone named Jürgen Forchert, thirty years her junior. She also filled me in on the fact that the part of town I'd come from had grown, and that the shack which I had called home for the first nine years of my life had been bulldozed into oblivion to make way for new housing. Although not surprising, it made me sad, nonetheless.

Mama's letters and photos kept me going during my senior year of high school because, not only did they remind me of my happy childhood but, between having her back in my life and loving David, things were finally looking up for me which surely meant that my life was headed towards "normal" again!

Meanwhile, I still had to contend with Bill's endless put-downs about my relationship with David, of whom he clearly didn't approve. This became clear late one Saturday evening when I came home from a date.

I knew something was up when I saw Daddy sitting on the couch, watching TV, because he normally went to bed fairly early, even on weekends. He stiffened when I stepped across the threshold to enter the living room. In an apparent attempt to block my path, he turned off the TV and then slowly and deliberately turned towards me, his face reflecting enormous agitation.

"You sure are late tonight," he said. "What have you been doing?" His voice was low and tight and it was obvious the dam was about to burst. He must have been sitting there for hours, stewing. I couldn't help but think that maybe he had had a fight with Goldie.

"We went to a drive-in movie and they had a double feature."

"Is that right?" Keeping his mouth tightly closed, Bill made a show of running his tongue back and forth across his top teeth and gums, which was an irritating habit he had whenever he was angry. It served to force his pointed, knobby chin forward and distort his face into more of a hideous visage than it already was. "What else did you do?"

None of your business, I thought, but I didn't actually dare to verbalize it because I knew it would get me slapped across the mouth. And so I simply mumbled, "Nothing," and attempted to walk around him to head toward the kitchen.

He grabbed my arm on my way past and said, "Hold up, little girl!....I bet a million dollars you did exactly what your mother always did whenever *she* was out on a date. I'm just wondering whether you're following in her footsteps."

His tense posture was reminiscent of the night I threatened to call the cops, and my breath caught. David had dropped me off at the house and was long gone by now; and so once again, I was facing Goliath and his rage alone.

Fear quickly turned to anger, however, and the "fight or flight" syndrome made me feel brave. I had an entire lifetime of rage bottled up inside me, and if Bill laid one hand on me tonight, I decided I would put him in the hospital! At 5′ 3″, I was nearly as tall as he, and certainly older and stronger than I had been on that fateful night years ago when he nearly killed me. If I couldn't hurt him in the physical fight that was about to ensue, then I would wait until he was asleep and beat him to death with a crowbar....

Glaring at him in defiance I said, "Well, I was wondering how long it would be before you accused me of being a whore. I'm a 'good girl' when I have sex with you against my will, but now since I found someone I actually *want*, it makes me a whore?"

The pain reflected in his evil, wrinkled countenance told me that my words had smarted; but he quickly recovered and seconds later his face twisted into a crimson mask of fury. Simultaneously, the realization slammed home that I had gone too far, and I both heard and felt the blood rushing in my ears as I braced myself.

"You two-faced little bitch!" I heard him growl over the pounding of my heart. "I told you I don't like that boy, but you never listen, do you? You're a smart-assed piece of white trash, just like your damned mother. I should have killed you both long ago...."

"Daddy, please...." I said, trying in vain to extricate myself from his grip. "Why are you mad at me tonight? What have I done?"

"Don't 'Daddy' me, you little hard-headed Kraut! You smart off to me one more time and I'll break your g---- d---- neck, you understand?"

My arm was killing me as his grip tightened; I began to feel like two separate people at that point. On one hand, I wanted more than anything to tell him off, but on the other, I was too busy fearing for my life. Whenever Daddy got this angry, you didn't dare talk back.

When I found my voice again, it sounded pathetic to my own ears, and I was secretly ashamed of myself. My earlier brief determination to kill him was already dissolved, right along with that short-lived feeling of courage. "Daddy, I – I'm sorry, okay? *God!*... I'll be out of your hair soon and then I won't be a problem for you anymore...."

"Don't use the Lord's Name in vain!"

"...because I'm getting married right after I graduate!"

I don't know what happened inside Bill's head but for some reason, his demeanor changed. He blinked and emitted a long, shaky sigh and then simply released his grip on my arm, giving it a short and angry thrust before he let go, as though I simply wasn't worth the effort anymore. When he spoke, he sounded old and tired.

"Damn you, sis," he said, "I don't want you getting married. What will it take to get that through that damned thick skull of yours?"

"But Daddy...."

"What hurts me in all this is your blatant disregard for my feelings. I've done everything in my power to raise you right and have taken good care of you, and now you're just using me for a roof over your head until you can move on with this immature little boyfriend of yours. That's plain stupid! You're a damned ingrate, you know that?"

So, there it was, out in the open: He was jealous! I wasn't sure whether to feel sorry for him or to smack him upside the head. My adoptive father was an expert at mind games and I was getting sick of the emotional roller coaster. Even more, I hated that I was helpless against this powerhouse who, in various ways, had a death grip on my very soul.

"I'm not using you, Daddy," I retorted weakly. "I'm paying for this roof over my head...I cook for you and clean your house, and...."

"Sis, if I charged you for your room and board, you'd be doing a hell of lot more than you're doing now. You don't know what work is...."

My jaw dropped and I felt as if I'd just been slapped! I didn't know the meaning of work? What had I been doing ever since he and my mother stole me from my foster parents in Germany?

"You could have made all this a hell of lot easier on yourself if you had just listened to me and done what I told you. I'll put you through college, and then, when you're older, you'll be more capable of making better decisions. Stop concentrating on boys and get an education, first...."

The thought of living with Bill Forrester for another four years made me hyperventilate; I couldn't have felt more trapped if he had literally locked me in the hen-house. "I don't want to go college," I snapped in defiance. "You wanna know why? Because you'll only expect me to repay you with sex, and I can't do that! I won't do that!"

"…Well, how the hell else are you gonna do it, then?" he responded with that horrible air of superiority he always wore like a cloak. "Or do you want to end up as nothing more than a waitress like your mother?"

Enraged now to a boiling point, yet feeling like a whipped dog, I didn't know what else to say. I just wanted to be left alone. In the back of my mind, I realized the man was crazy, and soon I would be free of him forever. I had to hold onto that thought just for a few more months.…

"I asked you a question, dammit!"

My throat was beginning to ache with tears of frustration and I wanted nothing more than to be away from his evil presence. Tossing him a perfunctory glance, I shrugged and said, "What I want, Daddy, is to go to bed. It's late; I'm tired, I don't want to fight with you, and I just don't want to talk anymore." And with that, I simply left him standing there, alone, in the living room. If he said anything, I didn't hear it because seconds later I slammed my bedroom door on my father, this night, and the whole sickening scenario.

That night, like so many other nights, I cried myself to sleep.

Chapter 6

The year 1969 proved to be interesting, not just because of the manned moon landing and world events, but because it was the year I graduated from high school and had just turned eighteen; and best of all, I would at last be legally free of my parents.

I found out through my brother Teddy that my mother and Oliver had re-married and moved to Indiana somewhere, and purchased a tavern with an upstairs residence in which they lived. I remember chuckling to myself, thinking that if Ollie was forced to leave her sitting in the bar for any reason, he could just go upstairs and leave her there without having to worry about how she was to get home....I couldn't help but wonder how long she would stay married this time, but it didn't really matter. I no longer cared about my mother and her soap opera life. Soon I would be marrying my own sweetheart and *my* life would be great!

Of course, for me nothing ever came easy, and so it came as no surprise that my happy marriage plans were put on hold. As it turned out, David, the one person on Earth I loved and trusted with all my heart, the person who would kiss all my boo-boos and make everything better, had decided to join the Air Force and was being stationed in Thailand after his Advanced Individual Training (AIT). I was crushed when he told me we should probably wait to get married until after his return because his tour of duty would be shorter as a single person. In the meantime, of course, I would have to remain at my father's house....

What hurt even more was when he told me that he had been dating while overseas, "just to pass the time" until we could be together again. That bit of information absolutely floored me! He loved me, so why would he even LOOK at another woman? To say I was shocked and devastated would have been an understatement.

Over the next month or so, as I tried to figure out what my next move should be, I kept thinking that David probably wouldn't have wanted another woman if I were prettier. As someone with kinky, curly dark hair, brown eyes and big "Kike" nose (as Bill Forrester liked to refer to it), I had never considered myself very pretty. *"With that big nose you'll never be Miss America"....*

So, really, it was no wonder I couldn't keep a boyfriend. If I could have changed my looks, I would have done so in a heartbeat, but plastic surgery was beyond my means back then.

The pain and feelings of inferiority gave way to anger one day when I concluded that men were all alike, and if I was to be happy and successful in life, it would be up to me.

And so in August of 1969, right after Hurricane Camille, I ended up in the Women's Army Corps (WAC) as a clerk typist. I had tried to enlist in the Air Force first, but by the time I got my adoption papers translated and my naturalization certificate, they had met their quota for the year and wouldn't let anyone else in. It would have been a great career because I had passed all the aptitude tests, including those for German, Spanish and French, which would have gotten me into Intelligence as a linguist. And so, broken-hearted but determined to get as far away from home as I could as quickly as possible, I went next door to see an Army recruiter – and before I knew it, I was in basic training at Fort McClellan, Alabama, headed for a career as a secretary, the only thing available to enlisted WACs at that time besides the medical field.

David was livid when he found out I had enlisted, but I simply told him that, since I couldn't depend on him to get me away from home, I had been forced to make my own way in this world. I told him I wasn't about to sit around waiting on some man who couldn't keep his promise to ride me off into the sunset. From now on, I told him, I was in charge of whatever happened in my life, and if he wanted to be a part of it, he would have to straighten up and put me first.

Over the next few months while David wrote letter after letter proclaiming his undying love for me, I was busy graduating from "Basic" and "Advanced Individual Training" at Fort McClellan, Alabama. It was there I discovered that, although I had physically removed myself from my parents, psychologically and emotionally I was still very much tied to them – an unfortunate detail that mostly manifested itself via night terrors, which was an extremely embarrassing thing to suffer in open bay situations where there were rows upon rows of beds.

I had been prone to having nightmares for as long as I could remember, but I didn't know the extent of the problem until one night when I sleepwalked my way into the latrine and nearly tripped over a couple girls lying and talking on a blanket by the showers. I woke up when one of them exclaimed, "Hey Forrester, you're sleep-walking again. Go back to bed!"

I was often teased about my restless sleeping habits, but the final straw that had my company commander sending me to the Post psychiatrist was when I dreamed one night that a huge spider had cocooned my bed and was about to have me for dinner. Screaming hysterically, I stood and took a flying dive onto the next bunk – waking up just in time to feel myself being tossed abruptly onto the floor by the bunk's startled occupant.

The following day, perched in front of the psychiatrist, I found I couldn't open up in fear that if I mentioned my past sexual abuse, they might contact Bill Forrester and he would come and kill me. With no other information to go on besides the fact that I suffered from nightmares and sleepwalking, the psychiatrist chalked my problems up as stress, prescribed some Valium, and sent me on my merry way.

* * * *

In early 1970, after completing my AIT, I was stationed at White Sands Missile Range, New Mexico, to work as a clerk typist for the SAFEGUARD Systems Evaluation Agency.

I was on Cloud Nine, partly because I was showing my father that I, without any help from him whatsoever, had not ended up as "trailer trash" or "just a waitress like my mother." I was earning my own living working as a secretary in the Missile Site Radar Division, where I worked for a couple dozen educated people who treated me with respect and helped me to move up the ranks. In the two years I was there, I made Soldier of Month and WAC of the Week and was promoted all the way up to the rank of Specialist 5. Moreover, I also took regular evening classes at New Mexico State University – and Bill Forrester wasn't paying for any of it!

Ironically, at the same time, I felt that my accomplishments were hollow. In my mind's eye, I could almost hear my mother asking, "What is a Spec. 5, in the grand scheme of things? You're just an enlisted person, not an officer in charge of something. And "WAC of the Week" – that's just a title given to a selected woman whose boss sent her name to the Post newspaper because she was doing a good job at the office. Sure, 'Soldier of the Month' is a great honor because you did a lot of studying to prepare for the board – but you *failed to win* the more prestigious honor of 'Soldier of the Quarter"....

Down deep, as much as I hated to admit it to myself, I desperately wanted my parents, especially my adoptive father, to be proud of me. My mother...well, I really couldn't care less about her, but for some reason I was obsessed with Bill's opinions. It pained me to the core whenever his tone revealed disappointment. Realizing that I was suffering from years worth of conditioning to yearn for the approval of this "macho man," I tried hard not to let it bother me; but yet, it hurt to know he was rejecting and dismissing me at every turn. The man was an expert at playing mind games designed to show me I could have done better had I bothered to do things *his* way. Therefore, just to spite him, I decided to keep my chin up, and continue pushing toward greatness because one day, by George, I would do something that *would* knock his socks off and *force* him to be proud of me!

In the meantime, whether Bill was proud of me or not, my career was soaring and, for the first time in my life, I was actually feeling good about myself. Plus, I was dating some cute guys, very much against David's will. In response to a scathing letter in which he forbade me to date other men, I boldly informed him that since he said he was dating girls in Thailand, there was no reason for me to sit around in the barracks here in America, pining away for him. Several months later, after a long dry spell with no correspondence from David, one day I received a letter carrying the news that he had married his Thai girlfriend....

The word "devastated" does not begin to describe how I felt. I truly wanted to die! The news sent me into a deep depression and I sat around in the barracks at night for months on end, crying and blaming myself because my brazen insolence had surely been to blame for pushing David into someone else's arms. Why had I not simply complied with his wishes to not date other men? Why was I not prettier? Why, why, why....

A million questions ran through my mind about why David and I ended up separated. But I wasn't to receive an answer to those questions until some thirty-five years later....

* * * *

Seventies comedian Flip Wilson had popularized the saying, "The devil made me do it!" and I truly believed that, that must have been what had happened to me. I certainly believed in the devil (thanks to my foster grandmother who had told me about God and Satan when I was a kid), but usually I didn't give God or the devil much thought. Assuming they were there, "somewhere behind the scenes," I felt that ultimately man was in charge of his own life. I knew this because God had never answered my prayers back when, as a little girl, I was hiding in closets from my father. Since God was more powerful than Satan, He could have stopped Bill at any time, but He didn't, and so, obviously, we humans were in charge of our own destinies. Maybe everything was just a test, after all, to see how well we could handle various situations. I had apparently failed this test with David, or else he wouldn't have married another woman. Bill Forrester had been right all along: I was just a hardheaded, smart-alecky *Kraut*....

When finally I snapped out of my depression, I concluded that the best thing for me to do would be to get married, as well. At 19, there was no reason for me to become a recluse just because I had been jilted by a fiancé who kept breaking my heart in one way or another. And so when a guy named Chuck from Pittsburgh, Pennsylvania, asked me to marry him, I didn't hesitate to accept his proposal.

Chuck, with his hair-trigger smile and quirky ways had a unique personality and somehow he seemed like a "real man" to me. With a crooked nose and wavy dark blond hair, he was ruggedly handsome and very rebellious, which I found kind of "sexy" at the time. He was an amateur boxer who performed on weekends at the Post gym, and he had supposedly played guitar with the Bob Seger System. I totally overlooked the fact that he was also a pathological liar, an egomaniac and drug addict with no education and no ambition – and that he just happened to bear a sharp resemblance to Bill Forrester, right down to the green snake eyes and manipulative nature....

But, Chuck was there to catch me while I fell out of love with David and together we decided we needed to be married to each other. It didn't matter that he treated me like dirt most of the time and gave me a steady diet of put-downs. We chalked up his mood swings to drugs, and found a way to make up after every fight. I was his saving grace, he said, because I would be the woman who could help wean him off drugs permanently.

While we were dating, Chuck, the drug addict constantly managed to get into trouble and, looking back, I wish I had paid more attention whenever people tried to tell me he was "bad news." If he wasn't making his bosses angry and being shoved from one job to another because no one wanted him working for them, he was getting into car accidents or ending up in the hospital from drug overdoses. He even ended up on the psychiatric ward after wrecking my car one night and severely injuring several people, including a woman with whom he was cheating on me. I had actually decided to break up with him after that incident, but when he cried giant horse tears in front of me and the Catholic priest he had asked to his bedside, I was seized by guilt pangs and decided to give him another chance.

And so we set a wedding date – which turned out to be the first of the many bad and stupid mistakes I would make in my lifetime.

Of course, a bride has to have someone walking her down the aisle, and so I asked Bill Forrester to do the honors – not because I necessarily wanted him to do it, but because I knew it would hurt him enormously to see me pledging myself to another man. But he declined to come at all, just as I figured, and that's how my brother Teddy, who was then fourteen, assumed the honors. Naturally, my mother had to tag along, and so we were forced to "kiss and make up" after not being on speaking terms for the last three years. I was secretly glad to know she would be there, though, because it would show her that I had become my own person in spite of her many attempts to rule my life. It was important to me to have her see her daughter in an environment where I was more than "just" a housekeeper or baby sitter, wordlessly simmering in the wake of her put-downs. My office job and this brazen move to become a married woman, I felt, would serve to let both my parents know they had forever lost their hold on me, and that I had "made it" on my own terms – despite Bill's predictions that I would end up as "nothing but a whore and a waitress"; and despite my mother's "you're ugly, stupid and lazy" speeches....

* * * *

My wedding day, like my life, proved to be bitter sweet, thanks, of course, to my mother.

To begin with, from the moment my mother laid eyes on Chuck at the airport, there was non-stop flirting between them. She was newly single again, having just divorced Oliver for the second time. And here she was now, free and single and ready to get her hooks into whoever happened along next – which, at the present, turned out to be my fiancé.

At one point during one of our many sightseeing tours that were crammed into the two and a half days my mother and brothers were there, Chuck insisted on crawling into the back seat to sit between her and my little five year old brother, Lonnie, while Teddy kept me company in the front. Hoping it was just Chuck's way of being a good host, I pushed away the creepy thought that he had an ulterior motive; but my intuition proved to be correct when I craned my neck to peer at them during some animated conversation, and caught the movement of their hands quickly separating.

I don't know why I didn't say anything, but for some reason I decided to swallow my pride and just let it go. Surely, these two weren't going to be able to consummate their desires in the short time my mother was here! Why would they even want to? Chuck was my fiancé, a twenty-four year old who would become my husband tomorrow afternoon; and Lonny was his soon-to-be mother-in-law, someone who was nearly twice his age....

No, I was absolutely sure nothing would happen between those two. By this time tomorrow, Chuck and I would be married and I would finally be a "respectable woman," which was something I wanted more than anything in this world. No longer would Bill Forrester be able to accuse me to being a whore!

It was *imperative* for me to ignore the little secret glances between Chuck and my mother, or the fact that they were holding hands. If something had already happened between them on the first night after her arrival, I didn't want to know about it, in part, because I wouldn't have been able to handle another heartache just yet.

And so I didn't make a scene over Chuck's suggestion of retiring early that night, using as an excuse the tradition of "the bride not seeing the groom the night before the wedding." I didn't open my mouth when he insisted on keeping my car and dropping me off at the "WAC shack" so he could take my mother and brothers to the Guest House. And I purposely didn't call his barracks that night, or check to see if my mother was at the Guest House, for fear that neither of them would be in...For, *surely*, there wouldn't be anything going on between Chuck and my mother....

In desperation for that "normal" life I was to have once I was married, I simply sat in my barracks room and watched TV alone, waiting patiently for my wedding day to arrive, and secretly stewing over the fact that my mother had had the audacity to expect Chuck and me to pay for everything while she was here. Providing food, gas and entertainment on the meager military salaries Chuck and I were receiving was no easy feat. As a Private First Class, Chuck – who was paying child support for two young children from a previous marriage – was only bringing in a total of $112 per month. And, as an unmarried Specialist 5 without dependents, my salary wasn't much more than that. Neither one of us had a savings account, and so having my mother there to see me get married basically broke our wallets.

To add insult to injury, my mother acted as though everything revolved around her. On my wedding day, in the hours before we were to be at church while I was trying nervously to get ready, she complained about her hair and the dress she was wearing, which had apparently become wrinkled in the suitcase, and so she expected me to drop everything to take her to the beauty shop and the cleaners. I nearly died when I saw that her dress was one of those "micro-mini skirts" like the ones worn by the "go-go girls" on TV....

The wedding went as smoothly as possible, but I felt no magic as Teddy was walking me down the aisle. In the back of my mind, I kept thinking this was a huge mistake – something that was absolutely confirmed when I saw Chuck's glassy eyes at the altar and realized he was high on Heroin. He told me later he had been partying all night with his friends who had insisted on giving him a big send-off into holy matrimony land. Although disgusted with him, I was relieved to discover that he hadn't spent the night with my mother.

After the reception, we put my mother's suitcases in the trunk and headed for El Paso, as her plane was leaving early in the morning and we didn't want to risk making her late. Since she supposedly couldn't afford to pay for a hotel room for herself and my brothers, Chuck and I were forced to rent a suite that could accommodate the five of us. So much for our long-awaited wedding night!

After we saw my mother and brothers off at the airport the next day, we took a brief honeymoon trip to the mountains near Alamogordo, and then returned "home" to a small trailer we had rented in Las Cruces, approximately 30 miles from White Sands Missile Range. Back in those days only E-5 and above were allowed to live in on-post housing and, although I was a Specialist 5, the rules applied to the male spouse as the responsible party, and so we were forced to find our own housing outside the Missile Range.

On our way to Johnson's Trailer Park after our brief and uneventful honeymoon in a tiny one-room mountain cabin, I was secretly ashamed that Bill Forrester had been right about my becoming "trailer trash" some day….

Chapter 7

The last time I ever saw my mother was in January 1972, seven months after Chuck and I were married. Chuck received orders for Vietnam and demanded I get out of the Army because he didn't want me "around all those men." Back in those days, women could get out of the Army on the grounds of marriage, and Chuck insisted that, while he was gone, I was to live with one of my parents or with his family. Naturally, I chose his family and obediently prepared for the move to Pittsburgh, Pennsylvania....

Our short marriage had already been full of strife and turmoil, as Chuck had a habit of straying with other women. Even though his driver's license was revoked and he and was barred from driving in the state of New Mexico, he often took my car and disappeared on weekends – fully expecting me to believe he had been "partying with the guys." No amount of crying, sweet-talking or tantrum throwing made Chuck realize how much his actions were jeopardizing our marriage. He simply didn't seem to care.

During those stressful days, my "egg/needle-in-throat" episodes intensified and it became common for me to wake from a deep sleep gasping for air every single night. I also had many sleepwalking and "ESP" episodes wherein I would wake up upon "feeling my soul had just returned to my body" and I literally sat up in bed proclaiming things that made no sense at the time, but which always came to pass. The one time that stands out in my mind is when my "soul" traveled outside our little trailer and I saw that the tire on the rear passenger's side of my little gold Plymouth Cricket was flat. Extremely agitated that we had another flat we couldn't afford to get fixed – and to prove once again that these strange visions weren't a result of an over-active imagination – I jerked my husband out of a deep sleep to make him accompany me outside and see for himself that we had a flat tire! Like my mother, though, regardless as to how many times I showed Chuck evidence of my "ESP" (for lack of a better term), he always downplayed it by insisting I was "just a strange chick."

But weird or not, my visions were always right on the money, exactly as they had been back in Springfield, Missouri, where at age eleven, I had told my mother that everything was full of fleas….

Anyway, on our way to Pennsylvania, which was to be my temporary home while Chuck was in Vietnam, we briefly stopped to visit my parents at their respective residences in Missouri. Bill Forrester was cordial albeit slightly cool to my new husband, but all went well during our visit with him in Springfield. The visit with my mother, however, turned out to be another fiasco on several levels, beginning with the fact that she wasn't home when we arrived at her house in Osage Beach – even though we had told her we would arrive around noon. My brothers informed me that she had gone bar hopping and "should be back shortly."

In those days before cell phones there was no way to contact Lonny and we had no idea where she might be, so we simply sat and waited – which turned out to be a good thing because it gave us all a chance to become reacquainted. I really hadn't had occasion back in New Mexico to talk to my brothers very much, and found that they behaved quite differently here, in their own home.

It was interesting to see how different both Ted and Lonnie had become over the span of just four years. The last time I had had any real contact with Lonnie was when he was just a baby no more than a year old, and it felt strange now to be able to see him as a boy and to have actual conversations with him. He had turned out to be a fairly boisterous and remarkable little boy.

And Teddy, who was now at least a foot taller than me, was no longer the same person I had grown up with. At fifteen, he was beginning to resemble the good-looking, statuesque man he would one day become. His voice had changed and the once bright blond, wavy hair was now more of a light brown and very curly. In all honesty, I couldn't see any resemblance between him and his father, and I secretly wondered if Ted was actually Bill's son. Knowing our mother, Ted could have belonged to any of literally dozens of men she had been with over the years.

What saddened me was that the connection I used to have with Ted was nowhere to be found. He was friendly and talkative, but extremely distant, and I was at a loss as how to fix that problem. The one thing he did admit was that he wasn't thrilled about being Lonny's babysitter and housekeeper, and that he was looking forward to the day when he, too, could leave home. It was obvious he felt trapped and manipulated, and so I offered to have him come and live with Chuck and me whenever Chuck returned from Vietnam and we had found a permanent residence.

We all craned our necks to watch our mother stagger through the door sometime around mid-afternoon. It would be an understatement to say that I was disappointed when I saw her, flushed and reeking of beer, and wearing a skimpy, purple polka-dotted "hot pants" outfit with a plunging neckline that accentuated her flat chest. Clearly, she wanted to look younger than her 40 years….

But, she made her grand entrance as if her late arrival was nothing out of the ordinary, and with a quick and perfunctory hug she blurted, "Where's that handsome son-in-law of mine?" When I told her Chuck was taking a nap on Lonnie's bed, she immediately made a beeline for the bedroom.

Curious, I followed at her heels and watched as she perched on the edge of the bed before bending down to plant a kiss squarely on my husband's mouth. Chuck, awakened from a deep slumber, flinched at first, and then wrapped his arms around her waist when he realized who it was. "Well, hello, Mom!" he croaked sleepily. The image left no doubt in my mind that something had definitely gone on "behind the scenes" back in New Mexico, and I bristled at the thought.

"Hey, son-in-law," she slurred and gave him another quick peck on the lips. "How you doin'?"

Behind me, Teddy called out, "Would you two like to come out to the living room and join the rest of us?" When I turned to gaze upon him, he shrugged his shoulders and gave me a knowing look.

"We're coming," Lonny replied as she clumsily reached for Chuck's hand to help him out of bed.

My brothers and I had already selected our respective seats in the small living room by the time my mother and Chuck entered. Still shaken from what I had witnessed in the bedroom, I pasted a silly grin on my face and hoped I would be able to control the anger in my voice. "So, where have you been all afternoon, Mother?" I demanded a little more testily than intended. "Didn't you remember that I said we would be here around noon?"

She gawked at me as if I had just slapped her. "I was out!" she snapped. "Is that all right with you? In all honesty, I was a little upset over the fact that you guys went and saw Bill first."

I wondered when she would bring that up. "Well," I said, "he was the first one we got to on our route!"

"I don't give a damn! Who came to your wedding? Me; I did. Not Bill! He doesn't care about you...."

"So, we were supposed to drive eighty miles out of our way just to come and see you first?"

"Ladies, ladies!" Chuck chimed in. With a wink in my mother's direction, he said, "We're all together now, and it doesn't matter who was first or last.

What matters is, we saved the best for last, right Lonny?"

"Absolutely," she replied, her face brightening. "So, what do you wanna do now? You wanna go bar-hopping, Chuck?"

He shrugged and, tossing me a quick glance, he said, "Sure. Let's go!"

"*NO!*" I quickly protested. "I don't want to go bar hopping. Let's just go out to eat and then come back here and talk or something. We never talk to each other...."

Lonny's lips tightened and I could tell she didn't like that idea.

Emitting a sigh of impatience, I threw up my hands and said, "Mother, look, I'm only twenty, and I can't legally drink in civilian bars yet. I truly don't want to sit there and watch you two get drunk....And neither do Ted and Lonnie!" I added, tossing a glance in Teddy's direction.

"Well, then," she replied matter-of-factly. "You guys can either come along and watch us drink while you nurse a Ginger Ale, or you can all stay here and you can play babysitter, just like in the old days."

Her words cut into my very soul. The world began to move in slow motion as I sat there glowering at her across the few shadowy feet of space dividing us. I had never hated my mother more than I did in that particular moment, and for a few seconds I just sat there, stunned, trying to figure out how to react.

And then the dam broke.

For the sake of my two brothers, I tried to remain calm, but my rage won out as I stood to face her. "You haven't changed at all!" I said, keeping my voice as even as possible despite the hot fury surging in the pit of my stomach. "You just keep making the same mistakes, over and over...No, I'm *not* going to stay and babysit for you now or ever again – and you'd better get that through your thick skull! Those days are over with!" Turning toward Chuck, I said, "Get up and get your coat; we're leaving."

Apparently realizing she had gone too far, Lonny stepped towards me. "Carmen, don't be childish!" she said. "I just want you all to have fun while you're here."

I tossed her an icy stare, secretly wishing looks could kill, and then turned on my heel and headed for the door, mumbling an apology to my brothers over my shoulder.

Outside, the late afternoon sun shone orange through the few scattered trees in the yard. The hot tears that spilled over my cheeks were quickly cooled off by the brisk winter breeze that assaulted me as I dashed across the lawn towards my car.

Nearly hysterical by the time I threw myself behind the steering wheel, I couldn't keep from shouting a barrage of curse words in sheer frustration when my shaking hands failed to locate the ignition. Out of the corner of my eye, I caught a glimpse of Chuck standing on the front steps of my mother's house, apparently wondering what to do. "Honey, come back!" he yelled. "Your mother was just kidding!"

Behind him, Lonny was peering helplessly over his shoulders.

I glared at him; in that moment and in that setting he looked more like Bill Forrester than ever, and I hated him for it. I couldn't figure out what on Earth I had ever seen in this loser.... "You either get in the car right now, or I'll leave your dumb butt here with her since that's what you seem to want!" I cried. At that moment, my car roared into life and I stomped on the accelerator and began to back out of the driveway.

The car was already moving forward on the road when Chuck jumped unsteadily into the passenger side. I slammed on the brake long enough for him to settle in and get the door closed, and before mashing the accelerator to the floor, I rolled down my window and tossed a searing glance at Lonny who was still standing in the doorway, appearing quite dazed. "This was the last straw, you b---!" I screeched, not caring who heard me. "I never want to see you again! *I hate your guts*, you hear me?" I'm not even coming to your g---- d---- funeral when you die!"

And without further ado, I pointed my little car towards the main road in my determined quest to leave Osage Beach behind in the rearview mirror forever.

Chapter 8

Moving to Pittsburgh to live with Chuck's parents while he was in Vietnam turned out to be another major mistake on my part. Not only was I unable to land a decent job during those dark days when the state of Pennsylvania was going bankrupt, but Chuck's family was no picnic to be around.

His poor father suffered from depression and often sat on the sofa, weeping bitter tears for hours on end; while his mother, a short, round bossy woman, felt the need to check up on my every move, never hesitating to ask where I was going or what I was doing, and generally driving me up the wall. And if that wasn't bad enough, his older sister who had severe mental problems, immediately viewed me as her best friend and confidante, as well as private chauffeur....

Without going into all the "gory" details, my life quickly went from bad to worse because living with Chuck's parents was worse than being incarcerated in some prison. With no money, no job and no support from Chuck, I was literally stuck in that "Catch-22" – and so I once again, albeit *very* reluctantly, opted to move in with my adoptive father.

There was a feeling of déjà vu as I picked up the phone to call Bill who, like before, he told me he would *love* to have me "back home"....

"Sis," he chuckled, "these days you can have your choice of me, or your mother and her new husband. She's over near Fort Leonard Wood married to some PFC named John Carter."

"I'd rather die than live with her," I said without hesitation.

A week later, not much happier, but relieved to be away from the Soap Opera in Pittsburgh, I was enrolled in a Business College in Springfield, Missouri, and had a job working as an evening cashier at a small department store. Daddy and I hardly ever saw each other, which suited me fine. I couldn't believe, that once again, I had been forced back into his world, and wondered if my destiny was to live with Bill forever!

* * * *

Just before my twenty-first birthday, I fell into a three-week "coma-like state" due to a misdiagnosed ruptured appendix. It seems no one could figure out what I had when Dad brought me in to the emergency room at Fort Leonard Wood on a Monday evening, even though I told every doctor who examined me that the onset of this excruciating pain originated with a "ripping" sensation in my abdomen. And so, I lay there, semi-delirious and in agonizing pain until Thursday afternoon, when the hospital commander finally decided to order exploratory surgery, despite the failure to get my sky-high temperature down. The last thing I remember before entering this "coma-like" state, was someone waking me to say I had had a ruptured appendix and should be "just fine now."

It was during these three weeks in a coma, that I had my first glimpse of God.

My strange adventure started with two "out-of-body" experiences (and, looking back, I truly believe that the first one served solely to remind me that the second one was real).

During the first experience, I remember "sitting up out of myself" and looking in confusion around the room. While I certainly felt like "me", I had no real attachment to my body which I noticed was "wired for sound" with tubes protruding from just about everywhere. That, in itself didn't bother me, and it didn't really faze me to know I was near death. What did bother me was that I felt heavy, chained and uncomfortable. My body was holding me hostage, and I wanted desperately to be free from it.

Looking around, I realized no one seemed to notice that I was awake and sitting up on my own; not even an orderly buffing the floor nearby bothered to look my way. And so, without giving it another thought, my "soul" took a flying leap toward the ceiling, and in the next instant, I was headed along Interstate 44 toward Springfield. Shortly thereafter, I was inside

Bill's house – wondering why on Earth I was bothering to visit him! – suspended in the corner of the ceiling above the tiny dining area, peering down on him and his girlfriend, Goldie. Their voices sounded hollow as though they were speaking into a barrel, and I could hardly make out what they were saying; but I was able to discern that Bill was discussing the possibility of selling his cows and starting a pig farm. This surprised me because he had told me in the past that pigs were a lot more trouble to take care of than cows, and that's why he only kept two at a time around.

While peering down at the couple, I was astounded to discover the lack of feelings I was encountering. Normally, I couldn't look at Daddy without feeling a modicum of disgust, but now I didn't feel much of anything; apparently my soul just needed to know he was okay. And as for Goldie, she was like a surrogate mother whom I had instantly liked from the moment I'd met her several years before, but in my present state, I didn't feel much of anything toward her, either. I didn't feel much about anything or anyone; rather, I felt more like an observer in this world, just basically passing through.

Believing I had accomplished my mission, I felt compelled to return to my ailing body back at Fort Leonard Wood. Although I didn't necessarily want to go back, I somehow knew I had to, and so when I arrived, I unhesitatingly sat down into myself as if taking a seat in a chair. It seemed a totally natural thing to do.

Sometime thereafter – several days later – I again found myself leaving my body behind. This time, I headed for outer space and floated around for what seemed like an eternity. Having no body, no arms, no legs, I was simply "consciousness" hanging out on a bed of swiftly moving air. What was I doing here? Where was I going? I don't know, but I felt I **had** to do it.

Although I couldn't see much, I distinctly heard sounds from somewhere below, on another plane; they were eerie sounds, comprised of a mixture of howling winds and human wailing. In my confusion, I was certain that, whatever I was hearing, I wanted no part of it.

Suddenly, to my great relief, in the darkness above me and off to the right, there materialized a silhouetted figure of a man dressed in white robes standing – or so it appeared – in front of the sun. However he happened to be there, I felt elated and literally willed myself to float in his direction. He was difficult to look upon because of the blinding bright light that spilled out from behind him, but the closer I got, the more I realized this man wasn't very good looking and I remember thinking he wouldn't be somebody I would ever want to date. He was rather Middle-Eastern in appearance, swarthy, with black, curly hair and a big nose. But he had the kindest eyes I'd ever seen. Regardless, he was another human being in this huge, strange void, and that's all I cared about at that moment.

"Please help me!" I called, somehow communicating via thought waves.

The man answered me, but his words were ripped from his lips by the awful howling winds that seemed to be growing in ferocity. The few words I did manage to catch sounded foreign and I wasn't able to comprehend what he was saying. But, nothing else mattered to me in that moment, except this one and only living being who, I hoped, would be able to pull me out of this strange and scary nothingness. I wondered why I couldn't simply will myself closer; after all, there was nothing in my way. Why was I stuck several yards below him in the middle of nowhere, an unwilling prisoner of some invisible force that kept me from getting too near?

Suddenly, the wind shifted and I was blown helplessly in the opposite direction! Horrified, I tried to will myself back, but it was no use; I was completely helpless. The man briefly reached out for me, and said something in a language I couldn't comprehend. His face reflected a mixture of anguish and sadness as I floated further away – and yet I got the distinct impression that he was *sending* me away! My eyes sought his as the chasm between us widened. Soon, there was nothing I could do except to watch him recede into the distance, a silent sentinel among the stars in the middle of the universe – a human silhouette bursting with bright lights and enormous energy.

Just before he completely disappeared from view, something inside me "clicked" and I recognized him! He was Jesus, that guy who was nailed to the cross for going around telling everybody he was the Son of God! I had heard of him through various "Bible thumpers" I'd met over the years and also from dear ol' "Dad" who proclaimed to be a Christian; but other than that, I had no clue as to the history behind the cross.

But here I was, beholding him with my own eyes! I couldn't believe it – he was really real!

Moments later, I bumped into something hard and unyielding. I winced as my head hit something sharp. In the pitch-black darkness of outer space and the confusion of the moment, I realized that I had a body once more – and it was clinging to what seemed to be the face of a cliff. My fingers found purchase on some sharp outcroppings and I let out a small cry. Beneath me, the shrieking, howling voices were growing louder and I knew I would be joining them if I allowed myself to let go. Beneath the terror of the moment, I couldn't help but wonder why Jesus wasn't willing to help me….

Suddenly and seemingly out of nowhere, from above a hand appeared. It was malformed, disfigured somehow, frozen into a cloven hoof, and I winced. "I'll save you," a disembodied voice told me.

Panicked yet relieved at the same time, I peered up at my unexpected rescuer through clouded and tear-filled eyes. I recoiled when I saw his face; it was wolflike, pitch-black like coal, and hairy – straight out of some horror story. His eyes shone red, while the twisted, sinister smile revealed teeth as white as snow. There was no doubt in my mind that I was staring straight into the face of Satan.

Below me, the wailing intensified. My mind whirled. What should I do? To stay here meant certain death, but if I took Satan's hand – where would I end up? Should I take the chance? In desperation, my eyes searched the horizon for Jesus, who was by now a tiny speck of light. **Why wasn't he helping me?**

Raw fear drove me to grab the hairy hand of Earth's mortal enemy. I had no other choice, if I wanted to live. Moments later, I realized I was back in my body....

"...Carmen?" someone yelled. "Carmen? Are you with us?"

I squeezed my eyes shut against the glaring, bright lights.

"Carmen, wake up!"

"What?" I mumbled stupidly. My tongue felt thick against the roof of my mouth.

"Are you with us, hon? Do you know where you are?"

Through the slits of my eyelids, I could see several people standing around my bed. Doctors, nurses, medics.….Memories came flooding back as I realized I was in the hospital.

"You've been in a coma," someone said. "But you're okay, now. You're awake. Your screaming and hollering gave us quite a scare!"

The lights were so bright; they made my eyes ache. "I saw Jesus," I whispered hoarsely as the confusion began to lift. "I saw Jesus.…" My world was quickly returning, and I didn't know whether to be glad or sad. On one hand, I wanted to return to that other plane to be near the Savior again, even if it meant doing nothing but groveling at his feet forever. On the other, I was glad to be back among the living.

For days afterward, I felt extremely close to God, praying constantly and without reservation, as if it were the most natural thing in the world. Until then, I had barely prayed privately, let alone publicly. But at that particular point in time, I didn't care who knew or saw. Whenever people passed by my bed and asked who I was talking to, I unashamedly replied, "God." For some reason, I had a connection with Him now, and it "felt right."

Of course, some people thought I had been affected by all the drugs that had been pumped into my body, but I was adamant that the experience had been real. This was actually confirmed later while talking with Dad's girlfriend, Goldie, who was astounded to learn that I knew about Bill's plan to sell his cows and starting a pig farm, for he had told no one else.…

Chuck showed up shortly after I came out of the coma. Since I was deathly ill, the Army had given him permission to return to the U.S. on emergency leave and he ended up staying for a couple of months before rejoining his unit in Vietnam. While I was learning how to walk again and generally trying to recuperate, my husband seized the opportunity, not to sit at my bedside for moral support, but to quickly make friends who could help to support his drug habit....

I felt ashamed and trapped in this farce of a marriage to a "junkie," but what could I do?

In the meantime, my health took a turn for the worse, and, as with the ruptured appendix, no one knew why. It all started with a severe pain in my mid-back that veered off to the left and around to the front, underneath my ribcage. Within a couple of days, any movement whatsoever resulted in excruciating pain and I could hardly get out of bed for my regular walks through the hallways. My fever spiked and the smell of food made me nauseous.

Making matters worse, I developed a severe allergy to Ampicillin. No one took me seriously when I complained of "itching in weird places" – behind my eyeballs, inside my tongue, between my toes – until someone injected another dose into my IV that caused my tongue to swell up and my throat to close. Thanks to my roommate, who immediately called a nurse, I'm still here today!

When my back pain, nausea and general condition worsened, my doctor decided to have some special X-rays taken; but all they revealed was that "something" was visible in my left lung. And so I was once again wheeled into the operating room where it was ultimately discovered that the generalized peritonitis I had suffered as a result of the ruptured appendix, had flared up in my pancreas....

After the operation, to everyone's surprise, my health immediately improved. My fever went down and my energy returned, and before long, I felt like my old self again. There was one small problem, however, and that is, the doctor made me aware that I was borderline anorexic because I cringed when he told me I needed to eat as much as I could in order to get past my present weight of eighty-seven pounds. I honestly thought that this illness had helped me get down to that "perfect size" – never mind that I looked like a concentration camp survivor who could count every rib!

Within a week or so, I was released to my husband who had rented an apartment near the Post on the doctor's orders, as I was to return to the hospital for daily checkups for one month. After that, the doctor said, I could return to Business College in Springfield, and Chuck was to return to Vietnam to finish his tour of duty.

Chapter 9

By this time, the reader is probably wondering if I ever had any happiness in my life. The answer is, of course, yes. There were times of happiness, but they were rare because "bad stuff" seemed to stalk me wherever I went. Some things I brought on myself because of certain dumb choices; others happened because I allowed myself to be influenced; and some things simply "happened" that were beyond my control. Such was the case in the events that happened after the doctor released me to move back to Springfield.

Living with Chuck outside of Fort Leonard Wood for a month before he returned to Vietnam to finish the three or four months he had left on his tour, had turned out to be a nightmare. He hadn't wasted any time finding other drug addicts, and our apartment quickly became their favorite hangout. Over my loud protests, Chuck spent nearly every evening getting "high" with his new buddies, and I found myself wondering how much longer I could put up with his criminal behavior. After all, my living with a drug addict and pusher made me an accessory – a fact that made me very uncomfortable.

That one month of personally witnessing Chuck shoot up Heroin and smoking Marijuana and bringing an endless parade of drug-addicted strangers into our home served to corroborate the huge mistake I had made by marrying him. There was no doubt I was paying the price for having made Chuck my "rebound" relationship designed to "get back" at David. I didn't even love Chuck! Initially, I had believed that he "needed me" to help him beat his drug habit, but that wasn't true. I was nothing more than a quick solution to his need for extra cash to support his drug habit....

Even so, after he returned to Vietnam, I was fully expecting my life to get back to "normal" in Springfield. In those days, after my most recent experience with my wayward husband, I often found myself daydreaming about being single again.

Little did I know in early 1973 that my dreams were about to come true – this time, because of a tragic twist of events that happened when I discovered Chuck had been kicked out of the Army for *murdering a fellow soldier.*

I was stunned when he called from the mental ward of the military hospital at Fort Dix, New Jersey.

"It was just a accident, babe," he whined. "We were both high and goofin' around with our M-16s, and mine went off. It was just one of those things."

The world around me seemed to slow down as I listened to him speak. "High on what?" I demanded as my anger rose.

"Heroin."

"Heroin…Well, that's just great, Chuck. I *knew* your stupid habit would get you into some real trouble one day! I told you!"

"Carmen, I said it was a *accident*!"

"'It was just a accident!'" I mimicked with all the sarcasm I could muster. When I first met Chuck I thought it was cute how he deliberately ignored grammar rules, but right now, I wanted him to know how stupid I thought he was. "Does that make you feel better to know it was 'just a accident'? Does it bring your dead friend back?"

"No, babe, but…."

"You know what, Chuck, you'd better be glad you're not within reach right now, because I'd love to slap the crud out of you! I've been trying to tell you all along how dangerous drugs are, but no – the great wise Chuck knows better!"

"But it was a *accident*…."

"**Shut up, moron**! You killed somebody, regardless as to how it happened!" I was absolutely livid. Never before in my life had I known anyone who had killed another human being, and the thought of being married to a murderer gave me chills.

The man I was married to was not only a drug addict, a liar, a user and an adulterer who kept getting busted down in rank because of his screw-ups, but he was also someone who, due to several accidents in which people had been seriously injured, was permanently forbidden to drive in the state of New Mexico. He was someone who cared more about getting his next "fix" than he did about providing a safe, secure and stress-free environment in which his sick wife could recuperate after nearly dying. And now he had *killed* another human being. This was too much....

While sitting there on my bed, listening to Chuck's explanation about the day he killed his friend it occurred to me that he wasn't in charge of his life; Satan was. His life was steadily heading downhill, going from bad to worse – and he and his demons were taking *me* down with them.

And so I decided right to get out of this predicament and begin to rethink my future. This was *not* the path I was meant to be on! This was a sign from God telling me I needed to get away from Chuck while I still had the chance because I would probably end up as his next victim.

* * * *

Even though I thoroughly hated Chuck after less than two years of marriage, the divorce still hurt, and I found myself very depressed. My greatest fear was that I was following in my mother's footsteps. Here I was, just twenty-one and already divorced. This surely wouldn't have happened if I had married David, the love of my life. I was so sad and lonely....

And, to make matters worse in my darkest hour (this couldn't have been scripted any better in Hollywood) Bill Forrester, rather than understanding and being supportive during my latest ordeal, didn't waste any time seizing the opportunity to let me know that, since I was to be unmarried shortly, he wanted "first dibs" on me. I was doing the dishes one Saturday afternoon when he casually sauntered up behind me and ran his hands up my shirt as a way of introducing me to his latest aspirations.

Outraged, I swung around and cried, "What are you doing? Get your hands off me!"

"You're back on the market and I want what's coming to me," he replied with a smug look. "I mean, I've taken you back into my house every time you're in a jam...."

My jaw dropped. "*What?*...Daddy, I thought we were long past that..."

"Past what? You know I love you and I've always wanted you. That's never changed."

I was livid. Bill had that certain look in his eyes that indicated he was going to "have me," one way or another, and I wanted to just sit down on the floor and cry. "*No!*" I said firmly. "I'm not going through this again!"

His eyes narrowed. "No? I think you'd better think again, little girl. Do you think I enjoy supporting your a--? If you want to continue living with me, and inherit this farm some day, you'd best start straightening up and becoming a little appreciative of your ol' Dad."

The mixture of fear and anger surging through my system made me feel faint; my body had not yet fully recuperated from the operations and I backed against the counter to steady myself. Gripped by an uncontrollable rage as old emotional scars were being opened within my soul, I reached into the dish rack and pulled out a paring knife to shove against his chest.

"*I hate you!*" I shouted angrily. "I will NOT be your sex slave again, and if you force me, I will kill you because I'm *sick and tired of this*!"

Bill didn't flinch. His lips twisted into a sneer as he eyed me with an air of cockiness: "Go ahead. Do it. I'll be dead and you'll be in jail. Is that how you want all this to end?"

Eyes welling up with hot tears of frustration, I slowly returned the knife to the dish rack and tried to think about what I should do or say next. I wanted more than anything to shove the paring knife hard into his gut, but I just couldn't bring myself to do it. Bill certainly was not worth going to prison over. And as ludicrous as it sounds, down deep, I felt a little sorry for him because in his screwed-up mind he honestly seemed to believe that love could be forced.

After some moments I emitted a long, shaky sigh and looked him straight in the eye. "You know what, Daddy," I said. "I can't do this anymore! You can take your desire for me and your wonderful farm and shove it where the sun don't shine, because as of this moment, I am through putting up with your crap. Have a nice life!"

And with that, I left him standing there by the sink while I went to my room and gathered whatever I was able to carry before walking out of his life for the very last time.

Chapter 10

Running, it seemed, had become a part of my life, and I was devastated to recognize that it had happened again. Not knowing where to go or what to do, I automatically headed towards Goldie's house for temporary refuge. When I told her what had happened, she was furious with Bill.

"I *knew* it!" she cried angrily. "I knew all along there was something about Sarge I didn't like."

"Goldie, I'm sorry," I said. "I never wanted you to find out...."

"Well, I'm glad I did, honey!" she replied. "Why, I'd love to castrate that son-of-a....well, never mind. You just stay with me as long as you want, until you can figure out what you want to do."

Knowing I had a temporary place to stay was a huge relief, but the problem was, I wasn't sure what to do next. Everything had happened so quickly that I hadn't really had time to process anything. All I knew was that I was now forced to make a quick decision, because at the age of twenty-one, I had no business being a burden on anyone, especially my father's girlfriend. Having no other choice at the time, I reluctantly remained with Goldie for a month while job hunting.

Although my goal at the time was to become a legal secretary, the "coma-like state" had impaired my mind to some extent, which resulted in a serious drop in my grade average. Luckily, at that time, I had earned enough credits at Mid-America Business College to graduate with a "Medical Secretarial Diploma." It would have to do, temporarily, until I was able to get back on my feet and figure out what to do.

Ironically, "fate" stepped in to thwart my plans once again. It came about when I happened to walk into the Army recruiting office to apply for their vacant secretarial position, and the sergeant at the front desk convinced me I would be better off going back into the service. He assured me that, since I had only been out of the Army for fourteen months, I would qualify to have my old rank back, and would be sent to the duty station of my choice.

The next thing I knew, I was back at Fort McClellan, taking three weeks of refresher training before leaving for Heidelberg, Germany, where I was to become a Magnetic Tape Selectric Typewriter and Composer Systems Operator (the precursor to modern Word Processing) at Headquarters, United States Army, Europe and Seventh Army....

* * * *

I could hardly believe I was back in my beloved homeland! It was the first time back in Germany since that awful day, many years ago, when I had been ripped from the arms of my foster mother, and so, naturally, one of the first things I did – as promised – was to jump on a train for a three-day weekend to visit her in Wietze, some 230 miles from Heidelberg.

Memories *came in waves* as the cab drove the eight or ten miles from the train station in Celle through the tree-lined Steinfoerder Strasse into my beloved Wietze. On the outskirts of town, we passed the "Villa Steinförde," the local "mansion" Mama and I had often viewed from a respectable distance, wondering how it felt to live in such grandeur and style. Moments later, off to the left I noticed that a densely populated new housing area occupied the place where once stood the old *Kolonie* apartment complex where we used to draw our drinking and bath water from a public pump.

By the time the cab reached the Wietze Bridge, I was fighting back tears, and I nearly lost all control when my old elementary school building came into view. How many friends had I been forced to leave behind, and did they ever know what had happened to me? And, where were they all now, and would I recognize them if we were to meet on the street?

Somehow, I made it through the next few minutes or so that it took the taxi to wind its way through my tiny hometown. My heart pounded in anticipation as we neared Mama's house – an ancient, dilapidated shack nestled in a grove of pine and birch trees just a short and bumpy jaunt from Wietze's main street. I had hoped that her lot in life had improved over the years; but I took a deep breath because obviously it had not.

A large, black dog tied to a stake barked furiously as the taxi rolled to a halt in front of a tall, wooden gate, and I noticed an old, haggard-looking woman peering tentatively from the door of the shack. It took me a few seconds to recognize her – my beloved foster mother – changed into an old lady after just thirteen years! Had she really been that old when she was raising me? It didn't matter - after all these years I was finally being reunited with the woman to whom I owed my sanity!

Mama let out a shriek when she realized it was me, and moments later, she was tearing through the dusty yard on short and pudgy legs. "Carmi!" she cried. *"Meine kleine Carmi!"* Seconds later, I was in her arms, sobbing tears of joy. An eternity passed before we were able to let go; finally, we just stood there staring at each other in awe. "You shrank!" I said with a nervous chuckle.

"No," she cried, swiping at a tear, "you *grew*! You're all grown up now, look at you! And you're so pretty!"

In her late sixties now, graying and wearing a dress that had seen better days, Mama appeared much older than I had remembered her. Her long faded strawberry-blond hair had been cropped into a short, frizzy 'do, but the alert olive-yellow eyes still sparkled with pure love for me. Neither of us had believed that we would ever see each other again, and this reunion was nothing if not a fairy tale come true.

The spell was broken when a gaunt, mustachioed wisp of man dressed in ragged, grimy brown slacks appeared. After a brief introduction I discovered that he was Mama's live-in friend, Jürgen, who – I soon found out – was a major know-it-all and non-stop talker who thought the sun rose and set on himself. Jürgen dominated the conversation on the way back to the house and the entire time we were having coffee and Strudel in the tiny, gray kitchen, shortly after my arrival. In between bites when he took an occasional breather, he and Mama enjoyed long drags from their cigarettes, while I did my best not to choke on the cloying blue haze that hung in the air and burned my nose, eyes and throat. I couldn't help but notice Mama's long, dirty, almost calcified fingernails that were stained from years of chain smoking and wondered what had caused her to take up that nasty habit, because she hadn't smoked during the years I enjoyed with her in my youth.

I balked at the filth all around me: Dirty cups, plates and silverware from a previous meal still occupied the table, while more dirty dishes were soaking atop an old kitchen cabinet in wash bowls filled to the brim with dark, muddy water. The sagging wood floors were covered with several layers of uneven, well-worn linoleum strips that were in dire need of sweeping, while entire cities of cobwebs blossomed along the ceilings of the prehistoric structure that Mama and Jürgen called home.

It didn't take long for everything to come back to me – the squalor, the old "stuff", the hand-me-downs, the Spartan lifestyle. Until then, I had long forgotten about the conditions in which I had been raised, and it finally dawned on me why the townspeople had made fun of us and accused us of being dirty. As much as I hated to admit it, it was a good thing that I had been removed from the Neumann household, because who knows how my life would have ended up....

Talkative Jürgen, I quickly realized as the day wore on, was "not quite right" in the head – *ein bisschen bekloppt*, as one would say in my native German. As he prattled on, I soon discovered he had been turned off toward sex in his early twenties when he had caught his girlfriend with another man, and ended up celibate and lonely until he met Elfriede at some card game. There was an instant "spark" between them, he said, that drew them together into a kind of mother-son relationship, which resulted in their eventual non-sexual co-habitation. Consequently, both their needs were met, and they made a life together despite the wagging tongues of the town gossips. Like my Papa, Jürgen was not one to keep a steady job, either. He seemed quite content to live off Mama's meager widow's pension, spending most of his waking hours knitting or crocheting pillow covers. His myriad multi-colored crocheted roses graced every room of the house and did their best to brighten the gray and dingy backdrop of this couple's drab existence....

That night, when they showed me the spare bed next to the kitchen, I prayed the spiders would keep their distance while I slept. There was no doubt I would have been better off to find a hotel room, but it was too late.

Over the next couple of days, we attempted to find some of my old school friends of mine – especially my favorite friends Reni, Annette and Wera, but it seemed everyone I remembered had apparently moved on to bigger and better things and were nowhere to be found. And so we visited some of Mama's old friends and neighbors and I ended up having to repeat over and over again the story of the day Lonny and her American husband stole me from the Neumanns.

Aside from dealing with the ordeal of the filthy surroundings, the visit was absolutely magical. Somehow, it brought me closure along with the realization that I was glad my natural parents had given me to Mama to raise during my formative years, but it was not necessarily a bad thing that I had been taken from her and Papa....

Rags to Rabbi

Chapter 11

The years 1973 to 1976 were some of the best years of my life, at least career-wise. Life in Heidelberg was wonderful. Not only did being stationed in Germany offer many terrific travel opportunities, which included some memorable trips to England, France, Spain and Greece, but I was also in love with my career. My superiors seemed very happy with me and at one point, I was given "hard" sergeant stripes and put in charge of Classified Copy Preparation for the Adjutant General's Office. Just as in New Mexico, my superiors at Headquarters USAREUR were happy with my work, and did everything in their power to help me learn and grow and generally "climb the ladder of success."

At one point, someone from Military Personnel in Washington, D.C. contacted me to ask if I would be interested in trying out for a German translator position with the U.S. Embassy in Munich. I was interviewed, accepted for the position – and then promptly turned down because someone at Military Personnel realized I wasn't trained by the Defense Language Institute at the Presidio of Monterey, California. Never mind that I spoke better German than someone with just twenty-eight weeks of language training....

But this incident served to show me that women were continuously being afforded more opportunities in the military and I tried several times – unsuccessfully – to change my career field to something more interesting, such as the fields of psychiatry or veterinary medicine. While I loved my present job as Composer Systems Operator, there seemed to be something missing…the excitement of actually making a difference in the lives of others. Somehow, sitting at a desk typing Army regulations and the like seemed like "just a job" to me.

During this time, I had another driving desire, which was to find my natural father, Franz Klekawka, the man whose name was on my birth certificate.

After ferreting out his address, I sent a brief letter of introduction assuring him that I wanted nothing more than to establish contact in hopes of getting to know my father's side of the family. The anticipation of a reply from my "real" father dominated every waking moment; I was the first person in line at the mailroom every day as I waited, wondering what he would say to me. Visions of how the initial meeting would take place danced in my mind: I would be getting off the train in Dortmund and be warmly greeted by Franz and his wife and any existing half-siblings who would be holding bouquets of flowers, and anxiously waiting to smother me with hugs and kisses and proclamations of regret over our lost years together….

But that was not to be. The reply I received from Franz a couple weeks later was not what I expected at all. As it turned out, Franz told me I was the last person he ever expected to hear from because, not only did he *not* desire to claim me as his daughter, but my letter "opened an old ulcer" he had acquired in World War II which made him so sick that he had to wait several days before he could force himself to formulate a response. His letter – which included a carbon copy of their messy divorce, complete with the testimonies of a couple of men who had witnessed my mother selling her body while she was "very pregnant" – consisted of *six pages* of painful memories about my mother, the "drunken prostitute" who had cheated on him and caused him to be humiliated in the entire town of Wietze; six pages that outlined their brief lives together which, thankfully, came to an abrupt halt when he met his present wife who helped him through the grief and misery of those days. I couldn't possibly be his biological child, he wrote, because my mother had her period the day he left, and this is why I was never, ever to contact him again. End of story.

Franz's letter literally knocked the breath of out me. To say I was devastated would be an understatement because I might as well have been slapped – no, kicked in the head by a horse or hit by a car. The knowledge that my father had unceremoniously rejected me hurt me deeply to the roots of my very soul!

Like a moth drawn to a flame, over the next few days I kept re-reading his words, holding them in my hands, touching his presence while my emotions rose and ebbed. I truly didn't know how to feel, until one day when I came to the conclusion that I simply didn't care. If this was truly how Franz felt, then, as far as I was concerned, he could go to hell. I had a life to live and, rather than to sit around lamenting what might have been, I needed to look toward the future and make sure that I would *never* bring unwanted children into this world. As a matter of fact, his rejection of me revealed, in no uncertain terms that this world was just too awful to bring children into, period. Men only wanted women for sex and, whenever babies were involved, they ran like scared rabbits.

No, I would never have children. I would never impose this world or my broken, dysfunctional self on an innocent child. **Never.**

While I was still "licking my wounds" from Franz's letter, out of the blue came another shocker: A letter from Bill Forrester, stating that he and my mother had re-married! He said they had sold the farm and they and my two brothers were living in a doublewide trailer on some adjacent wooded, recently acquired property. "We happened to run into each other," he wrote. "When our eyes met, we knew we should never have divorced and decided we were meant to be together forever."

I felt like screaming! Bill and Lonny together again, after everything they had put us kids through? The endless fights, the constant arguing, the put-downs of us kids and of each other, the awful physical and mental abuse they had inflicted on Teddy and me...I was furious as the memories came crashing back, beating me with left and right hooks as though I were in a boxing ring. After all that had transpired, they were together again – and in a *trailer?* Did they really think I was going to be elated over this bit of news?

The moment I got home from work that evening, I sat down and wrote the "happy couple" a searing letter filled with all the venom I could muster, telling them exactly what they could do with their happiness. My final words to Bill and Lonny Forrester were:

"YOU TWO ARE DEAD TO ME, SO DON'T YOU DARE EVER CONTACT ME AGAIN!!!!"

* * * *

While my career kept soaring, my personal life continued to remain in chaos – partially, because I kept making ignorant mistakes and decisions when it came to men. Try as I might to find "Mr. Right" I always ended up in one abusive relationship after the next. I simply had some innate and weird attraction to "bad boys" that I couldn't seem to shake.

Once, in the spring of 1974, I was even brutally sodomized by a doctor I briefly dated, a British citizen who worked at the military hospital in Heidelberg as a gynecologist. I was thrilled to be dating a doctor; someone I hoped would become my next husband – until a couple weeks later when I realized he had a drinking problem and some kind of a weird hang-up about his mother. Everything I did reminded him of his mother, and one evening after we returned to my place after doing some bar-hopping in the Heidelberg area, something I said apparently triggered the rage inside him, and before I knew it, he was on top of me, screaming, "If you are going to act like a man, I'm going to treat you like one!"

Too embarrassed to turn him in to the authorities afterwards, I attempted to deal with it on my own – which turned out to be a huge mistake because in the days after the rape, I came dangerously close to committing suicide. Life was just too much to handle, and after downing an entire bottle of Boones Farm wine, I tried to cut my wrists. Fortunately, I passed out on the floor before I was able to do too much damage.

The incident with Dr. Quinn, on top of everything else that had ever happened in my life, took a huge emotional toll on me, and it was the direct cause of my becoming hooked on Valiums.

At an all-time low one night, I happened to be sitting in the "Nine High" Enlisted Club, perched alone at a corner table, drinking and feeling sorry for myself and whiling away the time until I was to report for midnight duty in the War Room at Campbell Barracks. My life, I felt, couldn't get any worse. After all the men I had known and dated in my twenty-three years on Earth, I still had no one to love me, no one to hold me, no one to share my joys or sorrows.

I remember sitting there regretting that my suicide attempt had been a bust, when suddenly a young man ambled up and began to engage me in conversation.

Although I cannot recall his name nor remember what he looked like, I do remember being grateful for the company. For some reason, I immediately felt very comfortable around him and before long, partly because the Valiums and alcohol had loosened my tongue, I ended up unloading all my woes and sorrows to this perfect stranger.

Talking about the "stuff" in my life seemed very cathartic and, once started, I had a hard time stopping. By the end of the evening, I had told him about how my alcoholic mother had given me away and then stolen me back from my foster parents; I told him of the mental abuse she had perpetrated upon me over the years and how she had unwittingly forced me into a life of sexual abuse at the hands of Bill Forrester. I told him about the poisonous rage I felt toward both of them and how hard it was to deal with the memories of the horror they had put me through. I told him about how badly it hurt to have my natural father reject me. I told him about my own stormy marriage and divorce, and I even told him about – without giving specifics about who had recently raped me – some really bad and stupid mistakes I had made over the last year, especially when it came to men....

To my surprise, this stranger didn't judge me. In fact, he seemed to take in my every word, and I remember feeling so very safe with him, totally relaxed and free.

Somewhere around midnight, when I mentioned that I needed to leave so I could report for duty at the War Room, this stranger walked me the two blocks to my apartment so I could change into my uniform. Instead of calling a cab, he insisted we walk to Campbell Barracks so I could sober up, as reporting to work inebriated would only get me into trouble. While flattered by all the attention, I was also ashamed of myself because, if he and I were to become a couple, this is not how I wanted him to remember our first meeting – partly because it was too reminiscent of how my mother always met men....

At the entrance to the building that contained the "War Room" where I was to spend the night sorting "TWX's" (the forerunner to faxes), I remember how he gently looked into my eyes and took my hands in his. At first, I thought he was going to kiss me, but instead – to my utter surprise – he quietly started talking about my character flaws!

The words that dropped from his lips that evening beneath a starry summer sky to this day reverberate in my memory because they penetrated the fog in my mind and served to both anger and shock me into a stinging reality.

"Carmen," he said softly, "you're a wonderful and sweet lady who's had a very hard life. But I feel the need to tell you that you have to start letting go of that baggage because it's keeping you from being all you can be."

I was dazed, not to mention, slightly peeved! "Excuse me?" I said. "I AM all I can be! I have a very successful career, and...."

"No – please listen to me! Judging from the things you told me tonight, it's clear you are a confused person. It seems to me, all your decisions are based either on outright rebellion against your parents, or on what you think they would want you to do."

Mouth agape, I listened in horror as his words pounded their way into my consciousness. "Wha...What?....What do you mean? My parents don't rule my life!"

"Yes, they do," he went on, "You're a nice girl but you deserve better than this. You should really consider some psychiatric help because you have a whole lot of issues."

"No, I...."

"You need to concentrate on figuring out who you are and what you want out of life. You don't need to be hanging out in the clubs, picking up guys. You're too classy for that."

My mind reeled as his words, one by one, began to connect with my soul. Slowly, painfully, they hit home, and I blinked stupidly, like someone who had just been punched in the stomach. He might as well have come out accused me of being a whore, just like my mother!

Angry tears welled up as I stood there wanting nothing more than to slap him – but I refrained because some dark, hidden part of me knew he was right. And so, without saying another word, I tore myself loose from his grasp, turned on my heel, and disappeared into the building.

* * * *

My night in the War Room felt like hell on Earth, ruined by another guy who had fooled me into thinking he cared about me. I remember being glad that my duties consisted of mere menial tasks, because my mind was completely preoccupied. I was angry with myself, mainly for having gotten into the habit of sitting in the Nine High every evening, dreaming that some man would come into my life and whisk me off into that ever-elusive sunset where happiness and contentment abounded.

As the Valiums and alcohol began to wear off, and I sat there, suffering from a bad hangover, it dawned on me that I couldn't even remember the guy's name! I had spilled my guts to a total stranger whose name I couldn't remember. I could hardly remember what he looked like! How much lower could I sink?

But, the thing was, as much as I hated to admit it, Mr. Nameless had been right: I *was* often making decisions based on rebellion against my parents, and my personal life *was* in shambles, and I *had* been following in my mother's footsteps...And, unless I made some major changes, I was destined to end up just like her. There truly was no reason for me to hang out in the Club night after night. I always hated that my mother did it, and here I was, doing the same thing. Surely, there had to be a better way for me to occupy my free time....

By the time eight a.m. rolled around, despite a pounding headache, I decided that Mr. Nameless had been some kind of a guardian angel sent to point me in a better direction. Surely, this had been some kind of a strong message from God, and I would be a fool to waste it.

When I returned home that morning, the first thing I did was to flush my supply of Valiums down the toilet. And later that day, I took a cab to the Education Center to sign up for some night courses with the University of Maryland.

I waited for weeks, hoping to bump into Mr. Nameless again somewhere, but it never happened. To my knowledge, I never saw him again.

Rags to Rabbi

Chapter 12

My tour in Heidelberg ended in early 1976 when I reenlisted and headed for the Presidio of San Francisco in California. Six months before I left, I fell in love for the second time in my life; but in the end, it wasn't meant to be. The boy's name was DaCosta, someone I met in one of my evening college classes. The son of a retired U.S. Army soldier and a German lady, he was handsome, sweet and ambitious and, unfortunately, six years younger than me. By the time I was preparing to return to the U.S., I was convinced that our relationship would keep him from exploring his options, both in the career and personal departments. He was young and innocent; I was already a divorcee, a "woman of the world." It wasn't fair to him.

Letting go of DaCosta was one of the hardest things I have ever done but, to me, the age difference was simply too great. He was still innocent, whereas I, at the ripe old age of twenty-five, was a "woman of the world" who had already been married and divorced once. Plus, his mother didn't like me very much which was sure to present a huge obstacle some day.

And so, when the Army moved me to California, I viewed it as a brand new start; a pristine chapter in my life that was to help me with my goal of "becoming somebody."

The San Francisco area was just beautiful and I thought I had died and gone to heaven! Outside of my military duties, there was plenty of sightseeing, excursions to local wineries, Sausalito, Fisherman's Wharf, San Francisco Bay, the Golden Gate Bridge, the Oakland Bay Bridge – an endless profusion of things to do, see, and eat.

During the first year there, I worked as an administrator for the Post Adjutant, but was later promoted to Staff Sergeant and moved to a more exciting position as Non-Commissioned Officer (NCO) in charge of the Survivor Assistance Office, which assured the payment of death benefits to survivors of active duty and retired military people in northern California and the state of Nevada. Oddly, there were times when I wished that Bill and my mother were there to see first-hand that I was successful in my career because deep down, I still harbored a secret yearning for my family to be proud of me. Of course, that would never happen, now that I had expelled them from my life forever.

As usual, here in California – like everywhere else I had ever been stationed, I continued to excel in my career, but my personal life remained in an endless state of turmoil. Nothing seemed to help me "snap out of" the years of upbringing that had convinced me I was ugly, stupid, and a perpetual disappointment to my parents who were products of their own dysfunctional backgrounds. Over the years, I began to realize that I was a prisoner of my past because, wherever I went, whomever I dated, whatever I did, it always boiled down to, *would Dad approve of this man/place/situation?* It was truly maddening.

I tried everything I could think of to basically "heal myself" including taking every psychology class I could possible fit into my schedule at San Francisco State University. Naturally, it didn't work, but taking evening courses helped keep me out of the NCO clubs....

Without going into a lot of detail about my life in San Francisco, suffice it to say, that part of the country is full of some very strange and unusual people – and I believe I met the crème de la crème of eccentricity.

One couple that comes to mind was Paul and Nancy whom I met in a restaurant/nightclub in Sausalito, one Saturday evening in 1977. On that particular evening, the place was more crowded than usual, and sitting alone at my table, I suddenly felt a tap on my shoulder from a man who wanted to know if he and his wife could join me, as my table seemed to be the only one left with any empty chairs. The couple seemed extremely mismatched. He was short, bald, and pudgy, while she – quite beautiful in her micro-miniskirt, stiletto heels, and gorgeous long, brown hair kept in check by an expensive Indian headband. She was very tall and statuesque, and appeared to have stepped out of the centerfold of a Playboy magazine. As the evening wore on, I discovered I liked this obviously well-to-do, exceedingly eccentric couple and, by the time we parted company (me in my GMC Pacer, and they in one of their two Rolls Royces) we had become fast and seemingly inseparable friends.

Before long, I was treated like a family member, spending my weekends at their penthouse or partying on their yacht. I went everywhere with them including some private parties in upscale neighborhoods. Paul even introduced me to some of his rich friends, but I found them all too old, too pompous, or too boring; none of them was "my type" even though Paul insisted that "type" should nothing to do with it, as long as they were "rolling in the dough."

All in all, for a few months, life was great, and I figured that through my new friends, I would surely meet "Mr. Right" one day – someone who was not only successful, but also handsome and charming, and who would love me unconditionally.

But it wasn't long before I discovered that certain rich people in San Francisco did some very strange things to entertain themselves. Without going into the gory details, it turned out that Paul, who was an extremely overbearing and domineering person, forced his wife to participate in all manner of illicit and immoral sexual activities at the popular and numerous Bay Area "swinging parties" that abounded in those days – and, of course, he felt I should "loosen up" and join in, as well. Unfortunately for him, he didn't know with whom he was dealing, and I didn't hesitate to set him straight!

Nancy confided in me once while Paul was a way on a business trip that she was extremely unhappy and wanted desperately to get away from him. She said she had run away from home plenty of times, but he always managed to find her. It was at that point I realized that money wasn't everything because it truly couldn't "buy happiness."

Nonetheless, Paul, who liked to dominate anyone who got close to him, didn't give up easily once he set his mind on something, and he managed to trick me into attending a "swinging party" one warm summer evening – and in the process, he unwittingly triggered another one of my strange, supernatural "visions"....

It happened while Paul, Nancy, and I were sitting on the floor of the living room of a party host, partaking of the plentiful Smorgasbord food that had been catered in for the occasion. I was under the impression that we were at just another regular party thrown by one of Paul's rich friends. One minute we were talking and joking and enjoying the throngs of people who were milling about, and in the next, Paul – with an impish grin – pointed toward a far door that I thought would lead to the garage, and suggested I check out what was happening there.

Having no clue as to what I was supposed to be looking for, but agreeing to humor him, I emitted an exaggerated sigh and rolled my eyes as I got up to cross the room. Paul was like that; he often liked to get silly and frivolous, and on those occasions, he expected people to unquestioningly play along.

At first glace, the room seemed pitch dark, but once my eyes adjusted I winced and did the proverbial "double-take." The place was obviously once a three- or four-car garage that had been converted into a huge adult playroom, as there, in the darkness before me, to my great and utter horror, were undulating piles of sweating humanity performing every pornographic fantasy imaginable. Repulsed at first, yet mesmerized, as if examining some bug under a microscope, I couldn't force myself to look away. For several seconds I was absolutely riveted by a scene that can only be described as a set straight out a horror movie featuring satanic rituals.

What jerked me back to reality was an unexpected, ear-piercing shout in my right ear:

"OH, GOD DOESN'T LIKE THIS!"

Startled, yet also realizing I was "feeling outside of myself" again, I turned around, but there was no one there! I was standing with my right shoulder next to a wall, and so it would have been impossible for anyone to yell into that particular ear. The fact was, there was no one in my immediate vicinity at all!

Feeling a little spooked, I scanned the area to determine whether or not I might have overheard part of someone's conversation; but the room was filled with a noise consisting of music, giggles, laughter, and random animated conversations, none of which I was able to discern. Out of the corner of my eye, I saw Paul watching me from across the room, and when he realized I was looking at him, he waved and gave me a "thumbs-up" sign.

Amidst the undiluted confusion in my mind, I wondered why I should care that "God didn't like this." The last time I had had any dealings with God was during my coma back in Missouri, several years before. As far as I could tell, God never cared about the activities in my life at all.

Regardless, that episode brought that particular evening and my friendship with Paul and Nancy to an abrupt halt. Although I tried to maintain a friendship with Nancy for a while because I felt sorry for her, things were never the same between us after that.

Admittedly, that eerie voice and the entire experience haunted me for years afterward. It had been completely unlike all my other weird ESP-like experiences, yet I couldn't help but feel that God had somehow "touched" me that night to keep me from making a huge mistake. Moreover, it proved to me that there were, indeed, behind-the-scenes things going on in the spirit realm that the ordinary human wasn't aware of – and I was completely unsure as to what I was supposed to do about it.

After that incident, in my quest to find "Mr. Right" within my military family where I thought I would be safer, I ended up dating a lieutenant who worked in the Survivor Assistance Office. Although he wasn't necessarily my type, he was tall, blond, and "kinda cute" and when he asked me to dinner, I jumped at the chance.

The ensuing excitement, however, was short-lived because, little did I know that my "military family" contained some eccentric characters, too, and wasn't necessarily a safe haven in a place like San Francisco. As it turned out, my date, Lance, a low-key Army officer, turned out to be a Satanist, a high priest of some kind....

Lance and I decided to go out one Friday evening and since he lived in "The City" and I lived fifteen miles down the road in Marin County, I brought my civilian clothes to work so that I could change into them later, at his place.

From the moment I stepped through the door of his efficiency apartment, I felt "something" wasn't right. There was an odd chill as he gave me a brief tour – an "icky" feeling that came, in part, from the strange paintings that graced his living room walls. Although Lance named the characters preserved in the paintings, my nerves were too much on edge and I failed to hear what he was saying. I felt positively uneasy among the terrible mythical, ugly underworld creatures, one of whom seemed to follow my every move with its eyes.

I didn't fully realize what these characters represented until Lance returned from his shower, dressed in a long, red robe with the word MASTER stitched in large black lettering across the back. Unable to help myself, I snorted a laugh and mumbled something about macho arrogance being out of style – until I saw Lance's demeanor change.

"This isn't some joke, Carmen," he said calmly and with an air of superiority that made me want to laugh. "I am the high priest of our local coven. More to the point, I am a Satanist. I am married to seven women, and I *am* their master in every respect. I don't think that's anything to scoff at and I'll thank you to respect my position…."

Not knowing anything about Satanists, I was afraid that if I acted too shocked, or simply ran from apartment, he might put some kind of a spell on me. And so I pulled my lips into a smile and said something to the effect of, "Wow! I…had no clue this stuff really exists…."

Before the unusual, very awkward evening ended, I concluded that I had enough problems without deliberately inviting Satan in, and so I managed to excuse myself at a reasonable hour to go home. Luckily, Lance must have felt that we weren't compatible either, because he never asked me out again.

* * * *

One more important incident happened while I was stationed in San Francisco – my mother died in March 1977 at the age of forty-five.

I knew she had died before anyone told me, thanks to another one of my weird "visions" the night of her death; and so, when I walked into the office that morning and heard the phone ring, I "knew" it was my brother Teddy, calling to tell me she had passed away....

Although I thought I was prepared for the news, I broke down in a puddle of tears when I heard Teddy's voice on the phone. The reasons for my reaction were manifold because the events leading up to her death were "typical Lonny" designed to be "all about her" no matter who she hurt in the process.

It all started with a phone call from my company's First Sergeant in January 1977 following a week in Missouri where I had spent the Christmas holidays with Goldie, whom I had been referring to for years as "Mom."

The First Sergeant, not knowing my family history, called to say, "Hey, Carmen, didn't you just visit your mother in Missouri?"

"Yes" I replied, perplexed. "Why?"

"Well, then I guess you know she's dying, right?"

I was stunned. "What do you mean she's dying? She was fine when I left her!"

There was momentary silence on the line, and then, "Oh. Well...isn't your mother's name Lonny Forrester?"

It took a second for it to dawn on me that he wasn't talking about Goldie. "Oh, yeah," I finally responded. "Lonny's my *natura*l mother...."

"...Ooops! Sorry....I, uh, have a message that you're to call her."

"What's she dying of? She's only 45."

"Cancer, I think that's what she said."

"Oh, okay. Thanks...."

My first reaction was to pretend I didn't care, but suddenly I was overcome by a strange, unsettling emotion: As much as I thought I hated Lonny, she was still my mother. It was because of her, I was in this world. Somehow, the past didn't really matter right now; all the awful things that had transpired between us were irrelevant in the grand scheme of things.

Unable to grasp the well of emotions surging through my mind, I was stunned to discover that I was filled with an almost painful *love* for her. The fact was, although I didn't like her very much, I didn't want her to die! She was my *mother*....

Before I had a chance to wonder what was going on, I quickly headed outside to the telephone booth and dialed the number that the First Sergeant had given me.

"Mommie?" I said warmly. "I heard you called."

"Well, hello stranger! Yes, I called. I guess you heard I'm dying."

My throat filled with hot tears and I found myself struggling to speak. "My First Sergeant told me." I said. "What's wrong?"

"Colon cancer. The doctor said I have about six months left."

I swallowed hard. "Isn't that the same thing your mother died of?"

"Yeah. All the women on our side of the family die of colon cancer. But now there's a cure, and that's really why I'm calling you. I need nine hundred dollars so I can go to Mexico for Laetrile treatments. The Americans won't bother because they'd rather see us die than to spend the money on REAL cures that are already available. But the Mexicans are curing people with Laetrile and I want to go there."

My mind was stuck in neutral and I didn't hear much after her remark: *"That's really why I'm calling you."* In other words, she didn't want me; she just wanted my money. My heart sank as I tried to squelch the growing pain my gut. As if from a great distance, I heard myself say, "Why doesn't Dad send you to Mexico? Didn't you guys sell the farm a couple years ago?"

"We're divorced. I left that bastard over a year ago and now am living in Osage Beach again."

I rolled my eyes. "I should have guessed," I said flatly. "Well, how about Ollie, then? Do you ever hear from him?"

"Hell, no! And I don't ever want to, either! I don't have **anybody**; that's why I'm calling you."

"Well, can Ted help, too? Doesn't he have a job these days? Last I heard, he was enlisting in the Army."

"He's just a PFC and doesn't have any money. Plus, he just got a compassionate reassignment from Germany to Fort Leonard Wood because of my condition, and he comes down here as much as he can to take care of me and Lonnie."

Lonnie! My little brother. My heart ached for him as I stood there in the cool January morning, having a conversation with my mother – someone I thought I would never hear from again. It saddened me to think that little Lonnie and I had never had a real rapport. I was just somebody he knew as "Sissy." And now his mother was dying....

An awkward silence ensued as I tried to figure out what to say. "Unfortunately, I don't have nine hundred dollars, Mother," I finally managed. "I only make seven hundred per month, and most of that goes to pay for my rent, car payment and gas. I don't even have a savings account."

"Well, so?" she snapped icily. "Borrow it from the bank! You can do that, can't you?"

"….I can try. But the thing is, I just borrowed some money a couple weeks ago so I could fly to Missouri for the holidays, and I'm not sure how much more I'll be able to borrow."

"You were here in Missouri over the holidays?"

"Yeah, I, I uh…spent Christmas with Goldie."

"Who the hell is Goldie?"

"Dad's ex-girlfriend…She's been like a surrogate mother to me for the last few years."

A profound silence hung between us for some moments before she said, "A mother? Hmmm. Well, then, I guess I know where I stand!"

"Mom," I replied, knowing full well that logic wouldn't work on her, "you and I haven't had a relationship for years. Goldie and I ended up being close after I left Dad…."

"That's beside the point. "*I'm* your mother, and the least you could have done was to drop by and see me!"

The love I had experienced a few minutes before was all but gone, replaced by the old familiar feelings of resentment and anger. Reality was quickly returning. I raised my eyes towards the heavens and sighed as it dawned on me that her German accent was beginning to grate on me again. "I don't know what to tell you,"

I finally said. "If I had known you were sick, I would have made every effort to stop by and see you."

There was a small pause before she said, "Okay, well then, just see what you can do, and then call me tonight and give me your home phone number and whatnot. I really would like to see you some time."

Feeling heavy and despondent by the time we hung up, I reluctantly did as requested and hiked over to the Wells Fargo Bank to see what kind of a personal loan I could get. The bottom line was: Nothing!

Lonny was disappointed and angry that evening when I called to tell her the news, even though I had spent most of the day trying to find ways to get the money for her. "You're just not trying hard enough, Carmen," she cried. "I knew I couldn't count on you! Why don't you just come out and say you don't WANT to help me!"

"Mother," I said, "I *did* try! I even called around to various charities and the American Cancer Society…"

"I'm not going to be used as a guinea pig by the g—d—m American Cancer Society!"

"But, at least you wouldn't have to pay them anything.…"

"Are you going to help me out, or not?"

"I'm trying, but I don't know what else to do, Mom. I don't have any money.…"

Click.

Furious when she hung up on me, I immediately re-dialed her number, but when she answered, I got no further than, "Mom…" before she unceremoniously hung up on me again.

And that was my last contact with my dying mother. Every time I attempted to call after that, she hung up on me.

Just two months later, the night after I had my "vision" about Lonny's death, Ted informed me that our nine-year-old brother, Lonnie, had discovered her lying dead in her bed that morning in March 1977. He said that there would be no services nor any need for me to come home as he was, per her wishes, having her cremated and then planned to spread the ashes across the Lake of the Ozarks.

Ted said our brother Lonnie would be going to live with his father, Oliver, and that he and Lonnie would divide her belongings and then get on with their lives.

Chapter 13

My mother's death absolutely brought me to my knees and I cried for months afterward. Before then I never realized how much she meant to me. All I could think was: My mother is dead….My mother's gone…My mother, my mother….

I felt as though part of my body was missing. My mother – who had been through hell on Earth due to the actions of her own mother who had ruined her life by turning her into a young prostitute – was forever gone. Why hadn't I been nicer, more understanding towards her? What kind of a monster was I?

For some reason, instead of the negative, all I could remember was the positive, the times where she *had* been good to us kids and made an effort to participate in our lives. Granted, for me, they were few and far in between, but they had still existed and I felt bad because I hadn't tried hard enough to understand her. I could have been more patient and understanding, but I didn't even try, and so much of this was my own fault.

I wanted more than anything to have another chance to have a face-to-face "sit-down" with my mother so we could finally straighten some things out, but it was too late. Once somebody dies, any chance of reconciliation is gone, and I had let my chance slip away.

Ultimately, because I couldn't seem to get over her demise, I ended up seeing an Army psychiatrist. But that fizzled out after just a few months for two reasons:

- I received orders for Stuttgart, Germany.
- We were getting "nowhere fast" because I couldn't take the ridiculous "how does that make you feel" approach.

The psychiatrist visits naturally progressed to the core of my depression, which was rooted in the events of my childhood, but he gave me the impression there was nothing he could do for me, as I clearly had not repressed anything. As a matter of fact, he was delighted that I had remembered my entire life in such detail, and was able to process everything that had happened without losing my mind. He even kept reiterating that he was amazed at how sane I was. His very words were: "Carmen, I've never met anyone saner than you, and I don't know how you did it! Whatever you've been doing, keep it up."

For some reason I had made the erroneous assumption that psychiatrists could take away the pain and make you "see life through rose-colored glasses." But that's not what happened, and so I was glad when I finally received those orders for Germany because it would be yet another chance to "start all over again."

The funny thing was, right around the same time I received my orders, I had passed the board and all the tests, and was about to leave for Officers' Candidate School. But when my First Sergeant told me I had orders for Germany, "something" gave me an intense desire to forego OCS and return overseas, instead.

* * * *

Naturally, I was elated to return again to my homeland – partly because I would get to visit Mama again. But the city of Stuttgart seemed like just another big, dirty city to me, and the job I was given as NCO-In-Charge of the Adjutant's Office was, to put it bluntly, very boring.

Luckily for me, the Director of Engineering and Housing (DEH) was looking for an administrative NCO/German translator, and he offered me the job without hesitation. Little did we both know that ultimately this move would serve to change my life yet once again….and that once again, it would involve sex in some way.

My new job, to my great disappointment, had to be put on hold for a couple of weeks because the bizarre backaches and "female problems" I had been suffering for several years suddenly became unbearable. And so I underwent an emergency hysterectomy, which immediately resolved the problem. The backaches, it turned out, were due to the fact that my colon had somehow attached itself to my backbone, apparently after my appendectomy back in 1972. The good news was that I felt like a whole new person afterward.

In the days and weeks prior to my surgery, an odd thing happened in that a young, Bible-toting black gentleman who had somehow heard about my physical problems, began a campaign to "lead me to the Lord" in an effort to keep me from having the surgery. He stood before my desk at least once a day to witness that Jesus would heal me if only I just "believed." At first, I tried to be nice, but after awhile, I dropped the pretense when I realized he was not going to give up.

"Look, Sergeant Lassiter," I said one day after listening to him drone on and on. "As I told you before, I do believe in God and I believe He heals when He wants, but I also believe He gave us doctors for a reason. If God wanted me healed, He would have healed me by now, instead of letting me suffer for the last six years of my life."

"Have you gotten down on your knees and prayed about this?" he asked.

"No, and I don't intend to. Why should I beg Him?"

"Praying is not begging," he said with that benevolent, one-size-fits-all smile Christians paste on their faces whenever they're doing their best to be patient with the heathens.

"You know what?" I said, emitting an impatient sigh. "My adoptive father was a Christian and, although I never once ever saw him praying, I knew he was a Christian because he was forever admonishing me about using the Lord's Name in vain."

"Well, he was right - you shouldn't," Sergeant Lassiter proudly interjected.

Peeved, I gave him a warning glance over the top of my glasses. "I'm trying to make a point here, okay?

My adoptive father, the 'good Christian', happened to be a raving pedophile who sexually abused me from the time I was nine years old, so I don't exactly have a lot of respect for Christians and I'm not exactly chomping at the bits to become one, which means you're wasting your breath...."

The look on Sergeant Lassiter's face was a mixture of shock and compassion and, for once, he seemed at a complete loss for words. "Your father was no Christian," he finally said. "...He was doing the enemy's work. And after all that, you need the physical and emotional healing that only Jesus can bring. All you have to do is let Him in."

"Yeah, right!" I snapped, rising with a force that knocked my chair against the wall. In the back of my mind, I was grateful that no one else was in the office just then. "Where the hell was your Jesus while I, as a little defenseless girl, was hiding in the closets every night, praying that God wouldn't let my perverted father find me?"

Without batting an eye, Sergeant Lassiter calmly smacked me in the face with a pat Christian response: "He was right there beside you, helping you to make it through those awful times."

His level gaze enraged me to the boiling point, and the only reason I didn't crawl across my desk to scratch his eyes out was because the rational side of me warned that he wasn't worth my being court-martialed. I felt completely cornered by this man, mentally "raped" and excruciatingly vulnerable; and at that moment, I was dangerously close to coming out with teeth and claws bared.

Angry tears spilled down my cheeks as I stood there trying in vain to control myself. "He was 'helping me' make it through?" I said between clenched teeth and with unleashed sarcasm. "He was *helping* me? Pray tell, Sergeant Lassiter, how exactly was he helping me?"

"He helped you by just being there."

"Really? Seems to me if he really wanted to help, he would have stopped my father somehow. But he didn't, and that's what's making me angry with *you* for even suggesting it. He let that pervert rape me almost every night for four years! I guess that means I wasn't worth *helping*!"

"Well, you made it through all that and you're here safe and sound now, and it's all because of His mercy and grace."

The word "rage" cannot begin to explain what I felt at that moment. For a split second, I was thrown back in time where I was hiding in a closet at Fort Carson, filled with dread and helplessness over the inevitable forced sexual activity that always awaited me whenever Bill was "in the mood." If there really was a Jesus, he surely wouldn't have allowed that, and he certainly wouldn't allow this religious, tongue-talking fruitcake to open old wounds at this point in time in some office and in front of all my co-workers….

Livid to a boiling point, I walked around the desk and stood violently trembling just inches from Sergeant Lassiter's face. "I want you to take your Bible and stick it where the sun don't shine," I said lowly and forcefully. "And if you *ever* come near me again, I will submit a formal complaint against you do you understand? And if that doesn't work, I will think of something else to get rid of your stupid butt – and I promise, you don't want to push me to that point!"

Sergeant Lassiter seemed unfazed as he gave me another one of those patronizing Christian smiles that I had learned to despise over the years. "Understood," he replied. "But if you ever change your mind, just let me know. Jesus loves you and He's waiting."

And with that, he turned to leave, leaving me standing there to stew in a barely contained rage. "I'll never change my mind!" I yelled after him as he disappeared into the hallway.

Moments later, swearing under my breath, I stormed into the ladies room to throw some cold water on my face. I had run into pushy, obnoxious and arrogant Christians before over the years, but none had ever managed to get under my skin like Lassiter had. The man literally gave me headaches; I felt sick to my stomach whenever he was around! The kind of reaction he had provoked in me could not have come from God because whatever "spirit" or whatever was in Lassiter, it was exactly the same one I'd felt in Forrester. Both men, regardless as to their respective motives and regardless as to how different they were, had a way of making me feel oppressed and driving me so completely crazy it literally made me want to kill myself.

The next time some Christian approached me, I decided, I wouldn't waste my time trying to humor him or her; at the first sign of "witnessing", I would pry his Bible from his hands and hit him in the mouth with it. So help me God....

* * * *

After my surgery, my new boss, a lieutenant colonel, and his wife invited me to recuperate at their house, a kindness that made me think working for him would be an awesome experience. But, to my dismay, I soon came to realize that my new boss had ulterior motives because he was a womanizer who couldn't keep his hands off the ladies, and so my "awesome experience" ended just six months later when I walked out on him after he took one too many liberties....

I was literally shaking in my boots as I sat facing the Command Sergeant Major (CSM) in his office afterward because I figured that by "telling on" an officer, I could probably kiss my Army career goodbye.

To my utter surprise, the CSM, oozing with arrogance and self-importance – not to mention, very much reminding me of Bill Forrester, right down to the green snake-eyes – emitted a low chuckle after I finished relating my tale of woe, and then promptly proceeded to fill me in on the fact that *everybody* knew about this "womanizing jackass."

"Frankly, Sarge," he said, "I can't believe it took you so long, because you have a reputation for being straight up and making no bones about telling it like it is. I was beginning to think you liked being pawed by your boss!"

"No, Sergeant Major, I didn't like it one bit. He's just so nice, you know…and I didn't want to hurt his feelings…."

"Well, I'll tell you the truth," the CSM continued in a voice that, exactly like Bill Forrester's, came from deep within his diaphragm, "the only reason he hasn't been called on the carpet by the Post Commander, is because he's retiring soon, and then we'll be rid of him and he'll be nobody's problem anymore."

"Well, it seems to me, he should be reprimanded, regardless," I mumbled, feeling a little disturbed that my complaint, it appeared, was going to be swept under the carpet.

"Okay, so what do you want to do?" he asked brusquely. "You wanna submit a written complaint or what? We can do that, if you want, but it will present a whole lot of trouble for all concerned."

I could tell he really didn't want me to go that route and so I reluctantly shook my head and dropped my gaze to the floor. "I guess not," I finally said. "I just don't want to have to work for him anymore."

"Good choice, Sarge!" His eyes kind of glazed over as he watched me from behind his desk, giving the distinct impression that he was deep in thought.

Suddenly, his face brightened. Shifting in his seat, he leaned forward, cocked his head to one side, and presented me one of his "tough man" looks. At that point he could have been Bill Forrester's twin brother….

"It just occurred to me," he said, "since you've done so much volunteer writing for various organizations around here anyway, and you're good at writing, how would you like to go to work for Captain Maddox at the Stuttgart Citizen?"

"Yes!" I blurted without hesitation. "I would *love* that! I don't know a thing about the newspaper business, but I'm a quick learner."

"Well, the thing is, Captain Maddox had to return to the U.S. on emergency leave, and he may or may not come back. But his journalists are sitting over there right now without any supervision, and so why don't you just head on over there and let 'em teach you what they know and we'll see where this leads."

As it turned out, the newspaper business was "right up my alley" and within less than a year, the Army granted me permission to attend the Defense Information School to legally change my Military Occupational Specialty to Journalist. And from there, in early 1980, I was assigned as NCO-In-Charge of the Public Affairs Office at the United States Army Criminal Investigation Command Headquarters, which in those days was in Falls Church, Virginia, just a few miles from the Pentagon.

Down deep, I happily realized something very important had been dropped into my lap, because my first love, writing, had unexpectedly been restored to me. Thanks to the "womanizing colonel" back in Stuttgart, my life had taken a completely new direction – and it "just felt right." There was no doubt about it: The journalism field was exactly where I was meant to be!

* * * *

While attending the Defense Information School prior to my assignment at the Criminal Investigation Command, I got to see my baby brother, Lonnie, in Indianapolis. No longer a baby now at age thirteen, he already towered above me. And he was gorgeous! Lonnie, with dark blond hair and shiny brown eyes, had been blessed with all the "good looks" in our family.

Lonnie had been living with his father, Oliver, since the death of our mother three years before, and I got the strange feeling from some of his "body language," that he thoroughly hated his father – no doubt, because of the acrimony our mother had planted in his mind. In fact, there seemed to be no spark between him and Oliver, or any life whatsoever in that household, at all. Lonnie and his father, it seemed to me, were just temporarily cohabiting for mutual convenience because they had no choice.

Lonnie wasn't very communicative with me, either, and I figured it was because I was basically a stranger to him. He was five years old the last time I saw him, and I hadn't exactly kept in touch, so how could he have felt anything for a sister who had randomly passed in and out of his life?

Oliver, too, seemed somehow listless. His eyes revealed a deep sorrow and unhappiness brought on, no doubt, by the pain of life in general, including my mother's ill treatment of him. As a matter of fact, although thirteen or fourteen years had passed, I could still clearly hear my mother's voice angrily berating him with that hideous German accent: *I make all the money in this household! If it wasn't for me, we would be living in poverty. You're worthless; you don't contribute anything to this family!*

Oliver, no longer an accountant, had returned to college since the last time I saw him the day I ran away from home, and he was now a counselor at a local prison. While he had a girlfriend of sorts, he had never remarried and, from what I could tell, there was no desire to.

At one point during my weekend visit at their house, after Lonnie had gone off to the movies with some friends, Oliver apologized for having climbed into bed with me all those years ago.

"It's okay," I said, feeling slightly embarrassed at the memory. "You were drunk."

"That's no excuse," he insisted. "You were just a kid. Granted, I was angry with your mother that night, but that didn't give me the right to try to have sex with her daughter. I'm very much ashamed of my behavior that night, especially since I know what that Forrester guy did to you."

I hesitatingly reached across the table to place my hand over his. "Ollie, I can't tell you how much it means to me that you're man enough to apologize," I said softly. "If only Forrester would have the decency to do the same, maybe I would be released to go on with my life...."

I never got to see Oliver again after that. A few short years later, I heard he died, alone and unhappy in his mid-sixties, of colon cancer. In the meantime, my brother, Lonnie disappeared from my life as well. There was simply nothing holding us together.

* * * *

My personal life seemed to improve somewhat after my arrival at the Criminal Investigation Command, especially after I started dating Paul, a Chief Warrant Officer who worked in the Personnel department.

Paul was a lively, interesting character, with a keen curiosity about practically everything, from gardening to cooking, to fine art, to country music, running marathons and frequenting garage sales. At five-foot-five, this father of three boys by two previous marriages wasn't much taller than me, but he was successful and respected, and he struck me as the quintessential "real man" in every sense of the word. In short, Paul made me happy and he made me laugh. And after I married him a year later in a small ceremony in his house, I also discovered just how much he could make me cry – because, Paul, with all his varied and assorted interests, had an insatiable desire for women that went above and beyond the one he was wedded to.

Consequently, our marriage was not necessarily made in heaven, and we experienced many arguments that ended with me crying myself to sleep at night.

In spite of everything, besides my promotion to Sergeant First Class, a couple of very fascinating things happened during the time we lived in Springfield, Virginia.

One was that I decided to get a "nose job" – just because I had always hated my big *shnoz* – and the other was finding my long-lost brothers, Josef and Ingolf, the two boys my foster parents had told me about when I was little.

On a whim one day in mid-1984 – even though I didn't know their last names or the names of their respective fathers – I decided to see if I could find them using the incredibly sketchy information I had, and hoping that someone in my hometown courthouse could be of help. To my surprise, some weeks later, a woman named Ulla Mertens responded to inform me that she would be happy to give it a try!

One glorious Sunday morning shortly thereafter, I received a call from a man in Germany who sounded extremely anxious as he attempted to tell me in broken English that he was my brother, Ingolf.

"Ingolf!" I shrieked the second it hit me that my half brother was on the line. "*Ich kann Deutsch….*"

Ingo, as he preferred to be called, turned out to be a younger brother – almost a year and a half younger. He and I spoke for more than an hour, filling in the gaps of our respective lives in animated tones. As it turned out, in our early years when I was with the Neumanns, Ingo and I lived less than fifty miles from each other, as Ingo's adoptive parents resided in a small town called Lachendorf, not far from Wietze. He said he had, for years, been trying to find his mother, even when he discovered she had remarried and moved to the United States. Tears choked my throat when I told him she had died, because it was obvious he very much wanted to meet her. Since there was no father listed on his birth certificate, he had hit a dead end in every direction, and had basically given up, until Ulla Mertens contacted him to let him know his American sister was attempting to locate him.

Local newspapers and a television news team were on hand when Ingo came for a three-week visit over the Christmas holidays that year. Being in public affairs myself, I had contacts who jumped at the chance to cover the story about a brother and sister, aged thirty-one and thirty-three, respectively, on two separate continents, who had never met before. It was a magical time, wherein we were able to truly get to know each other and establish a strong bond that remains to this day.

What made it even more magical is that Ulla Mertens had also managed to find my other brother, Josef, who at that time lived in France. Josef called while Ingo was visiting and so we were both able to speak to him.

Unfortunately, the longer I spoke with Josef, the less I liked him because he was a rabid anti-establishment type who unashamedly admitted he had stolen someone's credit card in order to call me. Furthermore, he didn't bother to pretend to hide an obvious distaste over my being a U.S. soldier.

I discovered several things during that call, one of which was that Josef and I shared the exact same birthday. He was a year to the day older than me, but he had a different father. His father, he said, was in prison during Josef's formative years, and so he was raised by his paternal grandmother in southern Germany until the age of five when his father was released. For some reason, his father decided to relocate to Cameroon, Africa, where Josef lived until his late teens when he decided to travel the world.

Before hanging up, we promised to get together in Heidelberg the following year, as my husband and I were being stationed there. But Josef never made the effort and, to this day, we have never met.

Chapter 14

June of 1985 found Paul and me stationed in Heidelberg, Germany.

Being in Germany again was magical, in part, because it meant I could visit my aging Mama once more – even though, as the years passed we'd had less and less to say to each other. Truth be told, our relationship had been hovering dangerously close to the nonexistent level for a long time because our worlds were simply too different. Plus, I couldn't take Jürgen and his incessant chatter that always served to come in between Mama and me, as she tended to defer to his desire to dominate conversations.

As much as I begged Paul to come and meet my Mama after our arrival in Heidelberg, he kept procrastinating and insisting we had plenty of time. Right now, he said, he wanted to concentrate on his new job, and I should do the same.

As it turned out, I would ultimately discover that his procrastination had more to do with a British female co-worker, than his desire to please his new boss....

In the meantime, I was perfectly miserable at the Seventh Medical Command's Public Affairs Office because my boss, a high-ranking civilian, was an evil psychopath who liked to play silly mind games with his employees.

I didn't like J.D. from the very first time I ever laid eyes on him. His appearance alone was unnerving as he looked like someone who had stepped out of a caveman exhibit, complete with large lips nestled between pudgy jowls, and a pronounced forehead above sunken, shifty eyes. All that was missing from the picture was a wooden club in his spade-like hands. I'll never forget, after our initial introduction on my first day at work, he sank back into his overstuffed chair, nonchalantly put his feet up on his desk, laced his hands behind his head and, pulling his lips into a smile that made me cringe, he proceeded to warn me about what I was "getting myself into." I would be middle manager of an office full of incompetent, out of control civilians, including "that big, fat, faggot sitting near the door, whom we recently acquired as an intern...."

His entire demeanor struck me as oddly disgusting, and in the back of my mind, I kept thinking: *Watch out for this guy; he's bad news!*

My instincts, as usual, were right on. Thanks to the office scuttlebutt, I soon discovered that J.D. had, shortly before my arrival, been responsible for the hospitalization of an older employee who had returned to the job force because retirement had proved too boring. J.D. apparently resented the man for, among other things, his much higher education level, and consequently, as I learned, "harassed the poor old man to death" on a daily basis - purposely overloading him with work and deliberate taunts, which included menial tasks that should have been reserved for lower pay-grade employees. He also constantly poked fun at his hearing problem and made a habit of rummaging through the old man's desk whenever he wasn't around – anything to show the old man he "didn't belong" there.

In the fifteen agonizing months I worked for J.D., he managed to go through two secretaries, one of whom said she was quitting civil service altogether because of him. I personally witnessed him harassing her on a daily basis, calling her racially mixed children "Oreos" and other derogatory names and then pretending he was "just joshin' her"; and once he threw an inbox against the wall and publicly berated her in front of the entire office because she had forgotten to reserve his call to the U.S. through the military telephone system. The "straw that broke the camel's back" was when he turned her in to the authorities for child neglect. I distinctly remember how very carefully he had neglected to tell the authorities that *he* was the reason her children were left home alone because he wouldn't grant her a day off after she had been forced to fire her baby sitter for beating her children. Since she had no vacation leave time left and didn't want to risk a letter of reprimand from J.D., she decided to leave her kids, aged seven and eight, at home alone, while a neighbor from the apartment next door checked in on them from time to time....

Everyone, including me, was afraid of J.D. because of his extremely volatile temper. We all knew that you risked your career if you crossed J.D. or somehow got on his "bad side" because he was simply one of those people who thrived on harassing others. I knew that one day, my time would come.

* * * *

Over the course of the next year, while I tried to deal with J.D. and his attempts to ruin all our lives on the one hand, my husband's incessant infidelity was driving me insane, on the other.

It all started with his Friday night meetings with "the boys" for their weekly card games, none of which ever took place in our own home. Naturally, I had my suspicions, but they weren't confirmed until I returned earlier than expected from a temporary duty trip with a film crew from the Pentagon during the 1986 "REFORGER" exercise in Germany.

Paul made a show of pretending he wasn't happy that a Colonel from the Pentagon had requested me as a driver/German translator/personal assistant for his two-week film making tour, but he assured me he would "muddle through" in my absence. And muddle through he did, as I came to realize first-hand when I returned a day early.

Snow crunched softly beneath my tires late that Friday evening as I pulled up in front of our house. The neighborhood, for once, seemed unusually quiet, and at first, I thought Paul was probably out with his buddies, playing cards. But, as I approached the front door, I was stopped in my tracks by the sound of soft, ectoplasmic music drifting from the house. I thought that to be unusual because Paul's preferred music in those days was C&W. Plus, at night, we normally watched television, which meant something simply wasn't "normal" that evening.

I could hear our Miniature Schnauzer, Ollie, loudly sniffing my scent under the door, and I started to call out his name when "something" stopped me. Something – perhaps "women's intuition" – told me to quietly make my way around to the back and have a quick peek through the French Doors, just to be on the safe side....

What I saw shook me to the core. There, just a few feet away on the sofa was my husband locked in a passionate embrace with the young, curly-haired blonde I had seen once when I visited his office. There was no mistaking the "big hair" and I distinctly remembered that English accent.

Not knowing what to do, my first impulse was to head back around and let myself in so I could punch both their lights out. On the other hand, I could just stand there silently and take a picture with the Nikon I had used to take still photos with the film crew from D.C. Since adultery was an offense that could get one kicked out of the military, one photo of Paul making out with that home-wrecking twit would have meant the end of his career!

In the end, however, I did nothing. Feelings of shock and betrayal numbed my mind as I trudged back to my car. I was simply too tired to think straight, and so decided it would be best to rent a hotel room and get some sleep before making any major decisions.

Whatever happened, I would definitely leave Paul, though. The bimbo could have him, I decided, because *I* was done forgiving and putting up with his philandering ways! As far as I was concerned, they deserved each other. I had had enough experience in life to know there was truth in the old adage, "what goes around comes around." If Paul ended up marrying her, he wouldn't be true to her, either, so eventually, she would be in the same boat as I was in now. Served her right....

Driving down the mountain away from our home that evening, I felt as if my world had come to an end. The tears were flowing so hard I could hardly see the road. Why, oh why, could I not find a decent, moral man who loved me for myself and who wanted to participate in a real marriage? Why did I always end up with unfaithful jerks? Why had I not tried harder with David all those years ago? We had been so in love, and would probably be happily married with several children right now if my pride hadn't gotten in the way. And why hadn't I married DaCosta? He was a great guy whose only drawback had been his young age. Instead, I had chosen to marry idiots! What was *wrong* with me?....

Little did I realize that my personal problems with Paul were nothing compared to what lay ahead in my professional life with my boss, J.D. As it turned out, during my two-week absence from the office, J.D. had decided it was time to harass Carmen – and my upcoming divorce would serve as the perfect fuel for his fire!

* * * *

Although J.D. was well aware of the fact that my emotions were still raw, he decided I should go to the U.S. to participate in the capacity of a public affairs representative in an Army Medical Exercise that was being held in Wisconsin. Having just removed myself from Paul's life and barely settled into my own apartment had worn me out, both physically and emotionally, and the last thing I wanted to do was to participate in a military exercise six thousand miles away. But, it seemed, I had no choice, and so I attempted to tie up some loose ends in the office in the days before I was due to leave. Since J.D. hadn't filled the secretarial position yet, I was saddled with a lot of extra work, and I was truly baffled as to why he would send me away right now.

On the day before my departure, J.D. greeted me at my desk with a sheepish grin, and quietly handed me a note.

"Could you do me a favor and copy this?" he whispered. "I need a woman's handwriting."

Perplexed, I briefly scanned the note that consisted of a short nonsensical paragraph in his handwriting. "What is it?" I asked.

"It's a letter to my ex-wife. I wanna make her think her husband is having an affair."

My heart sank as I read:

Dear Mrs. Russell,

You don't know me but I been having a affair with your hosband. We love each other very much and altho I know this must hurt, I didn't want you to be the last to know. We plan on getting married soon.

Sincerely,

Thinking it was some kind of a joke, I made a face and handed it back. "J.D., this isn't very funny," I said. "Surely you're not serious."

His sunken eyes narrowed. "Oh, but I am," he retorted. "I really need you to copy this, grammatical errors and all. I want her to think her husband is having an affair with a dumb blonde who can't even spell properly."

I was horrified, speechless. "Why, J.D.?"

"Because I feel like it. I just wanna play with her a bit."

"…But, why me?" I finally managed. "There are other females in the office besides me…."

"Yeah, but you're the only one I trust. You know I can't trust anyone else around here."

"But, I…No, J.D., please, I can't do this," I said, trying to douse a rising panic. "This is a Federal offense! We could go to jail!"

He leaned forward and gave me one of those "knowing" looks that indicated I had no choice in the matter. "Look, Carmen, it's gonna be just between the two of us. Nobody will ever know, okay?"

"But, I really don't want to do this...."

Anger flashed in his eyes as he said, "Well, then at least think about it." And with that, he casually flipped the note into my inbox and told me he'd be back later.

Too shocked for words, I helplessly watched him turn on his heel and duck into his office. The entire conversation had been surreal and I couldn't believe this was happening to me. All throughout my life, things just seemed to "happen" to me; things I never asked for – and this was definitely one of them!

I cast a furtive glance around the room to see if any of my co-workers had witnessed the exchange between J.D. and me, but nobody was looking in my direction....For once, I wished somebody, anybody, had witnessed what just happened, and would come to my rescue. But no one did.

Throughout the day J.D. was relentless in his harassment, constantly coming to check on me and demanding over and over again, "Did you do it yet?" After about the fifth or sixth time, I was a nervous wreck, because I realized I had only two choices here: I could take the note down to my First Sergeant and Commanding Officer to tell on him – which meant I would ultimately risk the horrendous wrath that was sure to follow; or, I could just get it over with and copy the darn note to get him off my back.

In the end, I copied the note. But, in order to cover myself "just in case," I made Xerox copies of both his original and mine and stuffed them into the very back of my file drawer. If this ever came back to haunt me in any way, at least I would be able to show that it was J.D.'s idea and hope that someone would believe that he had intimidated me into being his accomplice.

Although I had managed to get rid of J.D. for the time being, my conscience continued to work overtime. I simply couldn't shake the fact that I had committed some horrible crime and in the process, perhaps ruined Mrs. Russell's life, whoever she was.

That nagging feeling followed me all the way to Wisconsin and back, and I "just knew" when I returned to Germany that all hell was about to break loose….

* * * *

J.D. behaved very strangely on the day I returned to Heidelberg. Although he engaged me in casual conversation about my trip and acted glad to have me back, I sensed that something was off.

That "something" was confirmed when my First Sergeant called to tell me that our Commanding Officer wanted to see me….

"Sergeant," she said with a grim countenance after returning my salute, "you're here because it's come to my attention that you're suicidal."

"I'm *what*?" I blurted out. And then, remembering it was April 1, I added with a silly grin, "Is…this an April Fool's joke?"

The look on the C.O.'s face showed that she wasn't kidding, and over the next couple of minutes she explained that J.D. had come to her while I was gone, to voice his concerns that I had mental problems and that I appeared to be suicidal. He had told her that my work had gone downhill, that I had been "behaving strangely," and that he had been forced to verbally reprimand me several times over the last few months since I left my husband.

My jaw dropped as she spoke; I could hardly believe my ears! Yet, in the back of my mind, I had known the day would come when it would be "my turn" and so, this shouldn't have come as a total surprise.

"J.D.," I mumbled. "Of course. It's my turn now. I should have known." Trying to squelch my rising anger, I said, "Ma'am, if my work has been going downhill, then how come the Commanding General himself a couple of months ago personally complimented me on my briefing at the Public Affairs Conference up north? How come he chose to take me along on his brief trip to Vicenza to do a story about our Army Hospital down there? How come my name is listed in the 1986 *International Review of the Armed Forces Medical Services* magazine that contains my articles on suicide prevention as suggested reading?"

The C.O. shrugged her shoulders. "I don't know," she said. "But according to J.D., your work has gone tremendously downhill."

"Well, J.D. is wrong!" An electric silence hung in the air as we eyed each other. I had the sinking feeling that down deep that she had conflicting emotions about this situation. J.D., after all, was a high-ranking civilian whereas I was "just" an enlisted person. I truly didn't foresee that the results of this particular predicament would end in my favor.

"What did you mean by your 'turn has come'?" she said.

It was a strange feeling to be standing in front of my C.O., tattling on my boss. On one hand, it was a relief to get it out of my system; on the other, I knew I was opening a "can of worms." Her eyes widened as I outlined the goings-on in the Seventh MEDCOM Public Affairs Office, and I could tell she was having problems believing some of the things I said.

"Can you verify any of this, Sergeant?"

"Oh, yes ma'am, I sure can!"

Seconds later, I was at my desk to retrieve the Xerox copies of J.D.'s "Dear Mrs. Russell" letter; but to my horror, they weren't there! My heart thudded like a jackhammer as I thumbed through the files, frantically searching for the evidence that would halt J.D.'s attack in its tracks – but it was gone! J.D. had obviously rummaged through my desk while I was in Wisconsin, and found them; and I felt faint when that light bulb in my mind came on to reveal why it was suddenly "my turn"....

My heels echoed through the halls as I made my way, empty-handed, back into the C.O.'s office. "The letter's gone," I mumbled, dropping heavily into one of the guest chairs. "J.D. found it, and that's why he's trying to do me in now. He's retaliating....I should have known he would root around in my stuff while I was gone. I should have taken those copies home....How stupid could I possibly be?"

Warily eyeing me, the C.O. said, "So you really have no proof to back up anything you said?"

"The only thing I can suggest right now is that you call the former employees who left because of him. I'd be happy to give you their home phone numbers."

"Well, Sergeant," she said, rising to indicate that our meeting was over, "unfortunately, since J.D. has brought the accusation that you are suicidal, I have no choice but to initiate a command-referred psychiatric evaluation."

"But, I'm *not* suicidal!"

"Well, the psychiatrist will determine that. In the meantime, if you think you have a case against J.D., I would suggest you open a formal investigation with the Inspector General's Office."

* * * *

My throat was full of tears by the time I left the C.O.'s office, and so, instead of returning immediately to work, I briefly stopped to see my friend, Master Sergeant Rudi Kreb, an Army Reservist with a German heritage who worked down the hall from the Public Affairs Office. Rudi, during his childhood in Germany, had managed to survive World War II and then later emigrated to Canada and the U.S. where he ultimately joined the military to serve his adopted country. We had become fast friends partly because we both spoke German, and partly because we both had weird histories.

Rudi was my "big brother" and he had somehow become my sounding board for everything. After I left Paul, Rudi was there for me to basically hold my hand in a fatherly sort of way, and to let me know I wasn't alone in the world. And never had I felt more alone than right now....

Rudi's face brightened as I walked into his tiny office at the end of the hallway, but it dimmed as soon as he realized something was wrong. "What's the matter?" he asked in his heavy German accent.

"J.D.," I told him over the lump in my throat. "He's what's the matter."

Minutes later, when I finished relaying the day's events, Rudi sat there, shaking his head in disbelief. "Who does that guy think he is?" he said slowly, in that soothing manner I had come to adore. "Well, at least this didn't come as a surprise to you. You knew this was inevitable."

"Yeah, I knew it. It's just that this is bad timing. I'm not over my rift with Paul yet, and here's J.D. trying to drive me crazy with his silly mind games...."

"Oh, now Carmen, you're too hard on him," Rudi said with an impish grin. "He's a 'good Christian' who parks his butt in the pews every Sunday. He wouldn't harm a fly..."

"Yeah," I said with a snort. "He's just as 'good a Christian' as my adoptive father was!...As a matter of fact, I'm starting to believe this guy is Satan himself, come to do me in...."

"Well, so what are you going to do now?"

"I don't know. Take that 'command-directed' psychiatric exam and hope for the best, I guess. I need to get out of his office. Maybe I can get reassigned somewhere else."

"Well, in the meantime, just know you have a friend down here, just around the corner, whenever you need a break from that lunatic."

"I know," I said smiling. "I have a feeling I'll soon be needing more breaks than usual!"

* * * *

On top of everything else in my life, the "egg/needle in throat" episodes decided to intensify during those days. Whereas I had the occasional episode now and then – always triggered by stress which, during the "J.D. days" was through the roof – it got to the point where I was afraid to close my eyes at night. I had had several episodes since my assignment to Seventh MEDCOM Public Affairs, but after J.D. started applying his pressure, the episodes became a nightly ritual. Often, they were downright painful, where I would literally "feel outside of myself" while feeling that I was actually experiencing the needles lodging themselves sideways in my throat. As always, sometimes it was needles; sometimes an egg. Either way, the pain would literally jerk me awake and they always ended with me sitting up choking, trying not to swallow for fear I might die. Although I had had thousands of those episodes by the time the time I was in my mid-thirties, I simply couldn't get my mind to recognize they were just "dreams."

I hated the idea that J.D. was literally touching every aspect of my life, and was baffled about his intentions. Where was he going with all this, and why? What had possessed him to insist I was suicidal when nothing could have been further from the truth?

I got part of the answer the following day in the psychiatrist's office. The gravity of the situation sank in when the psychiatrist, a full Colonel, slid across his desk a February 1986 copy of EurArmy Magazine, opened to page 27 with the title *I Want to Die*, written by a "USAREUR Soldier."

"Sergeant," he said, "did you write this?"

Perplexed, I glanced at the magazine and shrugged my shoulders. "Yes, sir, I did. Why?"

"So then you *did* recently attempt suicide?"

"Recently? No, sir. As you can see in the first line there, that was back in 1975, the first time I was stationed in Heidelberg. See the opening line? It says, 'Heidelberg, 1975'."

"And 1975 is correct? That's not a typo?"

"No, sir. Why would you think it's a typo?"

"J.D. told me that '1975' was a typo, and that you had meant for it to say 1985, just last year."

Confused, I gawked at the magazine for several moments before the realization finally slammed home. "Oh, my *God*!" cried. "Sir, I promise that is *not* a typo. As a matter of fact, I can produce my original copy; it's in the file cabinet at work...."

"So, are you saying you're not suicidal now?"

"No sir, I'm not – but I think I'm quickly becoming homicidal! J.D. is trying to ruin my career and, in all honesty, I would like to choke him to death!" Swallowing hard as angry tears began to flow, I scooted forward in my seat and cast a bitter glance at the EurArmy magazine. "Colonel," I said, "this is getting to be really ridiculous now. J.D. is trying everything in his power to ruin my life and I really don't need this right now!"

"What do you mean, he's trying to ruin your life?"

I yanked a Kleenex from the box on his desk and blew my nose, and then proceeded to fill him in on all the sordid details. My face was red and puffy by the time I finished. "Sir, I don't know how much more I can take," I said. "If this doesn't stop soon, I may actually end up suicidal. Suicidal or homicidal, I don't care which one. All I know is, this has to stop."

The Colonel presented me with a sympathetic smile as he reached across the desk to retrieve the magazine. "Sergeant," he said, "for your own good and to give you a chance to clear your name, I want to administer an MMPI, a Minnesota Multiphasic Personality Inventory, as soon as you can give me three hours of your time. If you're indeed not suicidal – which it seems to me you're not – then the MMPI will definitely clear your name."

* * * *

It came as no surprise to me that the MMPI proved beyond a shadow of a doubt that I was *not* suicidal. Unfortunately, that didn't resolve my problems with J.D. As a matter of fact, his deviousness seemed to have no limits....

Never was that made any clearer than on one fateful the afternoon when I happened to be alone in the office, trying to catch up on my overwhelming workload. J.D. was out of town on business and everyone else had gone home early. Just as I was tying up some loose ends, the Acting Command Sergeant Major entered and asked for the slide tray containing the Command Briefing.

"Does J.D. still keep it in his office in the usual place?" he asked. "You go ahead and keep working, Carmen; I'll get it myself."

"Well, he keeps his office locked these days," I said, rising. "But I know where he secretly keeps a spare key, so hang on a minute."

Seconds later, we were in J.D.'s office, eyeing the Commanding Briefing on the top shelf of one of the bookcases. Unfortunately, someone had set the carousel on a stack of manila folders and pushed it far back against the wall, and I was forced to stand on my tiptoes in order to reach it. When the Sergeant Major, who was a good foot taller than I, reached above my head to help me out, between the two of us, we somehow managed to pull onto the floor the slide carousel and several manila folders in the process.

I was down on my knees gathering the contents that had spilled from one the folders, when I noticed two extremely blurry, out of focus black and white photographs that featured a half-dressed, dark-haired woman holding something in her hands at belly-button level. She was standing by an open suitcase with clothes haphazardly strewn about, and in the foreground at her feet lay a huge, white stuffed polar bear – the exact same kind of a polar bear I had given my landlady's little grand daughter for her birthday....

My heart gave a lurch and I felt the blood drain from my face as a sick realization hit me: That half-nude woman in that photograph was me! "Oh my gosh!" I whispered over and over. "Oh, my gosh, oh my gosh...."

The Sergeant Major got down on one knee and jerked the photo from my hand. "What's the matter?" he said. "You okay?"

I could hardly breathe as I bent over and got on all fours. "J.D has...He has...Oh, Sergeant Major...." My mind was whirling. At first, I thought someone might have taken that photo through the window of my tiny basement efficiency apartment, but the angle was wrong; plus, I wouldn't have been standing there half-dressed unless the blinds were closed....

And then it dawned on me: It was the evening before I left for Wisconsin and I had been packing. I vaguely remembered coming out of the shower and, for some reason, had decided to load my camera. In the process, I must have caught my own reflection in the full-length mirror on the *Schrank* and that's why the photo was so blurry and out of focus, cocked at a crazy angle....

"What is it, Carmen?" the Sergeant Major demanded in alarmed tones. "What's wrong?"

"That's a photograph of *me*!"

"This is you?" he said after some seconds, his voice drenched with disbelief. "This naked woman is you?"

"Yes! I stupidly caught my reflection in the full-length mirror while loading my camera the night before I left for Wisconsin, while I was packing."

"So, what's J.D. doing with it?"

"That's what I'd like to know!"

"Well, how the heck did he get this?"

"I...I don't know. I guess our photographer gave it to him. She's the only one who develops our film." Hot tears began to blur my vision as I gawked stupidly at the photograph in the Sergeant Major's hand. "Oh

God, what is J.D. trying to do to me? Oh God...I can't take this anymore...."

The Sergeant Major, looking quite bewildered, gently touched my shoulder. "Take what anymore?" he asked. "Carmen, what the hell has been happening in this office?"

Angrily swiping at a tear, I decided to tell him about how my problems had all started with the "Dear Mrs. Russell" letter and how J.D. had stolen the copies I had made. "I let the proof slip right out of my hands!" I lamented. "How could I have been so stupid as to leave those copies in my desk, when I know for a fact that that moron goes through people's desks?"

A devious smile formed on the Sergeant Major's face as he rose and crossed the room. "Well, you know what?" he said. "You take those photographs home with you and just wait and see what he does when he finds them missing. In the meantime, two can play his silly games. Let's go through his desk to see if we can find your 'Dear Mrs. Russell' note."

Minutes later, as if by divine intervention, we found something quite unexpected; something better than just a duplicate of the note he had forced me to copy: We found a Xerox copy of a letter J.D. had sent to someone in Ohio, saying. *"I promise this is not a letter bomb or anything, but would you please forward the enclosed letter? I want it to have an Ohio postmark and it needs to get to Frau Russell soonest."* Stapled to the copy of that letter was a duplicate of my note to Mrs. Russell....

I was elated. "There **IS** a God!" I cried happily! "Sergeant Major, thanks to you, I'm going to beat that jerk at his own game!"

"You bet!" he said. "Go make yourself a copy of this so he won't know you've been in his desk, and then just hang onto it for insurance. On the day he tries to stick it to you, you can stick him back!...Just don't tell him I was involved in this."

* * * *

It would be a major understatement to say that J.D. was upset the next day when he discovered the photos missing. He knew, without a doubt who had taken them, and he was absolutely beside himself with rage.

"Get into my office, I wanna talk to you!" he demanded when he finally could stand it no longer. Turning to one of my co-workers, he said, "Dave, come along and sit in on this."

"Hold it!" I said loud enough for everyone to hear. All eyes were on me, including those of the photographer who had betrayed me. "You can't counsel me in front of a co-worker, J.D.!"

"I can do whatever I damn well please because I'm the boss. Now, get in my office."

"Fine," I said with all the sarcasm I could muster, "if you insist on Dave's presence, then I'm going to get my First Sergeant to sit in, as well."

"Your First Sergeant has nothing to do with this!"

"He has more to do with this than my *co-worker*!" I yelled over my shoulder as I headed out the door.

J.D.'s office was quiet as a tomb a few minutes later when the First Sergeant and I entered. The two men briefly greeted him, and seconds later, all eyes were on J.D. who was casually rocked back in his chair with his hands laced behind his head and his feet propped upon the desk.

"Well," J.D. said quietly addressing me, "I guess Zero Hour has finally come." And with that, he pushed three one-page documents across his desk. "My formal complaints against you, Sergeant."

I couldn't believe my eyes! Because Army regulations require three written reprimands for a military person to be relieved from duty, J.D. was attempting to give them all at once. One, I noticed, was for "poor work performance," one for insubordination and one for "misappropriation of government equipment."

"Hmmm!" I said, feeling oddly brave in his presence, even though the palms of my hands were already wringing wet. "You forgot to give me one for being suicidal."

"Don't get smart."

"Well, in all honesty, J.D.," I went on, "I don't see how you can justify the poor work performance, when just three months ago, you gave me the most glowing efficiency report I've ever had. You inferred that I practically walked on water! What happened between then and now?"

"Your work plummeted after you left your husband."

"So, you're saying, in just three months I went from 'terrific' and 'a real treasure' to 'dirt bag'?"

"Yep."

"But you have no proof of that. None! I've actually done some of my best work in the last six or eight months."

"You'd be surprised what I have!"

And you'd be surprised what I have, too, I thought triumphantly. Watching him sit there with his arrogant attitude and condescending demeanor was beginning to grate on me, and I felt my anger slowly rising. It took everything in my power to keep from crawling across his desk to scratch his eyes out. "Well, moving on then," I continued, "would you mind telling me, in front of our two witnesses, exactly how, when, where and what government equipment I supposedly misappropriated?"

J.D.'s eyes twinkled as he reached into his middle drawer and pulled out a black and white photograph, which he pushed towards me. "There you go," he said smugly. "But then, you've seen this already since you broke into my office and stole the first couple of copies."

With a sardonic grin designed to show him that I wasn't as intimidated as he obviously wanted me to be, I said, "I've got three questions for you concerning this issue. The first one is, how do you know this is a photo of me since you can't actually see my face, and the photo itself is so blurry you can hardly make out any features, whatsoever?"

His eyes narrowed as he warned me for the second time not to get smart. "I just know it's you!" he retorted. "It's on one of the rolls of film you took in Wisconsin."

"Well, okay, then my second question is, what are you doing with a nude photograph of me that was taken in the privacy of my own home?"

The exultant smirk suddenly faded as his eyes narrowed. "It's on government film, missy!" he snapped. "Are you even capable of understanding the implications of that?"

I made a small puffing sound with my lips and then sighed as if in deep thought. "But it was an *accident*," I said. "Which actually brings me to my third question, which is: How exactly is this misappropriation of government property? I'm sitting here wracking my brain, but am drawing a complete blank!"

J.D.'s color rose as he cocked his eyes toward my First Sergeant who had been silently observing the exchange. "Do you see what I'm talking about when I say she's guilty of insubordination? She talks to me like that all the time."

"No, not all the time," I countered. "Only during those times when I catch you in the act of trying to ruin my life."

J.D. turned a bright crimson as he unlaced his hands and jerked his feet from the desk. Leaning as far forward as he possibly could, he glowered across the desk. "You want answers, Carmen," he said between clenched teeth, "well, I got 'em. This photo," he went on, tapping it for emphasis with his index finger, "is proof that you have mental problems, lady. Anybody of your rank should know better than to have someone take naked pictures of them on a military camera containing military film." Having said that, he slowly and deliberately pushed himself against the back of his chair and laced his hands behind his head once more, in obvious attempt to show his confidence in the fact that I clearly been ensnared....

My jaw dropped as his words sank in. Until then, it had never dawned on me that he was under the impression that someone had taken that picture of me! But, what else could he possibly have thought, since he had never been inside my apartment to see that full-length mirror?

The situation might have been hilarious under different circumstances, but this guy was attempting to ruin my career and so it was anything but funny. Stifling another sudden urge to jump on his desk and kick him in the face, I took a deep breath and forced myself to remain calm. "Boy, J.D.," I said, "Has it ever occurred to you that you could actually be wrong about something? I mean, take another really good look at that picture and try to imagine how else it might have gotten onto that particular roll of film."

The muscles in his jaw were working fast and furiously as he glared at me. Finally, he said, "I don't have to take another look at that picture, Carmen. I've seen it plenty of times. Someone – your boyfriend perhaps? – took your picture on Army film….That's misappropriation in my book!"

"A boyfriend," I said in mocking tones. "I had just left my husband at the time this photo was taken, remember? I didn't have a boyfriend then, and I still don't."

"Well, *someone* took that picture, so your point is what?"

I half rose as I snatched the photo from his desk and held it up for him to look at. "The point is, J.D., *nobody* took this picture of me! I accidentally caught my own reflection in a full-length mirror while I was fiddling with the stupid camera! Last time I checked, loading a camera, with or without your clothes on in the privacy of your own home does not constitute fraud and it's *not* a Federal offense – as is, say, forcing an employee to help you harass your ex-wife through the U.S. mail system!"

The look on J.D.'s face was priceless. His chair crashed loudly against the wall as he rose from his seat. "OUT!" he yelled at the top of his voice. "Get her out of here!"

I stood and cast a shrewd smile at my boss, then strode confidently towards the door with my First Sergeant in tow. Before disappearing into the outer office, I turned to face him one last time, and when I spoke, my words were laced with acid. "There's something else you should know, J.D." I said. "I know all about that 'Ohio postmark' letter which needed to get to "'*Frau* Russell soonest'....Divine Intervention provided me with a copy – and I don't even go to church! Have a nice day."

* * * *

I was removed from the Public Affairs Office after that incident and temporarily reassigned to Seventh MEDCOM's Personnel Directorate as a "duty soldier" – someone who was on call to do whatever needed to be done – while the Inspector General's Office conducted their investigation of J.D.

During the seven months that the investigation ultimately took, I was literally treated by everyone like the quintessential "red-headed stepchild." After all, J.D. was a high-ranking civilian who played golf with the Chief of Staff and the General, while I was just an enlisted person – so, whom were they going to believe, especially since most people didn't know the whole story? It was an awful time, but I was determined to stick it out. I had no choice.

Thank God I had Rudi to help me make it through those terrible times! He stuck with me through thick and thin. Regardless as to what happened and whether he might have thought I was right or wrong, he remained loyal while everyone else basically turned their backs on me. Not one single other soul besides Rudi bothered to help me through those dark and dreary days. He stuck with me to the bitter end and, thanks to him, I discovered the meaning of true friendship. If it hadn't been for his constant encouragement and belief in me, I might have truly succumbed to J.D.'s accusations. As a matter of fact, Rudi was the reason I reenlisted when the time came because, after the way the Army had handled my situation with J.D., I was ready to throw away my sixteen years of service and my hard-earned retirement, and simply return to civilian life.

There was one other glimmer of hope during those dim days, and that came when the Colonel in charge of the Personnel Directorate called me into his office about a month after I had become a "duty soldier" to congratulate me for "doing a good job around the headquarters."

"Carmen," he said, "I know basically what happened with J.D. and I happen to believe you got the short end of the stick. I've seen the kind of work you do, and I've watched you closely over the last month, and so I'd like to offer you the position of Congressional Inquiries Liaison. Would you be interested in that?"

"Yes, *sir*," I said without hesitation. "I would love that!" His words were music to my ears and soothing balm for my aching heart because it showed that some people still believed in me. That act of compassion, all by itself, served to restore my faith in "the system" I felt had been failing me for months – a system that had blatantly allowed a Department of the Army Civilian to harass his employees without any repercussions at all, even when presented with raw evidence of his actions. J.D. had been allowed to continue as Chief of Public Affairs, while I had been basically tossed out on my ear and made to look like a troublemaker with mental problems. Well, I would have loved to have been a little fly on the wall when J.D. discovered that I was to be the new Congressional Inquiries Liaison!

* * * *

The completion of the Inspector General investigation several months later revealed that J.D. had, in fact, abused his authority by attempting to force me into helping him harass his ex-wife. It revealed that he was guilty of several incidents of "conduct unbecoming" for someone of his grade and position and that there would be certain consequences to which I was not privy. But the bottom line was something that made me extremely unhappy. Since it's nearly impossible to fire a Department of the Army Civilian, J.D. was, unbelievably allowed to keep his job. Not only that, but a year later, he took an assignment as Public Affairs Chief at the Pentagon. I couldn't help but feel that the "Good Ol' Boy Network" had somehow intervened to help him out....

When I heard the news, I not only felt betrayed, but I was extremely angry and disappointed that someone like him had been allowed to remain in the system at all! The man had, after all, been found to have committed a Federal offense....

My only consolation was, not only had the Department of the Army seen fit to promote me to Master Sergeant, but just before J.D. left for the Pentagon, I stealthily got word to him via the "friend of a friend" route that, despite his attempt to ruin my career, I had been selected to attend the prestigious United States Army Sergeants Major Academy in El Paso, Texas, with a report date of January 1990.

Oh, how I would have loved to have presented the news in person, but common sense told me to stay as far away from that man as was humanly possible! He was evil personified, someone who was driven to ruin the lives of everyone he met. By that time, things had begun to look up for me as the years went by and J.D. became but a bad memory. And so I consoled myself in the knowledge that it surely must have galled J.D. to know he *hadn't* succeeded in ruining *my* career or driving me to suicide. That, in itself, made it all worthwhile.

To this day I cringe whenever those horrible years at Seventh MEDCOM come to mind, including the day I learned that my husband Paul, shortly after our divorce was final, had married the woman I had caught him with. I cannot describe how much it hurt to realize I had been so easily replaced, discarded like some dirty old rag and forgotten....

But life went on and approximately a week before I left Germany in December 1989, I received an unexpected visit from Seventh MEDCOM's new Chief of Staff who said he had a message for me from the new General.

"Sergeant," he said, "the General has asked me to express his apologies on behalf of the Command for the way you were treated during your ordeal in the Public Affairs Office. I can assure you that, had we been here during that time, things would have turned out very differently.

"And while I can't tell you specifics, I can tell you that J.D. didn't get off scot-free. The General has personally sent a note to J.D.'s new boss to make him aware of the kind of person he is. That, we hope, will be at least some consolation for you."

I could hardly believe my ears! Although I would have loved to have seen J.D. kicked out of Civil Service, this news was just what I needed to hear! It was at least something to hold onto. Actually, it was like Christmas and New Years and winning the Lottery, all rolled into one....

Chapter 15

It felt good to be back in the U.S. after nearly five years in Germany. With the J.D. saga behind me, I just wanted to get on with my life.

And so, on my way to the Sergeants Major Academy, I stopped off in Missouri with my cat and dog, to spend a week with an aging Goldie whom I had been calling "Mom" now for nearly twenty years. Goldie had been my anchor throughout my career, the one person who had been a constant in my life besides Rudi; the one person I had always been able to count on. We had "clicked" from the moment we met and the friendship had just kept on blossoming as time went on. I always looked forward to our visits because her ancient rental house in a tiny town outside of Springfield had been "home" to me throughout my adult life – since the very day I had left Bill Forrester's house for the last time.

Something was "off" on this particular visit, however, and, try as I might, I couldn't put my finger on it until the day before I left for El Paso….

Goldie, I noticed to my dismay, seemed to be changing. No longer the sweet, cheerful lady I had learned to love and admire, she was steadily becoming increasingly testy and even hateful sometimes, prone to speaking ill of her neighbors and vacillating in her loyalties.

This became crystal clear during my weeklong visit when, after a few days I realized none of the neighbors had dropped by to see me. Goldie seemed just as baffled as I when I voiced my concern, and she suggested they were "probably all busy." Unfortunately, I was unable to call anyone on the phone, because Goldie had some kind of an aversion to having a telephone in her house (to talk to Goldie, I always had to call a neighbor's house, which was particularly irritating whenever I tried to call her from Germany....).

Anyway, a day or so before I left for El Paso, while Goldie was in the shower, I popped over to visit one of the neighbors to find out why she hadn't come to say hello, and her answer was quite surprising: Goldie had told all the neighbors that I didn't like company.

During the course of the conversation, I discovered also that Goldie had actually spread quite a bit of misinformation about me around the neighborhood, including a concocted story about how we met. For some reason, rather than to simply relate the fact that I was the adopted daughter of her former boyfriend, she had told this particular neighbor that she had found my little brother, Teddy, and me living in some deserted alleyway in Springfield, and taken us into her home.

Needless to say, it hurt to discover that my "adopted Mom" lived in some kind of imaginary world where fantasy was indistinguishable from reality! This new revelation completely rocked my world, as it meant the demise of yet another relationship I thought had been real and tangible. The Goldie I had known and loved for so long apparently was a myth.

As disappointed as I was, I couldn't fathom life without her; it was too much to bear. Not knowing how to deal with this situation, I trudged back across the street and entered the tiny kitchen where Goldie sat quietly drinking a cup of coffee. Her face turned bright crimson the moment I sat down and I knew that she knew.

"Mom," I said reluctantly, "why did you tell everyone that I don't like company?"

"Well, you don't," she replied matter-of-factly.

"What makes you think that? I love seeing your neighbors whenever I come to visit. You know that."

"Well…I just know you like to rest when you come here and so I thought you didn't want to see nobody."

"I see." My heart ached when I saw the confusion and embarrassment in her face. She knew what she had done, but wasn't about to admit it. I was sure she would be saying the exact opposite if her neighbor were here instead of me.

Clearly, she lived in some kind of a fantasy world wherein her convoluted thoughts ruled her every word and deed. It was obviously not something she could help, and so I decided I couldn't be angry with her.

"Oh well," I said, making an effort to sound lighthearted. "I guess it must have been just a silly misunderstanding."

* * * *

It was with a heavy heart that I left Goldie behind when it came time to leave, because I wasn't sure what our future held. Throughout the years I had seen certain signs that she had tendencies to twist the truth and make up stories; I just never realized she would be making them up about me, and it hurt because I thought we had been a team, Goldie and I. After all, we had enjoyed a certain symbiosis over the years: She was someone who gave me a place to call home, and I helped her out financially by sending her regular monthly checks to help her pay the bills, since she had no one else.

Anyway, when it came time to leave, I rented a car and drove to Houston, Texas, to pick up my own car, which had been shipped from Germany and was waiting for me at the port.

In a hotel room near Houston the night before, I experienced another one of my "visions" which, this time, consisted merely of a loud crash and the feeling of a horrendous collision. Normally when I had these episodes, they were usually accompanied by a visual manifestation, but this time it was just a loud crash that caused me to sit straight up in bed, gasping for air. Heart hammering madly in my chest, I said a silent prayer that this had just been a bad dream.

Afterward, sleep was nearly impossible because, deep down in my gut, I knew what was to come, and wondered why bad luck kept following me everywhere I went.

Just to be on the safe side and in hopes of thwarting any kind of collision on the beltway the following morning, I stayed mainly in the right-hand lane of the eight-lane freeway, keeping the car at a steady pace between 55 to 60 miles per hour.

Suddenly, amidst the sounds of screeching tires to my left, a brown car briefly appeared in my peripheral vision as it sped directly into my path. I didn't even have time to put on the brake before crashing head-on into its passenger side. To my horror, I heard the exact same sounds and experienced the same sensations as in my vision the night before; I heard the same loud crash and felt the same impact. As if in slow motion, I watched as my dog and cat – who had been contentedly perched atop some of my of the suitcases so they could see out – tumbled over the back seat and landed under the dashboard. Horrified, I realized the car was spinning round and round like some out-of-control carnival ride, and I found myself praying that no one would hit us. After an eternity of spinning, we came to a hard stop against a little hill on the side of the road.

It took some moments for me to realize I had been in a bad car accident, but my pets – while completely bewildered – seemed to be okay. At first, I couldn't find my cat, Cisko, but quickly discovered he had lodged himself beneath my seat. No amount of urging brought him out, and so I finally grabbed a hold of his tail and forced him. Both animals were wracked with trembling from the ordeal, and I held and petted them for several moments, grateful we were all still alive and there was no blood to be found anywhere.

Somewhere in the back of my mind, it dawned on me that Satan was trying to kill me off…

Infuriated over the thought that someone had nearly caused our deaths, I left my animals in the car to confront the driver of the other car.

"What happened?" I demanded of the two young black children who emerged, seemingly unhurt, from the back seat of the ancient, rusted vehicle.

"Mommy discovered we were out of gas and so she tried to take that exit back there," one of them answered excitedly.

"Are you guys okay?"

"Yes. But Mommy's laying down."

The entire freeway had come to a halt, but no one offered to help. Trembling, I opened the driver's side door to find a very pregnant woman lying across the seat with her head in the passenger's side.

"You okay?" I asked. She merely nodded as if in a daze. "How far along are you?"

"Nine months."

"Oh my God....Well, are you in any pain at all?"

"No."

Not knowing what else to do, I assured her that an ambulance was surely on its way, and I stood there, helpless, not knowing what to do except to keep an eye on the lady and her children until help arrived.

Less than half an hour later, my dog and cat and I were safely sitting in the cab of the tow truck that had come to pick up the demolished rental car. Still shaken from the ordeal, I began to realize as the shock began to wear off, that my whole left side was sore – and I prayed that whatever my injuries were, they wouldn't interfere with the strenuous physical training that awaited me at the Sergeants Major Academy in El Paso.

"I can't believe you weren't killed," the representative at Budget Rental said after the tow truck dropped us off. "This car is completely destroyed. Good thing it was a rental, huh?" he added with a giggle.

"Good thing I bought rental insurance!" I replied with a weak grin.

To my great relief, the people at Budget Rental were wonderful. For some reason I expected major hassles over the fact that I had just wrecked on of their brand new vehicles, but instead, I was treated with nothing but kindness and understanding. The representative who processed me even drove me and my animals down to the port where my own car was waiting, and then followed me to a gas station to make sure I wouldn't become stranded in case I ran out of gas before I got there.

Chapter 16

Seeing the Sergeants Major Academy for the first time was an awesome thing. It was a dream-come-true for every enlisted person who aspired to reach "the top."

I couldn't believe I had made it this far, especially after the saga in Heidelberg. But, as one of only ten women in the class of five hundred students, I made it through the grueling six-month course in flying colors. Goldie flew to El Paso to attend my graduation, and it brought tears to my eyes to realize it was the first time in my career that a parent (albeit a foster mother) had been present at any of my graduations or award presentations to witness the achievement. Deep down inside, I was sorry that Bill Forrester couldn't have been there. Somehow, even after twenty years, I was still tied to that man emotionally and, while consciously I hated the very thought of him, a part of me would have loved to have heard him say, "Good job, Carmen! I'm really proud of you!"....

I was ecstatic just before the graduation ceremony, when the Command Sergeant Major asked me to stay on as a lesson developer and instructor. And I was absolutely on top of the world when I made the Sergeants Major List, E-9, a year later because that's as high a rank as an enlisted person can obtain. I had "made the cut." Unable to keep from gloating a little, I sent a copy of the Army Times containing my name to J.D. at the Pentagon with note that said: *J.D., as you can see, I made it to the top despite your vainglorious efforts to ruin my career! Deal with it!*

Everything I touched during my twenty-two years in the Army seemed to turn to gold. Even in Heidelberg when it seemed my career was all but over, I somehow managed to bounce back. But it was my personal life that always remained in shambles and it was beginning to worry me. At the age of forty, I was no further along in love and marriage than I'd ever been. I was still single, still loveless and still childless – a fact that I had been forced to accept after my hysterectomy back in 1978.

Consequently, I think I married Larry out of desperation – because if I had been thinking clearly, I would have kicked him in the teeth the day he presented me with an engagement ring....

Larry had been one of my classmates who began wooing me just before our graduation from the Academy in the summer of 1990. A personality-less, quiet and very effeminate "recovering alcoholic" and the father of a rebellious sixteen-year-old boy, he wasn't even my type, and we had absolutely nothing in common. In all honesty, I don't know what possessed me to agree to marry him, but I figured "my type" had gotten me into trouble more than once, and so I would probably be "safe" with this blue-eyed, slightly pudgy, nondescript man with no personality who *surely* would never even think of having an affair behind my back.

Unfortunately, I had never been more wrong in my life! Like the others, this marriage, put in simple terms, was straight from the pits of hell, and it was the first one that truly drove me to the edge of suicide because, at this point in my life, I truly couldn't take anymore.

As it turned out, Larry the "recovering alcoholic" who had no opinion on most things and appeared rather dead inside, was exactly like J.D. I had no inkling before I married him that, inside that soft, flabby exterior, he was actually a conniving, backstabbing, manipulative psycho who quietly and subliminally controlled those who he was closest to. It also somehow escaped me that he was bi-sexual, which became perfectly clear at a barbecue at his boss' home one afternoon when he gently touched the shoulder of a man wearing a "muscle shirt" to tell the guy he had "a body to *die* for"….

Anyway, I truly tried to make the marriage work, but nothing I did satisfied my husband. While he never actually came out and said it, I could "just tell" he didn't like my food, or the fact that I was an extremely orderly housekeeper, or that I enjoyed an occasional glass of wine. He also didn't like that I was fluent in three languages or that I had more education than he; and he certainly didn't like the fact that I made the Sergeant's Major list when he didn't.

In fact, when the list came out and Larry discovered he wasn't on it, he decided to retire from the Army, get a civilian job, and start taking night courses at a local university. In the meantime, of course, he made sure I knew that the only reason I had made the E-9 list was because "they have to promote their token females." (Larry wasn't the only one who said it. Several other men at the Academy who hadn't made the list threw the same barbs. I should have been used to it after hearing the same mantra from the male soldiers throughout the years, but I wasn't, and it hurt every time I heard it. Promotions for me were always bitter sweet, thanks to the childish barbs of the insecure men of the world who feel threatened by women who are often light years ahead of them in many ways....)

And Larry's son – well, with a father like Larry, it was no wonder that the kid was very angry and neurotic and would punch the occasional hole in doors and walls to "express himself." Both father and son had their own respective ways of driving me insane, and I knew it was only a matter of time before this marriage, too, would be dissolved.

After the E-9 list came out, things between Larry and me went rapidly downhill, especially after he accepted that civilian job and started attending evening classes because, suddenly I was not only working during the day, but trying all by myself to handle a rebellious and hateful teenager every evening until his father came home around 10 p.m. The weekends were generally full of chaos and fighting between father and son, and the stress levels in our house were through the literal roof.

Life went from bad to worse when I decided to retire, as well. Even though I was about to be promoted, "something" caused me to want to call it quits with the Army as soon as possible. It was as if my very life depended on it.

Several factors actually came into play in my decision, including the fact that our Commander, in mid-1991, wanted to shut down the entire academy and send every one of us into the middle of the Gulf war. By that time, I felt I was too old and had been through too much in my life to go to war now – especially for a country that had spit on soldiers returning from Vietnam. No, as enticing as it was to pin on those E-9 stripes, I just didn't feel like sticking around anymore.

Although Larry didn't like the fact that his wife was being promoted to Sergeant Major, he liked it even less that I was about to become "a mere civilian" when I announced that I just wanted to stay home and be a housewife and mother to his son, and to write that book that I've been wanting to write all my life.

"That's not gonna work," Larry said. "I don't want to be married to just a housewife."

"Why not?" I retorted. "After all, I'll be a housewife with an income! I'll be receiving a monthly retirement check, remember?"

"That's not the point."

"Well, what is the point?"

"I just don't think you ought to be sitting around at home."

"I won't be 'sitting around at home'!" I'll be writing my book!"

"Well, I'd like you to get a job. You can write your book after work every night."

"Oh, right. I can write while your son's at home wanting help with his homework, or expecting to be taken to some after school activity, or while he's loudly entertaining a bunch of his friends upstairs. His Dad is never here at night, so I'll get to write my book in between my 'Mommy duties' while you're gone...."

Day in, day out, Larry and I fought like cats and dogs over one issue or another. The problem was simply, nothing satisfied him. To placate him, I began looking for a part-time job, but then he went berserk when I announced that I planned on applying for a secretarial position, because no wife of his was going to be a mere secretary. Furthermore, he didn't want me working part time; he wanted me to work *full* time. Round and round we went, until I truly felt like choking him to death. If we weren't fighting over my potential job applications, then we were at his son's school, smoothing out some problems with the teachers who wanted to kick his smart-alecky son out of their classes. And on the weekends, like clockwork, I couldn't escape the endless father-son shouting matches.

These fights would often end in cold wars at the dinner table, with the two either glaring at, or making a show of ignoring each other. At least once or twice a week, I would be mentally jerked back into my childhood watching Bill Forrester glare at my little brother, Teddy, before exploding into a violent rage because the poor kid hadn't held his fork right. More often than not, my stomach was tied in knots well before we all sat down at the dinner table.

After a year and a half of this, I landed in the hospital for ten days. Although the doctors never did figure out what was wrong, I knew it was my body's reaction to the constant stress. The "egg/needle in throat" episodes had once again become a nightly ritual, and I often found myself daydreaming about killing Larry and his son. Whether I would have actually done it is debatable because I can't stand to see anyone or anything hurt, but these two were definitely pushing me to my limits. I was truly to the point where I simply couldn't take anymore. Something **had** to give quickly, or I would surely end up in a mental institution....

The marriage came to an abrupt halt in the summer of 1992, when – lo and behold! – I discovered that Larry was having an affair with some woman at work. It came to light late one evening when he came home terribly distraught from one of his college courses. Apparently, the woman from work with whom he had fallen in love found out she had breast cancer and decided to try to dump Larry and patch things up with her husband. For some strange reason he thought I would feel sorry for him. When I asked him to please explain to me exactly *when* he had found time in his busy schedule to have an affair, he admitted he had only been taking one night course at a time instead of two, and had been spending the other two evenings a week over the last few months with his girlfriend.

I didn't know whether to laugh or cry. Larry's news was not only devastating but also incomprehensible! It was absolutely shocking to discover that this effeminate, personality-less, bi-sexual, neurotic sack of flab was no different from my previous, much more macho two-timing husbands! I felt like I had somehow traveled into the Twilight Zone! What made me really angry is that I had wasted a year and a half of my life on this sham of a marriage with a dysfunctional man and his dysfunctional son, putting up with all kinds of mental and emotional abuse….

Once the initial shock wore off, my first reaction was, naturally, to knock his block off. But, instead, I managed to find a tiny shred of rationality through the muck and confusion that clouded my mind, which said in no uncertain terms: *Hey! This is your ticket out! Get out while the getting's good and don't look back!*

And so I said and did nothing.

The following morning I packed as much as I could possibly cram into my car including my dog, Ollie, took half the money out of our joint bank account and headed for Missouri.

Chapter 17

There is an adage that says if you keep doing what you've been doing, you're going to keep getting what you got. In other words, unless you become aware of your problem and are willing to acknowledge it and to do something about it, you will never break the cycle.

I obviously had a problem when it came to men. Unfortunately, I had no clue as to what to do about it. I was just unlucky in love, that's all there was to it. Somehow and for some reason, I always ended up picking bad guys. That's why, after I left Larry, I pretty much decided I was done with men altogether.

Physically and emotionally exhausted after my tumultuous marriage I found myself at Goldie's house in that summer of '92, wondering just what I should do next. Goldie, as always, received me with open arms, and told me to stay as long as I wanted. I knew I would probably stay for a week or two, until I could figure out what to do next, but I also wasn't about to impose myself on her for too long, because I wasn't sure exactly where I stood with her anymore.

Unfortunately, she was all I had because I had no one else to turn to. And right then, God only knows how much I needed a mother because, not only was I going through yet another horrendous divorce, but just before I left El Paso, I had discovered a "lump" in one of my breasts that was an inch in diameter. While doctors in El Paso had told me it didn't "look or feel like cancer" they insisted on "keeping an eye on it" for awhile, and insisted I return in six months for a follow-up mammogram and possible biopsy. The lump felt huge to the touch, and naturally, I was terrified. All I kept thinking was how unfair it was that I might be dying without ever having known true happiness....

Goldie was my lifeline in those days, though. As much as I hadn't wanted to end up overstaying my welcome, depression kept me from finding the energy to do much of anything. Finally, after three weeks I decided to stop being a burden, and found a place to live, just outside the Springfield City limits.

During the weeks I lived with Goldie, she and a couple of her neighbors tried hard to sympathize and empathize and help me "over the hump," but I was absolutely inconsolable at first. One neighbor – a forty-something lady who, like me, was going through a divorce – thought she was doing me a favor by inviting me to her to a singles' group which met at some church on Sunday mornings. My first reaction was to angrily rebuff her for even suggesting I cross the threshold of a place filled with religious "don't use the Lord's Name in vain" hypocrites, much less hang out in a place designed to help people find mates. But, realizing she was just trying to be nice, I managed to pull myself together enough to mutter a simple "thanks but no thanks." A singles group was the last place I needed to be because as far as I was concerned, those places were basically "meat markets," and the last thing I wanted was to meet or get involved with yet another man....

All I really wanted to do was to sit around feeling sorry for myself. I had earned it. A year and a half with Larry and his son had done me in. As a matter of fact, it seemed as if the memories of all the horrible events of my life had collaborated to begin haunting me all at once in an effort to rip my soul apart. I felt trapped beneath the mental and emotional baggage of years worth of "stuff" – and no way out.

Adding to my depression was the fact that, after twenty-two years, ironically, I was right back where I started: In Springfield, Missouri, on Bill Forrester's home turf!

Anyway, within just a few weeks, I found a job as an assistant office manager at a local bakery, but I had to quit after the first day because my nerves were too frayed to deal with people and telephones and the daily grind. It was then I realized that my ordeal with Larry had done more harm to my overall health than I wanted to admit, and so working was going to be out of the question for now. Luckily, I had my Army retirement to sustain me!

Since I had already been hospitalized once for stress, perhaps some really deep healing was in order; the kind that would restore me from the inside out. In order to do that, I decided I needed to cleanse myself of the demons of my past, starting with the person who had ruined my entire life by sending me on a downward spiral of self-destruction when it came to relationships; the person who was responsible for my dysfunctional behavior when it came to choosing men: Bill Forrester.

* * * *

As "Fate" would have it, Bill had died of lung cancer on the very day I rolled into Springfield. His widow, Marguerite, gently broke the news to me on the phone when I finally got up the courage to call.

As she spoke, in my mind's eye, I saw him sitting at the breakfast table every morning, wracked with uncontrollable hacking and coughing fits while insisting that the cigarette he was puffing wasn't the cause. "I've been smoking since I was thirteen," he was always quick to say. "They've never bothered me! Cigarettes are my only pleasure in life and I'm not giving them up."

"Oh, honey," Marguerite said, "I'm so glad you called. I've always wanted to meet you. I'm so sorry your father died before you two could see each other again."

And with that, she promptly invited me to meet her for lunch in Springfield, after which, she said, we would visit the National Cemetery where he was buried. Although I didn't really want to see his grave or be anywhere near the man, I didn't have the heart to turn her down.

Marguerite was a chatty and handsome gray-haired lady with bright eyes and a winning smile. It took everything in my power to bite my tongue during lunch while she spoke incessantly and in glowing terms about my abuser, her dear departed husband. She obviously had no clue that she had been married to a raving pedophile, and I felt it wasn't my place to mar her memories of him with the truth.

"Oh, honey, your Dad was such a good man!" she kept repeating in a high-pitched, grating voice. I couldn't help but wonder if he had ever slammed her forehead against the dining room table....

"He was such an amazing man," she went on. "You should have heard him sing in our church choir!"

"Church choir," I muttered, managing a weak smile.

"Oh yes. He had such a beautiful singing voice."

"Uh-huh. I'll never forget his voice...."

"And he was a deacon, too, you know."

"Really? Imagine that."

"Oh, he was just the best husband. And, honey," she said reaching across the table to place her hand over mine in a motherly gesture, "he was so proud of you."

"Proud of me?" I said, trying to keep my voice level. "How could he be proud of me when he never knew where I was or what I was doing? We had a bad falling out twenty-some years ago and I never heard from him after that."

"Oh...well, yes, but your brother Teddy kept him informed of your whereabouts."

"Teddy?" I said, surprised. "Actually, Teddy never kept in contact with me, either." As I scanned her face, it dawned on me that she was making things up as she went along. Bill wasn't proud of me and he never knew or cared where I was; he couldn't have known. If he had, he would surely have found a way to contact me. I had the distinct feeling that Marguerite's own life hadn't been the rosy picture she was attempting to paint for my sake.

"I haven't heard from Teddy in years," I went on. "Our mother did a really good job of turning him against me back when he was still a teenager, and so there's been no real relationship throughout our adult lives."

Marguerite's eyes suddenly widened and she seemed alarmed. "Then you don't know about Teddy, do you?" she said.

"Know about him?"

Again, she reached across the table to take my hand in hers. "Oh, honey," she whispered, "...your brother is dying. I'm sorry to be the one who had to break this to you."

"Dying?" I said incredulously. "What do you mean? He's not even forty."

"Well, he's got a disease called Scleroderma. It's pretty bad, I guess, because I heard it was not only in his skin but also in his organs."

I was stunned. My little brother couldn't be dying, not yet! Memories tumbled over each other as I thought about the sad life he had endured at the hands of his father, and I wondered if Marguerite had any inkling. Probably not.

"The good thing is, he's at least not alone," she went on. "He's got a wife and stepson and they're apparently taking good care of him...."

Swallowing the threatening tears, I asked Marguerite for Ted's phone number and address, and she promised to call me later with the information. The least I could do was to keep in touch now, if he would let me. Perhaps we could, through this awful dilemma, rekindle the once close relationship we had had as children.

After lunch, although I suddenly felt tired and weak and every fiber in my being rejected the notion, I let Marguerite talk me into visiting my father's grave. For some reason she was under the impression that I had a burning desire to see his final resting place and I simply didn't have the heart to tell her otherwise.

* * * *

My heart pounded as I pulled up in the cemetery's parking area, next to Marguerite's car. Never in my wildest dreams did I think I would ever be in Bill's presence again, much less be standing at his graveside, but here I was, staring down at the tiny plot where his ashes were buried. There, at my feet, lay the remnants of the man who had made my childhood – my very life – a living hell. It took everything in my power to keep from kicking the little headstone and shouting, "I hate you, Austin William Forrester! I hope you rot in hell!"

But, for Marguerite's sake, I kept silent, allowing my tears of anger and frustration to flow without reservation.

Marguerite obviously mistook them as tears of grief and said, "Don't worry, honey, I'm sure your father is in heaven. He was a good Christian."

I bristled at her words and my breath caught when an instant rage slammed along my spine. And then, without thinking I said, "Marguerite, I'm sorry, but the original reason I wanted to see Dad was to have it out with him. I'm very angry with him and my initial response to your comment is that if he went to heaven, then I want to go to hell because I don't want to spend eternity with him!"

The look on Marguerite's face reflected genuine shock. "Oh, surely you don't mean that, honey," she said. "We shouldn't speak ill of the dead. Whatever happened, I think you should just forgive him and get over it. There's no point in carrying a grudge."

"Forgiving is easier said than done," I snapped. In effort to force myself to calm down, I raised my eyes toward the gray, overcast sky and took a long, shaky breath. It had been stupid of me to agree to come here. Even though the man was dead, my animosity towards him was not, and I needed to give myself time to deal with it. "You're right, Marguerite," I finally said, forcing a smile. "I need to get on with my life. I just wish I had been able to talk to him and clear the air before he died. It would have made things easier."

Her face reflected sweet concern. "Well, honey," she replied, "You know you can still talk to him. He'll always be with you, right there in your heart."

I felt as if I had been slapped. Her words were the typical "Christian" response, and they made my soul cringe. My face flushed a hot crimson and my knees went weak as the words dropped from her lips. I felt raped at the very thought that Bill Forrester could "always be in my heart." Every fiber in my being rebelled at the thought and I found it hard to breathe. Thoughts of slicing my wrists and bleeding all over his headstone crossed my mind....

"I have to go now, Marguerite," I said feebly, with all the strength and control I could muster. My hands were trembling as I leaned into her for a brief, obligatory hug. "It was nice meeting you. Thank you for showing me Dad's grave, but I'm feeling really tired right now. I have to go."

Moments later, I was in my car, wanting nothing more than to leave this place, never to return. Marguerite waved as she disappeared into her own car, but I pretended not to notice and headed for the cemetery gate as fast as the speed limit allowed.

Chapter 18

Life in Springfield, Missouri, was mind-numbingly boring. If I wasn't sitting at home, I was sitting at Goldie's house, drinking coffee and re-hashing the same old conversations consisting of the same old neighborhood gossip I had heard time and time again over the years. We had recently tired of verbally bashing, for the trillionth time, all my awful ex-husbands and damning them to hell, and so Goldie was elated to hear "something new" when I told her of my experience with Marguerite. The conversation quickly caught fire, and somehow we ultimately came to a conclusion that this Marguerite must have been the very person with whom Bill was having an affair back when he and Goldie were still dating.

"I'm positive that's her," Goldie said, after rummaging through a closet to produce an old photo she had taken from Bill's house years ago. I had to admit that the woman in the picture did bear a close resemblance to Marguerite; although, apparently she had been much heavier in her younger days. "He told me he was dating somebody when we briefly broke up once, and this was her, I just know it."

"Amazing," I said. "Who knew they would end up married? Guess he went back to her when you dumped him the second time."

And so the conversation went for the next several weeks as Goldie and I once again rehashed the days when she and Bill had been together....

Melancholy continued to weigh heavily upon me, but I had no real desire to pull myself out of it. Life was a drag – and to make matters worse, I had to put my little Ollie to sleep when a digestion problem worsened to the point where he threw up every time he ate. It nearly killed me because Ollie had been my baby, my loyal friend, my steady companion through two failed marriages. The poor dog had been through a lot, and I simply couldn't stand to see him suffer anymore.

Afterward, I cried for two weeks straight as it seemed my situation just kept going from bad to worse. I decided that, even if I were to come out of my depression, I would only end up meeting another man who would ultimately lead me into yet another failed relationship. Perhaps I was doomed end up an "old maid" like poor Goldie who had never remarried after her husband Walt was killed in a trucking accident when she was very young, and she and I would both sit here drinking coffee, day in, day out, for the rest of our lives, endlessly gossiping about the neighbors and days gone by.

Oh how I longed for my Mama in Germany back then! I would have given anything to get that "safe" feeling I used to have, back when I was a little girl. But those days were long gone, and Mama wasn't keeping in touch anymore. The couple of times I called her on the telephone, she was uncommunicative and even angry, and I got the distinct feeling she was losing her mind. As sad as it was, it was time for me to let go of her.

Anyway, my life was basically at a standstill for several long and tedious months, until one Sunday morning when I awoke from a dream that spurred me out of the rut I had allowed myself to get into. In the dream, I was sitting at the very top of a steep roller-coaster track with the wind blowing on my face, watching throngs of tiny people milling around below. No one seemed to notice that I was perched at the crest of the track, no one cared. I was all alone.

Somehow, a uniformed police officer materialized on a motorcycle that came to rest near my feet. "Hello, ma'am," he said. "What are you doing here?"

"I don't know," I replied lethargically. "I have nowhere else to go."

"Well, that's fine, but the thing is, you can't stay here, either. You need to move."

"Why?"

"Because you can't stay here, ma'am."

I awoke with a start. Although it hadn't been one of my "vision" dreams, I realized it must have been trying to tell me something. Minutes later, while sitting at the breakfast table with a hot cup of coffee, pondering the policeman's words, I recalled a passage from a book about Oklahoma's "favorite son" Will Rogers who said, among many other things, "Even if you're on the right track, you'll get run over if you just sit there."

"Sitting here" is exactly what I had been doing. For way too long....

As much as my mind rebelled at the thought, it occurred to me that, at age 42, I might still have some living to do. And so I forced myself to take a shower, get dressed, and check out that singles group Goldie's neighbor had mentioned weeks ago.

* * * *

It was with great apprehension that I crossed the threshold of Schweitzer Methodist Church that Sunday morning. The last thing I wanted to do was to meet a bunch of holier-than-thou Christians, but I truly needed a social life that included someone else besides Goldie and her aged neighbors. Christians would simply have to do for now.

The singles group calling itself the "Soaring Solos" consisted of several hundred members of mostly middle-aged people, like myself. The conference room in which they met, thankfully, wasn't a regular church setting. As a matter of fact, it had nothing to do with the Sunday-go-to-meetin' crowd who congregated in the sanctuary across the hall. That suited me just fine.

Furthermore – and much to my surprise – I wasn't, as I had feared, accosted by a gaggle of dirty old lecherous men looking for dates. Instead, I was greeted by a couple of smiling ladies standing at a table by the entrance, offering coffee and donuts to visitors and handing out flyers about the group.

The guest speaker that morning was a local female psychiatrist who talked about necessity of getting on with our lives after divorce and dealing with the emotional trauma, whether we were the "dumpers" or the "dumpees." No Bible verses, no sermon; just a regular speech full of good, useful and pertinent information.

Afterwards, there was some singing and praying, but I had to admit that overall, the experience had been very pleasant. Not one person approached to tell me how much Jesus loved me or gave me that fire-and-brimstone warning about how I would go to hell if I didn't "believe."

By the time all was said and done, I had made some new friends who invited me out to brunch afterward, and at some point, I realized my depression had lifted. And, for the first time in months, I was feeling "normal" again.

Within weeks, I was completely immersed in the group's activities – dances, picnics and outings of all kinds – and before long I was "manning" one of the tables at the door, and volunteering to hold weekly "TV nights" designed to invite a few people into our homes for fellowship and to watch movies, have popcorn, or just keep each other company. One of the group's mottos was that no one needed to be lonely.

I was with the Soaring Solos for approximately a year when I volunteered as a facilitator for their bi-yearly Singles Adjustment seminars. Based on the workbook, "The Road Less Traveled" by M. Scott Peck, M.D., the three-day seminars were intended to help the newly widowed or divorced adjust to their new "single" status through the application of Biblical principles. One of my favorite parts was when we tasked the group to write on a sheet of paper the names of everyone who had ever hurt them in any way – and then to set the paper on fire, which symbolically represented a forgiving and "letting go" and basically "turning them over to God." As a student of the seminar earlier that Spring, I had actually felt a very tangible sense of release from the hold Bill Forrester and my mother had on me, and I couldn't wait to become a volunteer facilitator so I could help others "become released." Of course, I realized it was merely psychological, but there is something about "doing" an action that helps our minds to "remember" the conscious effort to release ourselves from the demons of our past.

Little did I know that this act of volunteerism would kick off a chain of events that ultimately changed *my entire life*!

* * * *

It happened during the closing ceremony in the sanctuary on the last evening of the seminar while the facilitators and the seventy participants stood in a circle holding hands.

Each of us was to thank God for the seminar and for this time of learning and healing, and to take turns verbalizing "why I'm glad I'm me." When my turn came, I happily admitted I was glad to be me because I had been through hell on Earth and was still here to complain about it (which elicited several giggles), and that, although it had seemed that "Satan, or Fate or whoever" had been trying to kill me off all of my life, I had grown through every experience and somehow made it through, and I was – thanks to this group – glad to be alive again.

By the time the thirtieth or fortieth person had expressed "why I am glad to be me," my mind began to wander, and I found myself peering around the sanctuary, wondering why I had always hated churches. Churches themselves weren't necessarily a horrible experience, although, for some reason the few I had visited over the course of my life had always managed to make me "feel dirty" somehow, like my insides somehow needed washing. My biggest problem was with the general attitudes of Christians who seemed hell-bent on converting everybody, bugging people for their phone numbers and generally harassing them to death. It crossed my mind that I probably wouldn't mind attending this church sometime if I could only be assured I wouldn't have any holy rollers accosting me. After all, I did actually believe in God, even though He didn't much seem to care for me. I just didn't like the idea of anybody assuming they could just approach me at will in order to "lead me to the Lord."

Soon my eyes wandered to the lit cross on the wall directly in front of me, and I found myself pondering exactly who this Jesus was that Christians seemed to be stuck on. I remembered seeing him while in the coma back in 1972 when I found myself floating alone through outer space, but even then he hadn't done anything for me. I wasn't sure exactly what he was supposed to have done for me, if anything, but in all actuality, I was still smarting over the fact that he had left me all alone in there in the darkness to fend for myself. Satan was the one who had pulled me out of the "abyss" or whatever it was, just before I regained consciousness. Jesus hadn't moved a muscle – just like he hadn't stopped Bill Forrester from raping me....

*Who **ARE** you? I silently demanded of the cross. Why do you keep cropping up in my life? What do you want from me, anyway?....I wish you'd stop playing games and give me some kind of a sign for once....*

Not expecting any kind of response, I stopped concentrating on the cross long enough to allow my gaze to wander toward the high windows and into the night sky.

Suddenly, another one of my "out-of-body feelings" caught me off-guard and gave me a flashback to age five; and for just a few seconds I found myself sitting in my foster grandmother's lap, looking out at the night sky while listening to her soothing voice telling me in German all about God. Awed by the enormity of her revelation, the "me" that was viewing the vision from outside myself, remembered exactly how I had felt that evening; how I had readily accepted as truth everything she was saying because her words had made me feel all warm and safe inside.

In the next instant, the vision switched to approximately a year later to remind me of the presence of a "dark man" who had paid me a visit while I was asleep in my bed. In a déjà vu-like state, I remembered being awakened by a horrible stench in my nostrils, and I cringed in terror as my eyes focused on the silhouetted man staring down at me. An eerie silence hung in the room as he stood there simply peering through the darkness, oozing a raw hatred and animosity that literally paralyzed me. Unable to move or to yell for my Mama, I lay there, waiting to see what the devil had in store for me – for there was no doubt it was he. But seconds later, to my great relief, he silently turned on his heel and left. And I remained awake, petrified for hours, too afraid to move, wondering why I hadn't heard any footsteps....

Back in Schweitzer Methodist Church, I "came to" for a few seconds, long enough to realize that my eyes were once again riveted on the cross – when, suddenly, I found myself experiencing a second wave of visions. At another level of awareness, I was conscious of the fact that others in the room were still sharing "why I'm glad to be me." Nobody seemed to notice what was happening to me.

In the next instant – as crazy as it might sound – I suddenly felt myself slightly lifted off the floor as a warm, dark pink light engulfed my body. I remember looking around to see if anybody noticed, and I even checked my feet to make sure they were still on the floor – which, of course, they were.

Baffled and quite apprehensive while realizing I was experiencing another one of my "weird episodes," I knew there was nothing I could do, and so I decided to allow myself to be cradled in that light, to bask in its inviting, supernatural glow.

All of a sudden, I became aware of the fact that the light was God, and He was somehow holding me in His arms! He – a very nebulous yet simultaneously a quite tangible Being – was inside of me, filling my entire body, every nerve, sinew and organ, even my soul. It was a most unique and awesome experience, completely indescribable. I had never felt so safe and secure in my entire life, and I found myself hoping this "vision episode" would last throughout eternity.

I felt as if my soul had caught fire and melted into a warm glow that opened my eyes and helped me to "see" things more clearly. In this state I *knew* things! I knew God, I knew the purpose of life, I knew why man was constantly at war and I knew that He had made sure I had been given to the Neumanns to ensure that I would become a "normal" person. I simply understood everything. I also recognized that God was giving me some kind of a glimpse into eternity. He even spoke to me – not with a voice, but through osmosis! I didn't so much hear Him as *feel* Him speaking....

Part of me wanted to yell at God for the things He had done to me; the terrible things He had allowed without any kind of intervention. Yet somehow, I realized it wouldn't be necessary, because He already knew these things. Plus, these few seconds in His Presence made all those bad times worthwhile; they were simply irrelevant in the grand scheme of things. So, instead of being angry at God as I always thought I would be whenever I died and stood before Him, I found myself, instead, thanking Him for all the horrendous things that had happened in my lifetime. Oddly, somehow the bad seemed to be on an equal plane with the good, and it just truly did not matter because it all served as a learning experience designed to draw me closer to God.

Toward the end of the episode – which, unlike all the other visions I had ever had, was longer, lasting least two or three minutes – I felt God tell me that He had allowed me to experience a life of pain and agony for a reason. It wasn't that He didn't care or that I hadn't been worthy of His help; but rather, He showed me that He allows men the free will, the choice to do things His way, or not. Unfortunately, the choices of others often impact us, and that was why I had experienced so much turmoil.

His final words to me before the light left my body were: "Carmen, I'm going to use your experiences for My Glory." And then He was gone.

I felt excruciatingly empty when the light left my body. Suddenly I kind of "melted" back into the room where I was able to feel my feet on the floor. In the background, the last seminar participant was droning on about "why I'm glad I'm me." Nobody had apparently noticed anything unusual, and no one said anything to me when the meeting finally broke.

Filled with awe and excitement and feeling absolutely euphoric once I snapped out of the vision, I was dying to tell someone, to let everyone in the church know that I had been "touched by God" – but instead, I kept silent because I knew no one would believe me. But there was absolutely no doubt in my mind that God had touched me; He had touched *me*!

I wanted to jump up and down and shout **Halleluyah!** and dance out the door on my way to the car! I was on a huge "high" and it felt great! Something wonderful had happened in my life; and I could tell things were about to turn around for me. I could just *feel* it....

My first thought was to go and see Goldie to tell her about the vision, but then I realized, she wasn't a believer and most probably, she would laugh at me. And so, I figured, for now, it would be best to keep this to myself.

* * * *

The "God touched me" incident had happened on a Sunday evening. On Monday, I was still flying high on the idea. By Tuesday afternoon, I was beginning to ask myself, who was I to be touched by God? I was just "a nobody" who had done nothing but screw up her own life in one way or another. Maybe my vision hadn't been real after all. Maybe I had just been feeling euphoric on Sunday night because I had been a facilitator at a seminar that helped people to get on with their lives….

By Wednesday morning, I was totally depressed. Not only had my euphoria disappeared, but also I was dreading my appointment at the Mammography Center because, after two years of "keeping an eye" on the large lump in my left breast, doctors finally decided to do a biopsy after today's mammogram.

I walked into the office on rubber legs and prepared for the worst. The kind nurse assured me everything would be all right as she prepared to do my mammogram, but all I could do was to wonder how much time I had left on Earth.

It seemed like eons before she returned with the doctor's verdict, but the smile on her face told me that my worries were over.

"Carmen, the lump is gone!" she said matter-of-factly.

I was stunned, and unwilling to take her word for it, lest she had me confused with someone else. "Gone?" I replied cautiously. That couldn't have been true, because I had felt it last Friday evening while showering before attending the seminar. Granted, I hadn't bothered to touch it since then, because the very thought of touching the thing made weak, but was it really gone now?

"Yes," she said. "Look – see here? That white portion down there, that's the remnants of it. It's disappeared. Guess you won't be needing that biopsy, after all."

As I stood there gawking at the nurse in disbelief, it suddenly hit me that God really **had** touched me! It had not been my imagination or mere after-seminar euphoria; He **had** really been inside my soul, healing me with that warm pink light, and this was His confirmation! After two long years of worrying about that lump, it couldn't have been mere coincidence that it was gone right after that awesome God experience. I had received some kind of a second chance for some reason....

I wanted so much to say it aloud, but didn't dare for fear of looking like some religious hypocrite. Rather than take that chance, I simply thanked the nurse and left.

So, now what? I thought as I headed for the parking lot. Was I supposed to start attending church or something? If so, which church? Was God wanting me to become religious now, or what? I simply couldn't envision myself as a "holy roller," but surely He had given me that vision for a reason.

In the meantime, brimming with a kind of happiness I hadn't felt in a long time, I couldn't wait to drive out to Goldie's to tell her I wasn't dying. On the way, I stopped by the Humane Society to pick out a new puppy, a cute little Cocker/Lhasa Apso mix I named "B.J." after an old neighbor's dog....

Chapter 19

The "vision" at Schweitzer Methodist remained foremost in my mind over the next few months. I could hardly think about anything else. I lay in bed nightly, fervently praying for God to "touch me" again, but nothing happened. My daily mantra – *Dear God, what am I supposed to do now?* – remained frustratingly unanswered.

Christmas came and went, and as usual, the holidays had left me feeling alone and empty. Even though I now had new friends to spend some time with, the parties and the rituals of Christmas with all its bells and whistles and bright lights and gaily-decorated trees left me feeling like there was something missing.

I had actually had problems with Christmas since I was about five or six, when Mama in Germany had dropped the bombshell that there was no Santa Claus. What upset me more than anything was the discovery that my parents had **lied** to me. Until then, I thought every word out of their mouths was the gospel truth.

Be that as it may, ever since then, Christmas had held no real meaning for me. While I recognized the fact that it was supposed to be the birthday celebration of Jesus, you never heard his name mentioned in TV commercials or in malls where their main concentration was on Santa Claus; and most parties I had ever been to never acknowledged "the real reason for the season." For the most part, Christmas was all about buying presents for others you couldn't afford, and drinking and partying and feeling lonely and depressed when your own life didn't turn out like the in the movies with their fairy tale endings.

I harbored the same animosity towards Easter. Easter was supposed to represent the Resurrection, yet according to the TV ads and the stores in the malls, it was all about Easter egg hunts and egg-laying rabbits, buying candy, dressing up, and kids having fun. I was sure Jesus wasn't thrilled about either of those holidays!

During the course of the following year, I decided it was time to go back to work, and so I took a part time job as a receptionist at the KY-3 television station and did some free-lance writing for "*Springfield! Magazine*" on the side. It helped to while away the weeks while I waited for *something* to happen in my life, and/or for God's next "visit" – which I was beginning to think was nothing more than a pipe dream as the months passed, and spring turned to summer and summer to fall.

But, little did I realize that shortly my entire life was about to be turned upside-down, and in a way that I never in a million years expected….

The wheels of this upcoming life-changing event were actually set in motion on the night the Soaring Solos sponsored an "Oldies Dance" in November 1994, when my best friend and confidante, Rosemary, dared me to get up and ask a very shy man at a nearby table to dance. Rosemary and I had spied him sitting alone and appearing extremely uncomfortable; and since I was part of the Solo's greeting team, I used that as an excuse to introduce myself.

His name was Ellis. Dressed in a white western shirt and cowboy boots, he was tall and ruggedly handsome in a "country boy" sort of way. I discovered while we were out on the dance floor that he had a large beef farm in Seymour where he lived with his three teenaged sons, and that he was the owner and operator of a farm animal feed business. His wife, he told me, had recently left him for another man and so he was floundering about, trying to figure out how to be single again, and what he was supposed to do with the new life that had suddenly and unexpectedly been thrust upon him.

I have to admit my enthusiasm waned when he mentioned his three sons. It had been all I could do to handle Larry's *one* teenager, let alone allow myself to envision a future with a man who had three of them! At this point in my life, the last thing I wanted to do was get involved with another man who had kids from a previous marriage. Been there, done that, couldn't deal with the idea....

Ellis, it turned out, was a devout Baptist, and our conversations inevitably kept returning to Jesus and the Bible. To my dismay, he wasn't just religious; he was the quintessential "Bible thumper" – the kind of person who I knew would get on my nerves very quickly. And so, by the end of the evening, as much as I was drawn to him, I told him it would be best to part ways (and behind his back I jokingly told Rosemary she could have him). Not wanting him to feel completely dejected, though, I gave him my home phone number and invited him to call if he had any questions about the Soaring Solos.

Ellis did call a couple of times, but in the meantime, I somehow got sucked into dating some guy named Tom who – alas! – happened to be exactly "my type"....a confident macho man, complete with a domineering personality, unbridled arrogance and plenty of attitude. I was immediately smitten, which meant poor Ellis didn't stand a chance....

But, long story *extremely* short, Tom and I dated for a grand total of three weeks, which won him the booby prize as my shortest relationship ever. His idea of a good time was to hang out in local cowboy bars to drink beer, dance and "see and be seen" – something I wasn't exactly fond of, but chose to overlook, because – as you know by now – I was very gullible when it came to "my type" of man!

Amazingly, while the events that occurred to put a quick end to our relationship felt like a "twist of fate," at that point (thanks to my Schweitzer Methodist vision) I was beginning to think that **God** had more to do with it. Here's what happened:

Tom was a womanizer; there was no doubt about it. That's why I was surprised and completely thrilled to discover in the third week of our relationship that he had chosen *me* to accompany him to the Virgin Islands for the upcoming Christmas holidays. No man in the history of my life had ever offered me a paradise vacation before, and I thought it meant that he was getting serious. I should have known better!

Anyway, that evening, Tom took me to a country dance place to celebrate, and on the way in, he happened to see an old friend sitting at the bar. Giving me a quick peck on the cheek, he told me to find a table and order our drinks while he and the old cowboy caught up "with the latest gossip."

After ten or fifteen minutes of peering through the dusky smoke-filled room to watch Tom and his buddy laughing and joking and slapping each other on the back, I found myself becoming bored and slightly irritated that he could be rude enough to leave me alone for so long. Then, suddenly, a man who had been seated on the other side of Tom on a nearby bar stool, rose and crossed the room to approach my table. At first, I thought it was just some guy thinking I was alone and wanting to ask me to dance, but then a smile crossed my face when I realized it was Dave, a guy I knew from one of the Singles Adjustment Seminars. Dave, I remembered, was an extremely sensitive, sweet and shy man who had been dumped by an overbearing wife who had done some major damage to his fragile ego.

Appearing quite nervous as he addressed me from across the table, he tossed a quick and anxious glance over his shoulder and said, "Carmen, is that dark-haired guy with a mustache over there your boyfriend? I saw you coming in with him."

"Yes," I replied, beaming. "I guess you could call him my boyfriend. We've been together for three weeks now."

"How well do you know him?"

"Know him? Why? What do mean?"

"Well, you're planning on going to the Virgin Islands with him, right?"

"Yeah," I replied, perplexed. "How did you know that?"

Dave tossed another quick glance toward the bar where Tom and his buddy were still engaged in deep conversation. "Well," he said, "I guess I'll just come out and say it because you have a right to know....Your boyfriend is over there talking very disrespectfully about you. Without going into all the gory details, he's telling his buddy how he conned you into taking a vacation with him because he had bought a non-refundable package trip with his former girlfriend who apparently dumped him, and he didn't want to lose his money."

My eyes widened as Dave's words tore at me. "He didn't tell me that part," I mumbled.

"Well, the kicker is, he's over there bragging about how you weren't his first choice; that some other lady had turned him down earlier today, and so you are – to quote him – better than nothing."

I was floored, speechless. My mouth worked, but nothing came out, and I just sat there for a moment, shaking my head in disbelief.

"I'm sorry, Carmen, but I just had to tell you," I heard Dave say over the mad hammering of my heart. "You're a nice lady and you don't deserve this."

My mind raced as I watched Tom casually leave his barstool, slap his buddy's back for the last time, and then turn, with beer bottle in hand, to search for me in the crowded room. He grinned when he saw me, then casually sauntered over to the table and extended his hand to Dave. "Howdy partner," he said. "Who might you be?"

"He's a friend," I snapped, angrily rising from my seat. "A friend who's offered to take me home because you won't be."

Tom's eyes flashed as he gave me a puzzled look. "What are you talking about?"

"Ask your buddy over at the bar," I replied dryly. "In the meantime, perhaps you ought to consider taking your dog to the Virgin Islands. He would be better than nothing, too…."

And with that, I stormed from the room and left Tom standing in my wake.

* * * *

I awoke the following morning feeling unusually chipper. In all honesty, I knew that breaking up with Tom was the best thing that could have happened, and it was actually a relief to have it over with. The guy was another disaster in my life just waiting to happen.

Desiring to let Goldie in on my latest saga, I drove to Brookline after breakfast. I figured, after a conversation with my Mom over a hot, steaming cup of coffee, I would be good as new. Goldie would be more than happy to let me "talk Tom out of my system" – plus, it would give her some more fresh gossip as well.

I stomped on the brake and waved when I saw her coming down the alley from a neighbor's house. Oddly, she stopped in her tracks when she saw me, muttered something under her breath, and then without saying a word, she crossed the road in front of my car and continued walking towards her house.

Confused, I rolled down my passenger side window to ask what the matter was, but she simply ignored me and kept on going.

"Goldie?" I cried. "What's wrong?"

"Nothing. Just go away. I don't want no company this morning."

"What do you mean you don't want company?"

"I just don't feel like having company."

"But, I'm *not* company," I yelled after her, feeling slighted and confused. "I'm your daughter!"

At first, I started to make a U-turn and go back home. But then I realized I had finally had enough. Goldie had been acting strangely for months, and I wanted to know why.

Moments later, I was standing in the kitchen where she was in the process of heating a kettle of water. "You're not getting rid of me that easy," I said angrily. "I want to know what's bothering you all of a sudden...."

"You don't care about me," she said without turning around.

"What do mean by that, Mom? Of course, I care about you!"

"No, you don't!"

"....Could you please explain? I mean, exactly what makes you think I don't care about you?" I could feel my heart pounding in my throat because, whatever was going on here, it would not end well. It was clear that Goldie's deluded thought processes had concocted something, and in her mind, that made it real.

"You just don't care about me, that's all. I'm tired of being used."

I was stunned. "Used? Mom, how in the world am I using you?"

The whistle went off as the kettle started to boil. Angrily yanking it from the stove, she poured the hot water over the instant coffee in her cup, and then turned to face me. "I just don't think it's a good idea for you to come and see me anymore," she said.

"Fine, if that's the way you feel, but don't you think I have the right to know what you're angry about? I have absolutely *no* clue as to what brought all this on."

"You *use* me, Carmen!" she yelled. "You always want something from me."

"That's ridiculous. I don't want anything from you! I thought we were family, being there for each other."

"Well, I'm always there for you, but you're never there for me!"

"Oh," I said, with a dramatic wave of my hand, "now I get it. You and the gossip queen down in the back alley have been talking behind my back again, and came to the conclusion that I'm the bad guy for some reason. I should have guessed. You two have been at it for months because you've been decidedly chilly towards me. Thanks a lot, Mom!"

Goldie's face turned crimson. "I have a right to talk to whoever I want," she snapped. "It's my business."

"Oh, so it *is* true! I should have known it would eventually come down to this." I was livid, not to mention sick and tired of whatever was going around about me in the neighborhood gossip sessions, particularly with one old lady who had absolutely nothing nice to say about anyone.

"Mom," I continued as calmly as I could, "I love you, but if I walk out that door today, I promise you, I will *never* return, because I'm truly tired of this, do you understand? You have been treating me like dirt for months now and not even had the decency to tell me why. Is it because I've stopped giving you support money?"

"No."

"If so, I'd be glad to start giving you a monthly 'allowance' again. I have a job now, even though it doesn't pay a whole lot...."

"I don't want your damned money!" she yelled.

"Well, then what *do* you want from me?"

"Nothing! What do YOU want from me?"

"What are you talking about?"

"It doesn't matter. Just go away."

My eyes filled with angry tears as I watched her standing there in the scant light of the tiny kitchen. Outside, huge snowflakes were beginning to fall and I felt a chill course through my body.

"...Okay," I went on. "I'm guessing then, you just want me out of your life, is that it?"

Goldie's gaze fell to the floor as she turned slightly sideways and nonchalantly shrugged her shoulders.

"Okay," I said after a very uncomfortable pause, "I guess I have my answer. Thanks for everything you've done for me over the years. Goodbye forever, then."

I stopped short at the door in hopes that she would try to stop me, but she never made a sound.

* * * *

The Christmas holidays that year were basically ruined. Feeling as if I had just gone through another divorce, I sat around my rented townhouse, moping and crying and generally wondering what to do. I had never in my life felt more lonely, lost and forlorn than that day after my fight with Goldie. There had been no rhyme or reason for the rift between us. A friendship of almost thirty years was gone in a split second, doused like water on a flame – and I had no clue as to why. My efforts to contact her on the neighbors' telephones and through letters were in vain, and after awhile I stopped bothering.

To take my mind off Goldie, I thought about taking a trip to Florida to see my ailing brother Ted over the holidays, but since his fatal illness had failed to rekindle the sibling love we had once shared, I decided to stay at home and be content to simply continue with our occasional phone calls and letters. Ted, I discovered in our telephone conversations in recent months, had been harboring some major resentment against me – some of it dating back to the time when he allowed our mother to convince him to move back in with her after I ran away from home. Somehow, he had convinced himself that I was to blame for his lot in life as Lonny's babysitter and "chief cook and bottle washer" during those days. The years of festering hatred had basically taken their toll, with neither of us willing to put much energy into our relationship anymore. Our rare phone conversations were strained because we really had nothing to say to each other. And so I stayed home with my little doggie, B.J., the one living, breathing entity in the world who loved me unconditionally.

Although I spent New Year's Eve in '94/'95 with some people from the Solos, I felt alone. The party at a local nightclub I had been invited to did nothing to lift my spirits, and I lay in bed afterwards listlessly staring into the darkness and contemplating my sad life, and generally feeling sorry for myself because, except for my only real friend Rosemary, I had no one who was close to me.

As I lay there wide awake and lazily watching the occasional haloed car lights creeping along the ceiling, I thought of my old love David and wondered what my life might have been like had I not acted like a jealous, spoiled child and lost his love all those years ago. *Oh God,* I thought, *is there any possibility that David could somehow be restored to me?....*

I had been so sure that my life would change after the "Schweitzer vision" episode, but it hadn't. Things were the same as they had always been, and I was beginning to think God had probably forgotten all about me.

On the spur of the moment – thanks to my feelings of desperation, and thinking I had nothing left to lose, anyway – I folded my hands in prayer and tried to "tune into" Him somehow, hoping He might "touch me" again, to maybe help me figure things out, or tell me what to do....

"God," I heard myself say as if from far away, "I'm sure you know my situation; I'm pretty much alone in the world. Since I don't have Goldie anymore, I don't know where I belong. She was my anchor. As for men, I don't even know what to say because I can't seem to pick a decent one. All the ones I invite into my life end up being jerks and weirdoes. I hate this dating stuff, going from one guy to the next. And so, I guess what I'm saying is, if you're as sick and tired of my life and my lifestyle as I am, why don't you give me a good man for a change?"

Silence resonated in the room. The night was so still that I could hear my own heartbeat. There were no visions, no flashbacks, no weird "episodes" to lift my spirits or let me know that God was even remotely interested in my soliloquy. *I guess His line is busy*, I thought sardonically. *It's not fair God – You touched me a year ago, and then just left me hanging! Why did You do that?*

"Lord, please hear me," I begged as the tears started to flow. "My life is forever in the toilet, and I don't know what to do about it. I have no one, and I'm tired of being lonely…Please – I'm begging you – if you're really real and you care about me, please give me a good man for a change."

Frustrated, I swiped at a hot tear that had had made its way down my neck, and began crying anew. "…And for once," I added when the ache in my throat let up, "make me wise enough to know it…."

* * * *

I was shocked when Ellis, the Bible thumping Baptist, called the very next afternoon.

"Carmen," he said, "I don't know why I'm doing this, because I never bug a woman who's turned me down for a date. But something told me to call and try again."

I hesitated when I heard his voice, and was about to turn him down – when I remembered my request of God the night before. Rolling my eyes toward the heavens in hushed resignation that this must be God's will, I silently mouthed the words, "You've got to be kidding!"

Chapter 20

As much as my mind wanted to reject the idea of getting involved with a Bible thumping church goer, something deep inside told me Ellis' call had been a sign from God, and that I would be a fool to ignore it. And so mid-January, 1995, found me nervously seated in the pews of First Baptist Church in Seymour, amidst an entire congregation of Christians in a dumpy little town whose population - judging from all the horse-drawn carriages on the roads - seemed to be largely Amish. The whole scenario was quite surrealistic; especially the idea that I was actually in a *church* on Sunday morning.

Even though Ellis wasn't exactly my type, I found him irresistibly handsome in a country sort of way. He was funny and charming and very much a gentleman and, during our initial meeting a week earlier at a Village Inn in Springfield, I decided that perhaps God was trying to get me to change my taste in men. If that was to be the case, however, then I would have to work on getting him over the Bible thumping stuff and convince him to do something else on Sundays besides run to church and warm the pews.

In the meantime, I would simply have to deal with it and get to know Ellis' family and friends before trying to make any changes in their lives. As far as I could tell, his seemingly well-adjusted sons – ranging from ages fourteen through twenty-one – and their church friends all seemed like people I wouldn't mind being around. None of them seemed like the wild-eyed, hellfire and brimstone "Sergeant Lassiter" types who had caused me to hyperventilate.

Still – although I had been warmly greeted by Pastor Wil and his wife and some of the members of First Baptist – my apprehension level was quite high as I sat there nervously gazing around the church, because I knew it would only be a matter of time before these people started in with their "Jesus loves you" and "If you don't believe in Jesus, you're going to hell" speeches. Ellis, apparently sensing my uneasiness, gave my hand a reassuring squeeze.

The next twenty minutes or so, before Pastor Wil took the podium, were filled with the sounds of joyous singing and worship. I couldn't help but wonder how many people standing here with their rapt faces exuding holiness were actually *living* their belief and wholeheartedly *felt* what they were singing; and how many were standing there hypocritically thinking about their next illicit sexual encounters, or were waiting to go home afterwards to get drunk and end up beating their wives, kids and dogs.

For some reason Bill Forrester's wrinkled mug popped into my mind and I wondered how often he had sat there on Sunday mornings, singing with his own church choir pretending to be worshiping the

Lord while secretly fantasizing about the little girl he was currently molesting....

I breathed a sigh of relief when Pastor Wil finally took the podium and released my over-active mind from the grips of a downward spiral that had me wanting to make a mad dash out to the parking lot. Wil was a thin, bespectacled middle-aged man with dark hair and a wide smile. His demeanor – wise and alert, yet humble – came across as someone who truly "loved the Lord" and *lived* his faith without an ounce of hypocrisy.

When he spoke, it was in a surprisingly dynamic tone, and on that particular morning, he started his sermon with a question. "Let's suppose for a moment you died today and stood before the Lord God," he said, "and He asked you, 'Why should I let you into My heaven?'...What would your answer be?"

Peering up at Ellis, I grinned and shrugged. Until that moment, I had never really thought about it. I didn't recall God asking me any questions at all during my "Schweitzer Methodist episode." He had simply held me in His lap and allowed me to experience love on a plane I never realized existed. As far as I knew, I would automatically end up in heaven. After all, I was a good person who just happened to have lived through many misfortunes and been forced to endure hell on Earth.

In my peripheral vision, I saw Ellis stealing another glance at me and I blushed. Ellis, the sweet and innocent country boy from Smalltown, USA, really had no clue who he was with. While I had shared with him that I was a several times divorcee, he didn't know exactly how much of a "woman of the world" I was; or that, in my quest to find a husband, I had dated more than my share of men, and done many things I wasn't exactly proud of. He didn't know the extent of my sins which, in God's eyes, were probably pretty grave – although there was no doubt in my mind I would end up in heaven, anyway.

An uneasy silence hung in the air before the pastor spoke again. "Would your response be something like, 'I am a religious person trying to live a Christian life the best I can'?" he asked. "Or, 'I go to church, give to the poor, help people in need, and have always tried to be a good person'?"

Of course that's what I'd say, I thought. *What else can you say when you're standing in front of your Maker?*

But Wil's next comment knocked me for a loop, when he continued: "If your answer to any of these questions was 'yes' then you'd be wrong because **none** of those things would get you into heaven! **The only thing that gets you into heaven** is your belief on the shed blood of Jesus Christ – by your faith in Jesus Christ who was our Sin Sacrifice and died on the cross to pay the penalty for our sins...."

Sin Sacrifice. The words literally reverberated in my mind. Jesus was our *Sin* Sacrifice? What on Earth was that supposed to mean?

As if in answer to my question, Wil's sermon went on to explain why and how Jesus was the divine Being sent by God to forever abolish the need for the animal sin sacrifices required of God's people since the day Adam and Eve were evicted from the Garden. If you believed in Christ with all your heart, Wil explained, then you were "a brand new creature" who would be assured a place in heaven.

I couldn't believe my ears! Here was the answer to the question I had posed before the cross at Schweitzer Methodist a year ago: *Who are you?*

Jesus was our SIN Sacrifice; *that's* who he was. Somehow, this information satisfied me; it explained a lot.

As if guided by some unseen force that was telling Wil exactly what I needed to hear, he went on to explain that God, in His wisdom, grace and mercy, had provided the world an easier way to atone for sins and that was why, in the modern world, our priests and rabbis and pastors weren't required to kill innocent animals anymore....

A faint memory emerged from the archives of my mind about some book I'd read, or some movie I had seen that had included the idea of the Old Testament God demanding blood sacrifices for man's every little infraction. One thing that had remained with me was the idea that God had killed an animal in order to cover the nakedness of Adam and Eve who suddenly knew "shame" because of their blatant disobedience to keep away from the Tree of the Knowledge of

Good and Evil. I remembered thinking how awful it must have been for Adam and Eve to have an animal they had loved and named, killed in their presence.

As disgusting as the animal sacrifice thing was to me, it made sense in a way because God Himself had provided a "covering" for us, just as He had for Adam and Eve. Jesus, from what I had just learned, was the covering for those who actually believed in God and all those fairy tale-like stories in the Bible....

Somehow, I found it incomprehensible that a good and perfect person like Jesus – whom I had actually had the privilege of seeing while in my coma – had died in my place. After all, I was the one who had sinned; not him! On the other hand, as Wil was in the process of explaining, God always demanded a perfect, blemish-free, clean sacrifice – which meant I wasn't qualified to atone for my own sins.

In the next instant I had another thought, and it horrified me: If all this was true – that Jesus had died for everyone, and that the only thing required to obtain eternal life was to repent for our sins and "believe in Jesus" – then this meant that Bill Forrester *had* actually gone to heaven as Marguerite had suggested that day in the cemetery!

Once again I felt like dashing out of the church. The mere thought that I would have to spend eternity with that ghoul made me hyperventilate!

No, I couldn't allow myself to entertain that thought. Surely, God in His grace and mercy wouldn't allow a person like that into His heaven....

Plus, it wouldn't be fair that Bill, the "Christian" pedophile would go to heaven just because he "believed in Jesus" while my mother, the mixed-up child of an atheistic Jewish woman who had forced her into prostitution, went to hell. Like me, Lonny had been through hell and Earth, too, although she had caused her own hell for the most part and been responsible for the hell I had had to endure as a child. But to think she would be denied heaven because she hadn't been a "Christian" was ridiculous and unfair. I couldn't see a just God doing something like that.

"Nobody," Wil was saying, "is good enough to enter Heaven on their own. Nobody. Our works are like filthy rags to God. He is holy; He is perfect. Nothing imperfect can come into His presence. That is why Jesus took the sin of the entire world upon His shoulders. He *chose* to do it; He didn't *have* to. Thanks to Him, and Him only, we have a chance at eternal life. The moment He died, we were all forgiven, every one of us. When He died, He rose again and became the Holy Spirit. And all we have to do in order to 'be saved' is to repent and ask the Holy Spirit into our hearts, confess with our mouths that we know we are sinners, and then ask Him to guide our lives from now on. *That* is what will get you into Heaven. That is the *only* thing that will get you into Heaven."

Inside my head, something – like raising the blinds on a window, or opening a door and seeing what was on the other side – happened, and I felt strangely liberated. I "knew" the things Wil said to be true; just like I had "known" that my foster grandmother was telling me the truth about God. It was a feeling like the first time I figured out how to read or ride a bicycle: I just *"knew"*....

"...He is the Potter and you are the clay," Wil was saying. "He loves you and desperately wants to have a relationship with you. Realizing this, repenting, and getting down on your knees in complete surrender to your Maker is the *only* way you will ever be able to live your life to the full."

My throat ached as the urge to cry became overwhelming. I remembered enough of the "Schweitzer episode" to know that the things Wil was espousing were absolutely true. Some of the things he said lined up exactly with what I had "felt" that evening when I somehow, out of nowhere "knew" things.

Peering over the rim of his glasses, Wil slowly scanned the congregation and said – and I couldn't help but think he was addressing me – "Won't you give your life to Jesus today?"

I wanted desperately to go up to the altar to publicly accept Christ, but found I just couldn't do it. While I felt something special had just taken place inside my soul, the fact remained I was a stranger at First Baptist; I didn't know these people, and didn't know how they would react if they were to discover I was now one of "them." Just because I now believed, I didn't want to come across like some Bible thumper, even though I was sitting in a nest of them. Plus, I didn't want to make a fool out of myself by bursting into tears in front of all these strangers....

In the back of my mind I realized that the sermon had come to and end, and I suddenly felt tired and worn out. With the apprehension gone – along with some of the resentment towards Christians, I felt good and yet guilty at the same time, knowing that somebody else had died on my behalf. The thought was almost too much to bear. A million questions crashed through my mind, but they would have to wait until I had a chance to speak with Wil, one-on-one.

Ellis smiled and took my hand as we stood to leave. I believe he could tell there was a change in me; that something was different! I wasn't sure exactly what had happened, but something had changed inside my mind, my heart, my very being. It was as if a light bulb had been turned on and I could now "see" what God had been trying to tell me all my life.

I was a new person that day when I left that little white church in Seymour, Missouri. And I knew, beyond a shadow of a doubt, that meeting Ellis had been no coincidence.

Chapter 21

Life was never the same after that first experience in Ellis' church. I had begun dating him with the idea in mind that I would be making changes in his life; but, instead, it was the other way around. Ellis, the farmer, as it turned out, literally turned my world upside-down. And I haven't been the same since.

Not only did I become a regular at First Baptist, but before long, I was a member; and I even moved to Seymour – partly for Ellis, and partly to be closer to the church. And to my own astonishment (because, being childless, I was never "into" kids) by the time the summer of '95 came around, I was volunteering some secretarial skills at the church and had even ended up as one of the teachers for the children's classes at "Vacation Bible School."

My being involved in a church was the biggest paradox in history: Somehow, I – the former Christian-hating woman of the world - suddenly couldn't get enough of God! It was as if I had caught fire, reading and studying everything concerning this subject that I could possibly get my hands on.

During those initial months, one sweet little old lady thought she was giving me some sage advice by telling me, "Oh honey, this is just your honeymoon with Jesus. We all go through that. You'll get over it." Although I abruptly negated what I felt to be a strange comment coming from someone who supposedly "loved the Lord," it served to make me realize why so many Christians came across as hypocrites: They lost that initial thrill and cooled down eventually, forgetting the fact that there was more to their relationship with God than just "believing in Jesus." They ultimately failed to remember that God told us to be faithful and vigilant, continuously learning and *doing* His Word. They forgot that God has an enemy behind the scenes bent on our destruction; someone who lives to wreak havoc in our lives, using whatever tools necessary to get the job done. In my case, that enemy had repeatedly used sex in one way or another, along with raging animosity towards Bill Forrester and my mother, to keep me in bondage. As it turned out, I had dragged their "baggage" with me into every relationship – which explained why my career had always flourished, while my personal relationships remained in a constant state of chaos.

These things, I decided, were only understood by those Christians who made the extra effort and recognized the truth of the Bible. The rest of the world was oblivious to the goings-on of the spirit world. They saw everything in tangible and intangible, black and white, real and in fantasy. But I grasped the significance immediately. I could literally look back and see where Satan had tried his level best to kill me off. With God "on my side," however, I was a survivor of several things, including a ruptured appendix episode that would have killed most people, and a high-speed freeway accident!

Although it totally went against my "woman-of-the-world" mindset, I figured I could get used to Seymour and its residents with their friendly, down-to-Earth, simple country life by completely entrenching myself. And so I started by buying a modest "fixer-upper" since most of the rental houses in and around town were ancient shacks, and then eventually got a job as a feature writer and advertisement designer at the local newspaper, the Webster County Citizen. Life was actually pretty good and I was beginning to feel "in charge" again.

Unfortunately, my relationship with Ellis began to fizzle almost as soon as it started because the differences between us were simply too great.

While his faith was no longer a problem, his lifestyle was. Like most in Seymour, Ellis was a simple, hard-working, honorable man; the quintessential "country bumpkin" who was perfectly content to quietly live and let live, and to sit on his front porch chewing tobacco and admiring his cows or watching traffic pass on the ribbon of dirt passing by his house. I, on the other hand, needed more. I was a globetrotter, someone who had literally "been there and done that." I couldn't see myself sitting by his side year after boring year, lazily watching the paint peeling off the barn. There was a world out there waiting to be discovered; not the world I had already seen and experienced, but something deeper and more powerful that I couldn't quite put my finger on – something that seemed to have possessed me and was leaving me completely restless. Down deep, I knew I would never find "it" in Seymour and, after just sixteen months, my wanderlust kicked into overdrive.

One of the "straws that broke the camel's back" in my relationship with Ellis came one Sunday morning at church when, despite my vehement protests, both he and the children's pastor began pestering me about teaching children's Sunday School. By the time church let out, I was literally running out into the parking lot to take refuge in Ellis' car.

"What part of **NO** don't you guys get?" I yelled at Ellis when he slid into the driver's side. "I mean, ever since I started attending First Baptist, you people have been hounding me about doing things with children. I'm not *into* children, yet you guys just won't leave me alone. I helped teach Vacation Bible School, and that's *all* I'm going to do!"

"But you're great with kids," Ellis protested weakly.

"But I don't like kids!" I replied, fighting back tears of anger. "Kids worry me, I told you that. They make me uneasy because they bring up memories of my own childhood. I can't help but think that every man wants to have sex with little girls, Ellis. But yet, ever since I starting coming to church with you, I've had people trying to shove kids down my throat every five minutes, and I can't take it anymore! ***God*** knows how I feel about kids, and He wouldn't deliberately force them on me, so why are you guys doing it?"

Eyeing me soberly, Ellis quietly said, "Well, maybe God is trying to tell you something."

It would be an understatement to say that a blind rage overtook me when those words dropped from his lips. In that moment, I wanted to hurt Ellis, to tear out his hair, to scream bloody murder...It was all I could do to keep from dashing into the parking lot to find a rock and smash the car window. I felt as if I had been thrown into the past facing down that irritating fanatic, Sergeant Lassiter....

But realizing this was Ellis, I managed to control myself and just sit there, demanding he take me home.

Needless to say, I sulked for the rest of the day, crying and talking to God about this situation because I felt totally lost and helpless, demanding to know *why* He was allowing people to harass me about kids.

By the time Ellis came over later that evening to check on me, I had made up my mind that maybe, just maybe, he might have been right about God's trying to "teach me something." After all, you can't heal unless you first face the fact that you have a problem.

"Okay, you were right," I conceded. "I just hate the way you and Wil and the children's pastor have gone about this, literally trying to *force* me into participating in children's activities at church. It makes me feel raped, can't you understand that? There are plenty of women who love to play Mommy and to teach children, but I'm just not one of them, and I'm sick and tired of you guys trying to turn me into somebody I'm not."

"Haven't you ever wanted kids of your own?" Ellis asked after a solemn silence.

My face fell. "Yeah, I used to have strong urges when I was younger," I replied, "but I just couldn't bring myself to perpetrate this awful world on innocent children. I couldn't perpetrate ME on innocent children!"

"What do you mean?"

"You know exactly what I mean. I'm a broken person with an abusive and dysfunctional past. I wouldn't be a good mother, and I'm certainly no role model for kids! Being around kids isn't healthy for me."

Ellis eyed me sympathetically. "I think there's more going on than that."

"What do you mean?"

"Well, I don't know how to put it, exactly, but you're …well, moody."

"Moody?"

"Yeah. You're either up or down. I never know what to expect whenever I come to see you."

I blinked stupidly. "I'm not moody!" I said a little louder than intended. "I can't help it if you make me mad all the time."

Ellis grinned and rolled his eyes. "Honey," he said, "trust me when I say you're moody!"

In an effort to see if Ellis might have been correct in his assessment, I decided to perform an experiment over the next few days by charting my moods at certain times throughout the day – and what I discovered left me speechless. It turned out that he was right: I was definitely "moody." According to my crude chart, I learned that my moods would switch for seemingly no reason. They switched whenever I watched a TV show that evoked some memory, or when I smelled a certain scent, or heard a certain word or a song that reminded me in some way of my childhood. Even cooking with my Corningware tended to enrage me because it reminded me of the baking dishes my mother used. I went through many different moods throughout the day that left me angry, sad or depressed. Some were subtle, others were almost manic. I had never before realized that virtually everything and anything had such tremendous impact on me.

Rather than to try to deal with this situation myself, I decided to make an appointment with a psychiatrist at the Veteran's Hospital. Unfortunately, this woman didn't seem to want to hear my story, and decided after only twenty minutes in her office that I was "mildly chronically depressed," and wrote a prescription for a strong antidepressant that nearly killed me after the first dose, even though I had cut it into quarters, just to be on the safe side until I could see how it would affect me....

After that, I immediately sought out someone else; this time I ended up with a counselor in Springfield who was referred by a friend of mine. This lady was wonderful, listening to my story with genuine care and concern. After three or four months as her patient, I felt like a new person because she helped me to come to grips with many issues, including some I had never deemed important.

"How do you feel today, this very minute, about the fact that you were given away as a baby?" she asked me one day.

My initial reaction was to blast my parents, but then I felt a "nudging" from the Holy Spirit that caused me to rearrange my thinking. "Honestly," I replied, "I'm actually *glad* I was given away because that act kicked off the events that ultimately landed me in your office! I mean, I have God now, and I probably would never have become a believer had I been raised by my natural parents. Germany isn't a very religious nation. I certainly never 'felt' God in the twelve years I was stationed there....

"Plus," I went on, "I can understand why my parents chose to give me up. My mother was a young prostitute spurred on by her own dysfunctional alcoholic mother. They were both 'lost' people trying to deal with God only knows what was going on in their lives, including the death of my grandfather and the post-war world in which they were living. And my father, Franz, seeing only my mother's beauty, chose to overlook the fact that he had fallen into a hornet's nest, until it was too late and a child was on the way. The letter he sent me years ago outlined the terrible things he was forced to endure while caught in the web that my mother and grandmother had woven, and so, I can't really hold it against him that he eventually ended up with another woman. I don't like it because it affected me, but I can't judge either of them for their decisions.

"I think I will always have mixed feelings about my parents, but the bottom line is, I *forgive* the sins they committed in their youth. Their sins aren't for me to judge. After all, I've made plenty mistakes of my own. Luckily, I don't have any kids who can hold my sins against me!"

The counselor, gazing at me across the room, shook her head in disbelief. "Carmen, you're amazing," she said. "You're brutally honest with yourself and seem to have *no* suppressed memories, whatsoever. I've never seen anyone learn as quickly as you do. You're basically healing yourself, here; I haven't had to do much of anything at all. You simply deal with the issue and move on to the next quicker than anyone I have ever counseled. As a matter of fact, you've accomplished in just a few months what it takes most people years! I would even go so far as to declare you the sanest person I have ever encountered...."

"Well," I said, realizing the time had come to finally broach a subject that had plagued me for years. "There is one issue I haven't been able to deal with, and that is, I have this recurring dream, or vision, or whatever, in which I awaken with a start and feel as though I am choking on one of two things. Sometimes it's a whole egg in my throat, and other times it's needles lodged sideways. Although I have had this dream all my life, I always find myself sitting up in bed, wracked by violent trembling and trying not to swallow because I know I'll die if I do, and I'm all alone and won't be able to get myself to the hospital in time."

"Do you have any idea at all what might have caused this?" she asked.

I shook my head and braced for whatever was to come.

"Well," she said gently, "since you've had these dreams all your life, I'm guessing something happened to you as a baby or a toddler. Since babies and very young toddlers can't yet express themselves in words, they normally see things in pictures.

"So, let's start with the egg. What might have caused little toddler Carmen to think she was in danger of swallowing a whole egg?"

"As awful as it sounds," I replied with a slight tremor in my voice, "I've often wondered if perhaps I might have been sexually abused as a baby....I mean, maybe someone performed oral sex on me...."

"Do you know who?"

"Not really. In my early days could have been anybody. My mother was a prostitute who had many men wandering in and out of the house, and so maybe it was one of them. But, I rather doubt it because she gave me to a foster family when I was only six weeks old, and so maybe it could have been my foster father. I...hope I'm wrong because I loved my foster parents. But the truth was, Max Neumann was a drunkard who once raped my foster mother in front of me when I was about five or six years old. I ran to the neighbors for help...." A hard lump formed in my throat as I heard myself accusing my beloved Papa of such a heinous deed, but at the same time, it felt good to get it out of my system.

"Actually," I blurted in effort to take the spotlight off him, "he probably didn't do it. I mean, my dream doesn't always include the egg; I often have the 'needles stuck in my throat' thing going on, which negates the possibility of oral sex, right?"

The counselor's eyes softened as she watched my transparent efforts to maintain control of my emotions. "Carmen," she said, "pretend you're a baby and someone is performing oral sex on you. Describe to me what it would feel like to have someone's penis shoved into a baby's tiny mouth and throat."

Every fiber in my being shunned the thought, and I entertained the idea of just going home and never returning to this place. But something held me on that couch and I knew I had to go through with it. The thought that somebody could or would sexually abuse a tiny baby literally stole my breath away.

My hands were shaking when I finally said: "…There would be a ripping or tearing, maybe a stinging sensation. And to a baby it would probably feel like…needles."

My heart skipped a beat as the realization finally slammed home that I had not only been a sexually abused child and teenager, but that these things had also been perpetrated upon me years before, when I was just a baby. Suddenly, my resolve was gone as I felt my face crumble into a twisted visage of sorrow. I simply sat and cried for several minutes, until finally my counselor reached out to hold me in her arms.

"How could anyone do that to a baby?" I cried. "What kind of animal would do such a thing?"

"This world is full of sick people," she replied.

*****

I literally cried for days after the revelation in the counselor's office. Of all the issues we had managed to resolve together, that particular one sent me into a bout of depression from which there seemed to be no escape. It was an awful, sinking feeling to finally admit that I had been *a sexually abused baby* – possibly at the hands of the one man I trusted the most during my early childhood years.

But, knowing the origin of those hideous egg/needle in throat dreams helped put that particular issue to rest once and for all, and I haven't been plagued by them since.

In the meantime, I realized more and more that I wasn't meant to stay in Seymour forever. I was only passing through. This was meant to be a mere pit stop where I "tanked up" on the things of God.

Pastor Wil, my very patient and kind Bible mentor, had been more than happy to help me "tank up." As a matter of fact, he gave me the religious education of a lifetime when he discovered he had a "hungry babe in Christ" on his hands. Taking me under his wing and inundating me with his own knowledge and various Bible study workbooks, he taught me how to have a relationship with God and how to hear His "voice." Wil was extremely patient with me and my endless questions about God and the Bible, some of which he wasn't prepared for and admittedly had no answer for – especially those concerning the writings of the Apostle Paul who, on one hand, seemed to be negating "the Law," while on the other hand, insisting, "On the contrary, we *establish* the Law"....

Wil and I had endless discussions about God and the Bible, and I learned much from him. Throughout my tutelage, however – although I had never read the Bible before – I kept feeling as though "something" wasn't right in the church as a whole. It bugged me that God the Father, the God of the Old Testament had **commanded** a seventh day Sabbath, yet

Christians were keeping the first day (Sunday). It bugged me that we celebrated man-made "holy days" of Christmas and Easter, when God had been very specific about keeping *His* holy days, which were the seven Biblical Feasts. The only thing I could get out of Wil concerning these issues was they were "part of the Law" which had supposedly been abolished at the cross. Something about that train of thought, however, simply didn't sound right; but I figured I would just have to live with whatever Wil told me. After all, I had just found my way to God and was no Bible scholar, by any stretch of the imagination!

* * * *

While my religious education was flourishing, my relationship with Ellis ultimately came to a halt and, in the months after we agreed that we weren't suited for each other and had decided to "take a break" from our dead-end relationship, some serious thoughts of selling my house and moving began to enter my mind. For some reason, the idea kept coming to me that I should move to Colorado Springs. As much as I dreaded the thought of another brand new beginning, this one, I felt, would be different. Plus, Rudi, with whom I had remained good friends over the years, lived in the Colorado Springs area, and so at least I wouldn't be totally alone.

But the mere thought of Colorado Springs made me nauseous because it evoked horrible memories of the sexual abuse that Bill had perpetrated upon me in at Fort Carson. I really didn't want to move there; every nerve ending in my body fought against the idea.

Unfortunately, the "nudging" kept after me day and night, and I was beginning to think that this was God's way of telling me what He wanted me to do next. He wanted me to move there, for some reason. I remembered that the workbook, "Experiencing God" mentioned the fact that, whenever God gives us a God-sized task, it always leads us to a crisis of belief, and that what we chose to do about it shows how we really feel about God. My life had literally been turned upside-down since I found Him, and so, even though I was totally distraught about the very idea of moving to Colorado, I wasn't about to be disobedient.

During those lonely days while I was trying to decide what to do next, a lady from First Baptist kept insisting I join her for a Wednesday evening service at a Pentecost church in Lebanon, Missouri, which her brother-in-law pastored.

"Carmen," she told me one day after church, "John has the gift of prophecy, and I've just been feeling for a long time that he has a word for you. I think you would be wise to come with me...."

When I told Wil about this, he was less than enthusiastic, warning me to watch out for those tongue-talking Pentecost types, because "there's no such thing as prophecy anymore," as that particular spiritual gift had, according to Wil, been relevant only during Old Testament times. I was amused to hear him say this, in view of the fact that, only about a month before, I had experienced another one of my visions (which I, after discovering the reality of a spirit world, I no longer considered "weird"). Anyway, this particular vision had taken place one Sunday morning as I was entering the church and happened to "see" transparent flames shooting from the roof of the sanctuary. Wil chuckled when I told him First Baptist was going to burn down, insisting then, too, that there was no such thing as modern-day prophecy. Deciding not to engage in an argument, I simply kept mum and figured he would discover soon enough that he was wrong....

* * * *

The lady from First Baptist had been correct in her assessment. As it turned out, Pastor John had more than just "a word" for me. In all honesty, the events that transpired at the little Pentecost church that evening proved to be beyond belief. I still get goose bumps whenever I recall how Pastor John, an extremely short and stocky man, seemed to be looking right through me during the introductions. As a matter of fact, I could sense he changed his entire sermon on my behalf when he suddenly switched subjects at one point, and began talking about the "baggage" in our lives.

"Baby foxes are so cute when they're little," he said. "They'll grab hold of your pant leg and just growl and pull and tug, hangin' on for dear life as you pretend to walk away, because they like to think they've got you over a barrel. They're tough, boy! And you let 'em keep thinkin' they're tough because they're so cute.

"Well, as they grow, it gets harder to move whenever they're hangin' onto that pant leg, and eventually, you can't move at all. Unless you get mean and slap them away, you're stuck standin' in that barnyard forever with all these foxes clamped onto your pants, holdin' you down.

"That's how our baggage is. Every time something happens in lives that we don't thoroughly deal with, it weighs us down and keeps us prisoner because Satan likes to use it against us, and he'll bring it up, time and time again until you're blue in the face."

A shudder grabbed my spine when John's eyes finally met mine because there was absolutely no doubt that he was referring directly to me! Although the word picture he was painting was simple and crude, it was extremely powerful, reaching deep down into my very being.

"The thing is," he continued, "if you're a believer in Christ, you have ammo against Satan. Jesus Himself will take care of you, whether you're aware of it, or not. He will intercede on your behalf and heal you from the inside out, if you'll let Him. He'll take all that pain and hurt, and anguish along with all your sins and toss them as far as the East is from the West, and heal your soul. He'll remove those little foxes from your pant legs, and teach you how to walk freely again."

I literally felt weak in the knees when John stopped speaking, because his words had awakened a sleeping awareness. I knew I had been holding onto the baggage of my life – not that I wanted to, but because it just seemed to follow me wherever I went, destroying many relationships before they even had a chance to blossom. Bill Forrester and his hold on me was the biggest culprit, because I subconsciously measured all men against him. Again, not because I wanted that, but because his personality and his ways had been part of my childhood imprinting process. My psyche was convinced that this is how men were supposed to be, and so I was stuck in a cycle of constantly searching for someone like Bill, and then being utterly repulsed when I finally did. This caused a continuous, endless cycle of searching, finding and then fighting against the resulting inevitably abusive situation, and the ultimate breakups. It was a psychological game that constantly kept me in a place of turmoil and discontentment – which explained why I found good and stable men like Ellis boring! I had become aware of this over the years, but seemed helpless to do anything about it.

To my surprise there was to be more to this evening than I had anticipated. After the sermon, while sitting in a fast food restaurant, Pastor John hunkered down beside my chair and allowed the prophecies to flow. He spoke quietly and conversationally, treating me as if I were the only person in the room, while his wife and sister-in-law looked on.

"Sis," he said, opening the dialog. (I caught myself cringing because that's what Bill Forrester had always called me.) "Does the name Viesbo or Wiesba or something like that mean anything to you?"

"Wietze," I responded incredulously, peering down at him. "I think you're talking about my hometown, John! No one could have known that...."

"Well, that family was very poor, almost destitute, but God took care of you. I hope you appreciate that He put you with those people for a reason."

I nodded in wide-eyed amazement. In less than thirty seconds, he had managed to sum up the early years of my life! As far as I was concerned, this man already had me convinced he was the real deal.

"Okay," John continued. "I see a small, dark-haired girl standing under an arched gate or something. Do you know what I'm talkin' about?"

"Yes. My foster father built some kind of a weird awning-like covering over the entrance to our shack. He used to sit under there to smoke, regardless of the weather."

I was stunned to feel a tiny jolt of electricity pass between us when he reached out to gently place his hand on my arm. Deep in concentration, he allowed his gaze to fall to the floor somewhere near a neighboring booth, and I, too, felt as if I were experiencing another one of my "episodes." There was no doubt that something supernatural was going on here.

"Sis," he finally said, "I guess you know Satan's been trying to kill you since the day you were born. You have literally been through hell on Earth, living with illness and painful situations beyond your control. Am I right?"

"You have no idea," I said in a hushed whisper.

"Actually, I do…But, the good news is, all that stuff served to make you who you are today. God's already told you that, hasn't He?"

"Yes.…"

"He allowed you to go through those things in order to make you a stronger person, someone He could use for His glory some day. Because of what you endured, you're a sane, strong and independent woman who doesn't really need anybody."

"Well, that's true," I interjected. "But in all honesty, I don't want to be alone. I've always wanted a good husband.…"

"Well, just be patient," he continued, "because God is gonna give you a good husband – somebody that's gonna blow your mind because he'll be unlike any man you've ever met. The rest have all used and abused you – and truth be told, you allowed yourself to be used, too.…But there's a good man in the future for you. Somebody who will support you and take care of you, instead of the other way around."

A large grin crossed my face. "Really?" I said. When?"

"Well, now I don't know that. That's all in God's timing. But what I do know is that He will give you that man you've been a-wantin', and you will be amazed because he'll be like no other man you've ever had. He'll be a true helpmate in every way. And also," he went on, slightly rearranging himself in his seat. "I see God moving you away from Seymour. He's going to move you right back to where you started – and I'm not exactly sure what that's supposed to mean."

"Back to Germany maybe?"

"No, not Germany. Somewhere here in the U.S. Somewhere you've actually lived at before."

My eyes widened as I remembered with a jolt my unusual desire – and simultaneous revulsion – to move to Colorado Springs. Although I had entertained thoughts of perhaps moving there, I had told no one, and so once again, I was taken aback. "Well, I started life in the U.S. at Fort Carson, Colorado," I said with a grimace. "But I truly don't want to go back there. God knows how I feel about Colorado Springs, and so I'm not sure He'd force me...."

"Well, now," John said in soothing tones, "you will move there if He wants you to. He chose you for something special, and He knows you'll obey...He does things for a reason that we often can't understand at the time, sis. We often don't know the reason until we can look backwards, so don't be too quick to say no."

Rising slowly and painfully, John rubbed the backs of his knees as he stood, and then took a seat directly across from me.

"Two things, wherever you end up," he said, once he was seated. "One is, I see you in Israel, on television, doing something creative. I don't know what, but I know it's something God finds very important. And the second thing is, I see you around a lot of little kids, like a camp, or something."

I instantly cringed. "No, no…No, I don't think so, John," I said, making face and vehemently shaking my head. "First off, I'm a print journalist, not a television type. And secondly, I'm not into little kids, so I couldn't imagine what I'd ever be doing with children. *No way*!"

John eyed me with a slight grin and shrugged as he shifted in his seat. "Well, okay, sis," he said with a knowing grin. "Just remember this: I definitely see you either on TV or in front of one, doing something creative for God. And as for those kids, you'll know you're on God's path when you're around a whole bunch of kids and you see hand puppets – something like the Muppets or whatever. It's gonna come to pass, I promise you that because God has a lot planned for you…."

Chapter 22

The Sunday before I left Seymour in September of 1996, Pastor Wil – who clearly feared that I would go astray if "the world" was to get a hold of me, handed me a year-long Bible study to keep myself busy during the idle times, along with well-meaning the fatherly advice to "find yourself a good Baptist church when you get to Colorado Springs, and stay there!" With great love and admiration in my heart for this dear man, I promised I wasn't about to allow the world to turn me back to my "old ways," and agreed to give him regular telephonic updates on my new life.

And so, it was with mixed emotions that I left Seymour. On the one hand, I was excited to be moving out of "Hicktown, USA" but, on the other, I was leaving the place where I "got saved" and discovered that there was more to God and the Bible than I'd ever dreamed.

Moving to a new state and leaving all my friends behind was no easy undertaking at this point in my life, especially since I was comfortable in Seymour and had many friends both there and in Springfield, left over from my old Soaring Solos days. During my Army days, I never feared moving because I knew there would be other people at my new destination in green uniforms who were automatically "family."

And when I left Larry and moved to Missouri, I knew I wouldn't be alone because my Mom, Goldie, and her neighbors would be there for me. But this move to Colorado was different because I was going to a strange place where I knew no one, except for Rudi. The only thing that took the edge off this particular move was that Rudi had told me on the telephone that he had a room ready for me in the basement of his house, where I would be welcome to stay until I found a place of my own.

Everything went surprisingly smooth as far as the move was concerned. Several of my neighbors had bought my furniture, and all "loose ends" were tied up on the day I was to depart. But then, two hours before the closing on my house, my realtor called to inform me that the deal fell through because, it turned out, the couple wasn't qualified.

"*Not qualified?*" I screeched into the receiver. I was livid with my real estate agent who had already talked me out of taking another offer because she didn't want to share her portion of the profit with the other agent who happened to be her toughest competition in Seymour. "How could the closing fall through because someone wasn't qualified? Shouldn't that have been established early on?"

"Well, yes," she stammered, "but someone gave me erroneous information, and so I didn't know."

"You didn't know," I said sarcastically. "You told me you were the best around!"

"I'm sorry, Carmen. I'll tell you what I'll do, though. I happen to know a lady who just got divorced and is looking for a temporary place. She could rent it from you until it sells. Is that okay?"

"Well, what other choice do I have? I've sold all my furniture, and was sitting here on the front porch, waiting for you to bring my two thousand dollar check to me, so I could leave. My dog and the U-Haul attached to the back of my car are ready to head out of Seymour!"

My only saving grace at that point was that, after a quick phone call on the realtor's part, I learned that the newly-divorced lady agreed to rent my place, and so I was free to leave "without worry." The realtor promised to keep trying to sell the house, and promised that it probably wouldn't take too long since the market was good....

Although I didn't say anything, I made a mental note to fire her as soon as I got to Colorado Springs, and hire her competitor.

Anyway, I realized that the first of John's prophecies was coming true while saying my final goodbyes to Ellis who briefly dropped by my house just as I was getting ready to pull out of the driveway. It was a tearful departure, but we both knew that we weren't meant to be. His brief appearance in my life, we both agreed, was to "lead me to the Lord." I was happy to discover during that brief meeting, that since our breakup several months before, he had already found a new love, someone he was "getting serious with."

Ellis was the type of man who needed a good woman in his life, and I was somewhat saddened that that woman couldn't have been me. But the fact remained, God apparently had other ideas for me, and I wasn't about to disappoint Him. I had spent most of my life without Him, and I certainly wasn't going to mess up this wonderful gift of a "second chance." Life was going to be different from now on, that was for sure.

* * * *

Something unusual happened when I arrived at Rudi's house in the Colorado Springs area late on a Friday afternoon in 1996: Whereas I had been filled with tremendous apprehension about this move, I suddenly felt at peace; as a matter of fact, I felt as if I had "come home" – not necessarily at Rudi's house but, strangely, in Colorado Springs. It seemed as if a page of my life had been turned, and it was time to rest my weary soul – at least for the weekend.

Rudi, who had sadly been widowed since we last saw each other in Germany, was one of the very few people in my life that I had bothered to keep in touch with, and as we talked incessantly into the wee hours of the morning, I began to realize that our friendship had not been an accident. God had sent him into my life, not just to help me make it through those terrible days in Heidelberg during the "J.D. incident," but to help me transition into the new life God had apparently planned for me here, in Colorado Springs – the last place on Earth I ever wanted to see again....

Rudi not only welcomed me into his house with open arms, but he also introduced me his three grown children and his longtime girlfriend, Paula, with whom I felt an instant rapport. All in all, it was a great weekend, and on Monday morning, despite his urgings to the contrary and reminder that I could make his house my home for as long as I wanted, I persuaded him to drive me all over town so I could find a place to rent.

Colorado Springs, I noticed while we were apartment hunting, hadn't grown much over the years. Much of it appeared run down, although there seemed to be some efforts at renewal. I wasn't sure how long I was to remain here, but I figured I would stay until God told me to go.

Toward the end of the day, as we were about to give up, we happened upon a small townhouse in the foothills of the Rockies with a FOR RENT sign in front, which was just perfect for me and little B.J. It wasn't the greatest, but I figured it would have to do for the time being.

Because the cost of living was much higher than in Missouri, I knew I would have to find work quickly but, unfortunately for me, the jobs in the journalism field were scarce and didn't pay all that well. Therefore, to help make ends meet, I took a temporary position as a receptionist with a software development company.

Oddly, as my new life began to take shape, I began to feel less and less at home and I began to wonder if I had made the right decision in coming here. People in Colorado Springs weren't the friendliest I'd ever met. None of my neighbors bothered to say "Hello," much less, welcome me to the area. It seemed as if everyone preferred to keep to themselves, even at my new church where most everyone my age was married, and those who weren't spent all their time complaining about their ex-spouses and coming across as excessively needy.

One afternoon, while working on Wil's year-long Bible study, I received a surprise phone call from him. "Hey Carmen," he said, "I have some bad news for you. First Baptist burned down last night."

There was a slight pause as I remembered my vision of the transparent flames emanating from the sanctuary. Not being able to help myself, I blurted: "I told you so."

After a very pregnant pause, he went on as if he hadn't heard my comment. "Well, actually it wasn't the whole church," he said. "It was just the sanctuary. There was a short in one of the electric lines. Anyway, we're all sad about it. Guess we'll build a new church, now....Well, so, how are you doing up there in Colorado? Are you liking it?"

"Honestly, Wil," I replied, "I think I'm beginning to hate it. People are so unfriendly here, and I haven't made one single friend yet. If it wasn't for Rudi, I'd have nobody."

"Well, you know you're always welcome back here in Seymour!"

"I might just take you up on that. I don't know how much more I can stand."

Another awkward silence passed before Wil said, "I guess you heard that Ellis got married."

"No….No…I didn't." The news stung, even though I knew Ellis and I weren't meant to be. "I'm truly happy for him," I said, forcing the words and trying not to cry. "He deserves a good woman…."

"Yes, he's a good man. It's too bad you two couldn't make it together, but I totally understand. But I do hope you'll find yourself a good man one of these days. You deserve every happiness, Carmen."

"I don't even want a man anymore!" I retorted almost angrily. "I haven't had the best experiences with men, Wil. I gave my life to God and I think for now, I'll just concentrate on Him."

"Great idea! You just keep that up. And don't be a stranger. Keep in touch, okay?"

"Will do," I replied. My heart was filled with a mixture of sadness and gladness for Ellis as I hung up the phone. *Dummy*, I thought ruefully, *you let another good one get away….*

Chapter 23

There was no doubt that God had moved me to Colorado Springs, in part, to heal some old wounds. And so it was with a heavy heart that I, after a doctor's visit at the Fort Carson Hospital one day, decided I had no choice but to swing by the old quarters where we used to live when Bill brought us to the States in 1960.

As nothing much had changed over the last thirty-six years on that side of the Post, I was able to locate the building on Pershing Drive, with no problem. The only difference was, whereas in 1960 the quarters had bordered an empty field, there was now some kind of an activities center directly across the street. And so I took the opportunity to park in one of the slots, and from my perfect vantage point, as if it had been waiting for me all these years, I sat there and scrutinized the dirty dark red brick building that had once served as my torture chamber.

Tears began to flow freely as I beheld the black railing attached to the few steps that led up to the front door. With hand cupped over my mouth in horror, I allowed my gaze to roam upwards, to the small bedroom windows just beneath the roof. My old bedroom was the one in front, above the front steps. God only knew what kind of things had taken place in there so long ago…

From where I sat, I couldn't see the back of the building very well, but I wasn't interested enough to get out of my car to check it out. I couldn't have walked on my rubbery legs, anyway, even if I had wanted to.

I noticed storage areas had been erected behind all the buildings now, which dramatically changed the views I remembered so well. Without needing to actually see it, I also remembered there was a window in the second floor bathroom on the back side of the building – the place where Daddy had once violently introduced me to oral sex until I nearly passed out. Afterward, with a satanic grin, he asked me if I had liked it and then he said, "Your whore of a mother *loves* to do this...."

The mere memory of what all had transpired in that place literally sickened me. I wanted more than anything to just get out of my car, lie down on the pavement and will myself to die on that very spot.

But that, I figured angrily, was exactly what Satan wanted. And I wasn't about to give it to him.

＊＊＊＊

One day, not too long after my ordeal at Fort Carson, I received some devastating news from my new realtor in Seymour. The tenant who moved in after I left, she told me, was not cooperating with her efforts to sell the house, and the woman had gone so far as to change the locks and keeping the window shades drawn so no one could see in.

"I don't know what we're going to do, Carmen," she said, "but I promise to keep trying."

Depression threatened to engulf me after we hung up because at this point, it looked as though I might lose my good credit standing if the house were to end up in foreclosure.

Oh, dear Lord, what had I done to myself?

This move to Colorado, I decided, had been a terrible mistake. Perhaps it hadn't been of God, after all. Nothing had actually gone right since that first weekend at Rudi's. It was now several months later and, besides Rudi, I had no friends, no happiness, and no real job. As a college and business college graduate, not to mention a graduate of the prestigious Sergeants Major Academy with twenty-two years of military service under my belt, the *only* thing I had managed to snag in the way of a job in Colorado Springs, was as a receptionist at a software development company. I had gone from newspaper and magazine editor to receptionist; it was truly a new low for me! Who would have ever thought I would end up being the archetypal personification of "over-qualified and underpaid?" To supplement my meager income, I took a job cleaning houses on Saturdays. How much lower could I possibly sink?

Consumed with hopelessness, I clicked on the evening news, which served to depress me even further. Nothing good was happening in the world. Wars, fighting, famines, starvation, murders, rapes, abortions, man's inhumanity toward man. In frantic desperation, I folded my hands and asked God to "do something" to cause my house to be sold; to "do something" about my feelings of doom and gloom. ***Something*** had to happen for me and soon....

The following morning, still depressed, I dove into my daily Bible study before reporting for work. Seconds after seating myself, I felt "slightly outside myself," and I realized I was about to have another one of my "experiences."

Each episode was different from the last, and this time, I had the feeling that "something dark and devious" was attempting to influence me because, out of nowhere, "it dawned on me" that this Bible stuff was all for naught! During that "episode" I strongly felt that I had been duped into "believing in God" by all those Seymour fanatics. It dawned on me that I would surely have made friends by now if I were still the "old" me; that the people where I worked – who were mostly unbelievers – would like me better, and I would be having a good time dancing in the bars, or doing something besides sitting home alone every night, feeling sorry for myself.

A thought, like banging cymbals, crashed into my mind and made me realize that, although I had indeed become a "new creature in Christ," it was all just fantasy. There was no God, there was no Jesus; it was all just Christian myth. If there really was a God, I would be happy, wouldn't I? Life would be a lot easier. What had this "new life" gained me? Nothing! With no friends or family here, I had never been more lonely! What social life did I have here? If I wasn't at work, I was out taking my dog for long walks in the foothills. On Sundays I went to the Baptist church down the road – and then came right back home to work on Wil's Bible study. And now, on top of everything else, I would probably lose my house in Seymour along with whatever credit rating I had left. Being "a new creature in Christ" had turned me into nothing more than a lonely, bored, middle-aged woman....

When the uncomfortable out-of-body feeling receded, I sat there, staring down at my Bible as if it were a foreign object. After some moments, I concluded that I *hated* this thing! It was a symbol of those hypocritical Christians I had ever met – the Bill Forresters and Sergeant Lassiters and JD's of my life; all those who had physically, mentally or emotionally raped me. It was even a symbol of that little old lady in Seymour who had told me I would "get over" my joyous feelings once the "honeymoon with Jesus was over." How had I, an intelligent "woman of the world" allowed myself to become so completely bamboozled?

But yet...I couldn't deny that I loved Jesus with all my heart. He changed my life....

It was maddening. On one hand, I was feeling peculiarly released from the "religious stuff" and yet at the same time, I was on the verge of panic.

Not knowing what else to do, I decided to take B.J. for a walk in the nearby foothills. I just wanted to get away, to run, to scream, to hide…to be swallowed by the Earth.

My mind felt like mush as I watched B.J. frolicking through the tall grasses and weeds, frantically tracking the scents of other animals. Right then, I envied his carefree life. He had it made with no cares in the world. He had never known a day without food, water or love, and his biggest concern was getting Mommy's attention whenever he wanted to go outside.

Oh God, I thought, *will this confusion, this torture, this limbo **never** end?....*

Tears clouded my vision as stood on the side of the mountain, gazing dispassionately across the rooftops of the myriad houses lining the valley below. Was anybody down there, I wondered, as unhappy as I was?

It felt terrible, after having been a believer in Christ for more than two years, to come to the conclusion that He might be a just figment of my imagination. If He was a mere fantasy, then why did I feel as if my body had been completely vacated of everything I had ever held near and dear? And where had that "God experience" at Schweitzer Methodist come from? And had that disappeared lump in my breast truly been just a coincidence? What about the coma experience back in 1972 where I had seen Jesus? Had it really been "just a dream?"

Even the loss of Goldie and my beloved foster parents, and all my husbands put together couldn't come close to the emptiness and loneliness I was experiencing at that very moment in time. The loss of Jesus was a literal physical pain that radiated into my soul with a force so powerful that I wanted to commit suicide.

One thing was certain, I decided after awhile, regardless as to whatever else was going on in my mind: While the idea of getting rid of "religion" seemed liberating, letting go of Jesus was not. As a matter of fact, it felt downright painful. It was as though I had just lost my best friend, and that was simply *not* acceptable. **Religion** was the culprit, not God.

"Lord," I cried out loud, "*what is going on here?* Why am I suddenly torn like this?"

The answer, like lightening from heaven, came when a realization slammed home that literally stopped me in my tracks: **Because this was exactly what Satan wanted!**

My jaw literally dropped as I sank to my knees, and suddenly, it was crystal clear that I had just been privy to one of the many behind-the-scenes spiritual battles. I had just been afforded a first-hand glimpse of what life without God was like. Yes, I was unhappy in Colorado Springs, and yes, I was basically friendless. But it was just a temporary situation, designed to "grow me" in my knowledge of the Bible, and in my relationship with God. It was for a reason, and I needed to be strong in order to survive. God had kept the Israelites wandering in the desert for forty years to reacquaint them with Himself, and to teach them to rely solely on Him. And now He was doing the same with me....

Yes, this was exactly what Satan wanted! Wil had warned me this might happen – that Satan would try to tempt me away from God, and back into my old ways.

"Oh Father," I chanted like someone possessed as I knelt there on a grassy, deserted knoll, with hands tightly folded in prayer. "Oh my God, oh my God....Please forgive me! I'm so sorry. I don't want to be without You!"

Keeping my eyes toward the heavens, I made a solemn promise aloud, not caring whether anyone saw or heard: "Jesus," I said, "I don't want to return to who I was before we met. If it means remaining lonely and poor for the rest of my life, then so be it. I'd rather be lonely and poor in Your arms for the rest of my life than to ever risk being without You again. *Please, please forgive me!*"

Almost instantly, I felt a warm glow filling my soul, reviving my sensations. The Holy Spirit had come back full force, and instantly, everything seemed back to normal.

Blinking away the tears, I noticed that B.J., with a comical look of concern on his face, was licking my hand, and I automatically reached out to pet him.

"Everything is okay, sweetie," I said, smiling brightly. "We're going to be all right!"

Believing my divine lecture to be over, I returned to my apartment in hopes of finishing my daily Bible lesson. Unable to properly concentrate, however, at one point, I remember leaning back in my chair and allowing my gaze to lazily roam around the room as I pondered the morning's unusual events. For no apparent reason, my concentration began to focus on the refrigerator; specifically, on a magnetic frame containing a photo of me in long hair.

And then something very strange and unexpected happened: I was overcome by a sudden wave of nausea that nearly had me dashing to the bathroom. But oddly, the sensation left as quickly as it had come, and I stood, wondering what had happened, when my gaze once again, for no reason whatsoever, fell onto the photo – and I recoiled in shock when I saw that it was upside-down!

My only thought as I was dashing from the room was: *Satan is angry....*

Gripped by raw terror, I found myself cowering in the tiny living room, trembling near the staircase by the front door. At first, I thought I was possibly experiencing another one of my "episodes," but quickly realized I wasn't feeling "outside of myself."

Satan is angry! I kept thinking, while at the same time glad there no one was around to witness my apparent insanity....*This is Satan's doing because he is mad!* I could literally *feel* him! As crazy as it sounded (but with God as my witness that it really happened), there was no doubt in my mind that I was experiencing first-hand rage from the spiritual realm: Satan, God's eternal enemy, was furious with me for spurning his advances, and he had given me a visible, tangible sign!

After some disquieting moments during which I contemplated turning myself in to the nearest insane asylum, I slowly made my way back into the kitchen to investigate the possibility that, perhaps, my eyes had just played a trick on me. After all, I had been through a harrowing morning.

But it turned out that I wasn't crazy; the photo was definitely upside-down. Gathering all the strength I could muster, I bravely attempted to turn it around and, to my surprise; it felt very warm to the touch, indicating that this had *not* been mere coincidence....

Rather than to try to continue my Bible studies, I decided to get ready for work early. My nerves were shot and I needed to get away from the apartment as soon as possible!

* * * *

Still trembling while on the way down the mountain on that gorgeous Spring morning in 1997, I took my time driving the few miles to work. For once, I actually looked forward to going to work because it would serve to get me out of the house – and God only knew how badly I needed to get away from there that day! In attempt to put the strange events behind me, I focused my attention on the beautiful Colorado sky, which was a perfect rhapsody in blue, without a single cloud to mar God's canvas. A good sign, I decided, one that surely meant that the rest of my day would go better.

My gaze was drawn upward as I turned from Rockrimmon onto Mark Dabling Boulevard, and what I saw made my spirits soar: There, in the sky above me, like some divine omen, was a tiny cloud in the shape of a cross!

When, seconds later, I pulled into the parking lot of the company where I worked, I noticed the cross had already begun to dissipate and now resembled a fluffy little angel; and then, within the blink of an eye, it became a mere ball of fluff.

Things were going to be better now. I was sure of it.

Chapter 24

Everything began to change for me a few weeks after I saw what, for me, was some kind of an omen. This change was kicked off on the day I received the phone call I had been holding my breath for: Discovering whether or not I got the job as associate editor of the Colorado Springs Business Journal.

"Carmen," the owner said cheerfully over the phone, "I've got just one more question for you. When can you start?"

I was thrilled! My days of answering phones, stuffing envelopes and taking messages for people who often treated me as though I were an uneducated imbecile, were finally over with.

One of the first things I did after starting my new job was to take action to stop paying the high rents in Colorado Springs, and so I immediately hired a realtor to help me buy a small condo or townhouse. Once I found that perfect little place, however, I discovered, to my dismay, that I would need a five thousand dollar down payment to be able to make a valid offer. This was money I didn't have, and had no way of getting because of my large debt load. Since I hadn't been able to work for almost two years after leaving Larry in El Paso, in order to make ends meet, I had used my credit cards more than I should have. That, plus the fact that I still owned that blasted house in Seymour which was being held hostage by an evil tenant, seemed to indicate I would have to keep on renting for at least another couple of years....

But then, as if on cue, a miracle happened: A couple of newly-weds in Seymour who, even though they had never set foot in my house, bought it "site unseen" because they liked the outside and the fact that it was situated in "the right" neighborhood. And the best part was: My realtor called to tell me, after her cut, I would be receiving a check of five thousand dollars – *the exact amount* I needed to purchase my little condo!

At that point, someone truly could have "knocked me over with a feather!" This clinched it: God was definitely real and He was with me; He had been all along, battling Satan for me, even when I wasn't aware of it. It was simply amazing! Things were suddenly going my way, and there was no doubt it was because I had chosen to keep God in my life, and to obey Him. As a matter of fact, *obedience* seemed to be the key to having that special relationship that Pastor Wil always talked about. "You don't say 'no' to God," he repeated, time and time again. "If ever you can't feel God in your life, it's not because He moved; it's because *you* did."

The fact that my Seymour house had miraculously been sold coupled with my "God is a myth" and cloud cross experiences, along with the sudden turnaround in my job situation...it all served to confirm that I was not crazy; that God *was* indeed real (as if my coma and Schweitzer Methodist experiences hadn't been ample proof!). There were simply too many miracles in my life to keep pretending they were all just "coincidences." Even that silly thing that had happened with Tom, the guy whose Christmas present was supposed to be a trip to the Virgin Islands – that was a God thing as well because, what were the odds that he would have been "busted" that night while sitting at the bar? If I had taken that trip with Tom, I would have never met Ellis, who was directly responsible for leading me to the Lord and changing my life. I would most certainly still be a captive of that same rut I had been in all my life, seeking out men who reminded me of Bill Forrester....

With this knowledge in mind, I walked on Cloud Nine for months. I loved my new job and for the first time since I left the Army, I felt like "somebody" again.

It turned out that the Colorado Springs Business Journal was also responsible for the production of the Pueblo, Colorado, and Madison, Wisconsin Business Journals, and so my new job as associate editor kept me fairly busy. After a year, when our editor quit, I naturally applied for the job – and I was absolutely devastated to discover the two owners had chosen over me a twenty-two year old college grad with no experience!

When I confronted the owners about this, citing my lifetime of military newspaper and magazine experience, along my with year's experience as an ad designer/feature writer for Seymour's newspaper, the Webster County Citizen, they basically shrugged it off, insisting they had felt they should give this young college graduate a try, instead.

This "young college graduate" turned out to be a mean witch who couldn't get along with anyone, and she ended up fired after only seven or eight months. By that time, however, I was long gone. I put up with her nonsense for less than two months before finally walking off the job.

Gone also, as I discovered a couple months later, were the original owners. "Hey Carmen, guess what," one of my former co-workers told me on the telephone one day. "They sold the newspaper right after you left and we've been under new management ever since. Nobody knew. They just called us into the conference room on a Friday afternoon and dropped the bombshell that, on Monday we would be under new management."

I was elated to hear that one of the first accomplishments of "the new management" was to fire the illustrious "young college grad" for various reasons, including the fact that she didn't know what she doing.

"Now we know why you weren't selected for the editorship," my former colleague said. "It was all about saving money before they decided to sell, because they got her dirt cheap."

This news, of course, made me jump for joy, mainly because I had felt like a whipped dog when I was rejected for the editor position. At least now I knew it hadn't been because of my qualifications or performance!

And so, once again, I had to repent because it dawned on me that God's hand had been in this all along. I was positive that, while He had allowed me to become the associate editor so I could begin rebuilding my self-esteem, He now needed me to be at my new workplace for some reason, and I would simply have to patient and wait to find out why.

Anyway, my "new job" was an admin position at System Technology Associates (a defense contractor) which I managed to "fall into" while participating in a "spiritual gifts "class at Radiant Assemblies of God Church one Sunday. It just so happened that I mentioned in passing during a break, that I was searching for a new job. As it turned out, a man in the class happened to be one of the managers at STA, and when he discovered I was former military with both journalistic and administrative skills, he advised me about a particular job opening there, and the next thing I knew, I had been hired.

* * * *

Before leaving Seymour, Wil had been adamant about me finding a "good Baptist church." Unfortunately, the tiny congregation I attended for nine months when I first settled in Colorado Springs, seemed "dead" to me – not to mention that, as a single, middle-aged person, I felt totally out of place because most everyone else was married. Hardly anyone took the time to make me feel like a part of the "family," and so I started church hopping.

Although I ultimately landed in an Assemblies of God church for a while, I consistently felt "something" was missing in the church. All the sermons I had ever heard in every church and in every denomination seemed to be missing something. They preached, not necessarily God's Word, but rather, their opinions about selected Bible verses, supposedly designed to show us how to apply God's Word in our lives today. Their sermons were normally simple, heart-warming, ear-tickling messages that felt empty to me, as if the real message was missing somehow. It was truly upsetting to me that man-made "sermons" never felt quite right, and so I began to beg God to show me exactly what I was missing, if anything.

"Lord," I said one afternoon while walking B.J., "could you please tell me who I am to You? Could you please show me my purpose? I just feel like I have some kind of a purpose besides warming the pews on Sunday; you know what I mean?"

In those days, I also began to be nagged by the feeling that I was supposed to *do* something for God. I couldn't figure out what that might have meant, because Pastor Wil had made it perfectly clear that I didn't have to *do* anything but "believe in Jesus" but that simply didn't sound right to me. If I were a man, I decided, I would have no doubt been a pastor. But, as a woman - according to the Baptists - that was impossible, so I would just have to keep asking God clarification because I definitely *felt* I need to do something for Him....

And so, for the next three weeks, the name "Eliezer" kept coming to mind. I thought of Eliezer upon waking, while eating lunch or having dinner, or while walking the dog. I thought of Eliezer at work and at play and while lying in bed at night. My life was plagued by that name until it came out of my ears – until one day it finally dawned on me that perhaps God was trying to tell me something.

Since I knew Eliezer was mentioned somewhere in the Bible – specifically towards the beginning of the Old Testament, I began to read until I found him. And what I found astounded me because it answered the question I had posed to God: *Who am I to You?*

Of course, at first, I didn't recognize it as my answer because, upon investigation, I found Eliezer in Genesis 15 and 24, where I discovered he was Abraham's main/senior servant, whom Abraham eventually sent to his homeland to fetch Abraham's son, Isaac, a bride. Unable to figure out what significance that was supposed to hold for me, I finally closed my eyes in prayer to ask God for guidance.

What "came to me" was surprising as I realized God was apparently telling me that I was a type of Eliezer, His willing servant whom He had chosen to fetch a "bride" for His Son! The "bride" of Christ was everyone who accepted Him, including those hard-to-reach types like the "white supremacists" and "Ku Klux Klan" on the internet whom I had occasionally engaged in email conversations on the computer during lunch and my breaks at work. Although I had promised myself that I would never become one of "those pushy Christians," I couldn't seem to help myself, and was becoming more and more brave in my witnessing attempts, especially in the wonderful anonymity that the internet provided.

I was overjoyed! Ever since I "got saved" in Seymour, my biggest goal in life – although I was still very shy about doing it – was to witness to people about Christ, and so *that's* who I was to Him. Now I knew; and it "felt" so right!

* * * *

I had a couple more of my "episodes" in the summer of 1997. The first one happened two weeks before Princess Diana was killed that August. I was making my bed one morning when suddenly, I felt slightly "outside of myself" and the thought came to me: *Princess Diana and Mother Theresa will be dead shortly. The world will deify Diana and her carnal lifestyle for years to come, while Mother Theresa, who has done so much for humanity, will be nothing more than a tiny footnote.*

Once again I was right....

Around that same time, as if I was being shown that my "visions" were, in fact, some kind of a gift, I happened to have one while driving down Union Boulevard one day when I noticed a small, red sports car being driven erratically, with the driver weaving in and out of traffic. For some reason, when he suddenly appeared in front of me, my eyes were drawn to the personalized license plate, "JOYZ-TOY", and I remember having two thoughts: One, it was odd that I would have noticed the license plate, because I'm not normally one to do that; and two, I absolutely *knew* this car would be in an accident that same day.

Later that evening while watching the ten o'clock news, the anchors mentioned a one-car accident in Black Forest. My heart fluttered when they showed a close-up of its license plate, because it was "JOYZ-TOY."

The following day I made an appointment with the pastor at Radiant Church to discuss these "episodes" that had plagued me all my life, and find out whether or not he thought I had some kind of a prophetic gift from God. In short, he did not, simply because my visions were of random situations that had nothing to do with the Bible. But he did suggest that I start praying every time I have one, in order to prevent them from coming true.

These strange words from my pastor left me feeling simultaneously angry and guilty, even devastated – to think that I might have prevented the deaths of Princess Diana and Mother Theresa, had I prayed after that vision!

Somehow, his answer just didn't "feel" right....

* * * *

It was winter in 1997 when I received the answer to my second question, the one that kept nagging me to "do" something for God. It unfolded when a new person named Michael processed through my office at STA.

Michael and I landed on the topic of the Biblical end times scenario because the office buzz that day centered on the seventy or eighty tornadoes that had decimated the Midwest during that particular week.

"I honestly believe," I said in hopes of starting a conversation about God, "that this is just one of the end times signs."

"I agree," Michael replied.

My face brightened. "....You're a believer?"

He nodded. "I'm actually a Messianic Jew."

"A Messianic Jew?"

"Yeah. A Jew who believes in Jesus."

"Really?...I'm Jewish by birth through my mother's side....but I don't really know much about Judaism. I know enough to know that Jews don't normally believe in Jesus...."

A knowing look crossed Michael's face as he said, "Come to the Torah study we attend every Wednesday evening at the Radisson Inn, and you'll see what the Bible is REALLY all about!!"

"....Torah study? What's that?"

Michael smiled. "You'll see!"

* * * *

I was "hooked" after the very first time I attended that Torah study; and just weeks later, I became a member of Kehilat Sha'arit Yisrael, the Messianic synagogue that Michael and his wife attended. This "chance meeting" with my co-worker opened up a whole new world because, it was in these Messianic settings that I found confirmation for my gut feelings about how Christian churches were "missing something."

What was "missing," I discovered, was Torah – God's original divine instructions to humanity. For some reason, Christians were under the erroneous impression that "the law is a curse" and "Jesus nailed it to the cross" without realizing that, what was nailed to the cross was our certificate of debt, *not* Torah! I learned that Jesus was our Final SIN Sacrifice, who came to proclaim the Kingdom of God, not someone who came to abolish His Father's commands.

Pastor Wil and every other pastor I'd encountered since the day I "got saved," all insisted that the Old Testament "stuff" was abolished at the cross, including any further need to obey God's divine instructions. The death of Jesus somehow supposedly negated everything, including the Father's commanded *seventh* day Sabbath (day of rest) and the seven Biblical Feasts/appointed times – the very Feasts which foreshadowed Jesus, and which He is actually still in the process of fulfilling today….

Among the things that astonished me was my discovery that God the Father had a Name – YHWH, pronounced "Yahweh," and that His Son's real name was Yeshua, which in Hebrew meant "YHWH is Salvation." Also, I was amused to learn that my uneasy feelings about Christmas and Easter had been valid, all along, as both "holidays" were man-made and steeped in paganism! Easter, from the name Ishtar, has its origins in the mythical pagan goddess who had turned a bird into an egg-laying rabbit and started the tradition of coloring its eggs with the blood of sacrificed babies; while much of the "Christmas" customs were borrowed from the Druids who worshipped trees and brought one into their houses once a year to decorate and worship. God, I learned, had even warned us about these things:

Jeremiah 10: *2 Here is what Adonai says: "Don't learn the way of the Goyim (Gentiles), don't be frightened by astrological signs, even if the Goyim are afraid of them; 3 for the customs of the peoples are nothing.* **They cut down a tree in the forest; a craftsman works it with his axe; 4 they deck it with silver and gold. They fix it with hammer and nails, so that it won't move.** *5 Like a scarecrow in a cucumber patch, it cannot speak. It has to be carried, because it cannot walk. Do not be afraid of it - it can do nothing bad; likewise, it is unable to do anything good!"*

While there is no doubt many Christians "love the Lord" with all their hearts, I soon discovered they were actually following the much-misunderstood writings of the Apostle Paul who, according to the off-the-mark teachings of Catholicism and Protestantism, supposedly taught that "the Law" was abolished at the cross. To my chagrin, I found that Christianity had been based more on the writings of Paul than on the things Jesus had taught! Nobody seemed to bother to ask *why* Paul, a Torah observant Jew and loyal follower of our Jewish Messiah, would have taught that God's original divine teachings were abolished just because Jesus died....

So much about the Christian belief didn't make any sense – and apparently "something" in me had realized that all along, and my myriad questions were finally being answered now! While Christians had part of it right, they were missing the bigger picture: That without God's Torah, man would have *no blueprint* for moral, holy living. Torah outlined exactly what constitutes sin – and tells us that *sin is transgression of the Law*....which Christians insist was abolished....

Christians were even somehow overlooking the huge mistake in the King James Bible that renders Acts Chapter 12 completely ineffective because of its use of the word "Easter." The man-made term "Easter" was not coined until well *after* the death and resurrection of Yeshua!

These were the types of things that had bugged me from the beginning, when I first began to study the Bible, beginning with the question I had posed to Pastor Wil about why Paul would have said in Romans 3:31, *"On the contrary, we establish the law,"* while appearing to suggest that it had been done away with, in his other writings.

After all, Jesus Himself had even said in Matthew 5: *Don't think that I have come to abolish the Torah or the Prophets. I have come not to abolish but to complete. Yes indeed! I tell you that until heaven and earth pass away, not so much as a yud or a stroke will pass from the Torah – not until everything that must happen has happened.*

Every Christian I had ever known insisted that "fulfill" or "complete" in that particular scripture meant "put an end to." They never seemed to read the rest of that verse which says Torah would stand until *everything that must happen* **had actually** happened. And judging from the fact that heaven and earth are still here, it would seem that Torah is still valid....

I even learned that Bill Forrester had been wrong in his accusation that I had been "using the Lord's Name in vain" because "God" just a *title*! His Name – which you'll rarely, if ever, hear in a church – is YHWH! Plus, he was wrong in his assertion that "money is the root of all evil." What 1 Timothy 6:10 actually says is the *love* of money is the root....

The Torah class enlightened me to many things, none of which I had ever before received a real answer to. I was overjoyed to discover that this class and my new synagogue were helping to put to rest the nagging feeling about what I was supposed to "do" for God. *I was to obey His commandments by doing His Torah!*

For awhile I was torn about letting go of "the church," and so I kept attending Radiant every Sunday, while visiting Kehilat Sha'arit Yisrael on Saturdays. This arrangement ultimately (in 1999) came to a screeching halt because the two theologies clashed on many levels, and after several weeks of begging God to tell me what to do, I heard a clear voice during my Wednesday evening Torah study which insisted I *"Come out of her!"* There was no doubt in my mind that this meant the church.

Chapter 25

Meanwhile, in the Spring of 1998 – it came as no surprise – the children's pastor at Radiant Church began to hit me up about becoming one of the counselors at their yearly Royal Family Kids' Camp, which took place in a Rocky Mountain retreat approximately an hour's drive from Colorado Springs during the month of June.

I couldn't believe it! Here was that kid thing again that I was hoping to have left behind in Seymour.

"Come on, Carmen, you'd be great at it," I was told. "You're a natural with kids; the spiritual gifts test you took proves it!"

"But, I'm involved in the prison ministry," I protested, hoping against hope. "I visit the women's prison in Canon City at least once a month...."

"This won't interfere with the prison ministry, I promise. It will only take five days out of your busy schedule."

In the end, I gave in, remembering how Ellis had reminded me that perhaps God was trying to tell me something. Plus, at one point, the pastor said the magic words that pushed me over the edge: "This camp is for abused and neglected children from the area; kids who have been severely abused, sexually and otherwise...."

It was with mixed emotions that I awaited that dreaded week, and I virtually hyperventilated my way through the months of April and May, often wanting to back out. When the day finally came for the forty-nine children to arrive by bus at the mountain retreat, I found myself fighting the urge to get into my car and go home. Forty-nine "screaming meemies" to babysit for five whole days in the great outdoors and a couple of drafty, dusty cabins! What on earth had I been thinking?

Each counselor had two children for which they were responsible; "one for each hand," we were told, with the male counselors watching the boys, while the female counselors got the girls. The counselors had reported the day before to "bond" and fellowship, and to be amply coached by some representatives and professional counselors from Child Services who laid down the law about how to properly interact with the children.

On one hand, I was excited; on the other, I was terrified.

Okay – so the day was here, and since nothing in my life has ever come easy, I should have guessed ahead of time that I would end up getting stuck with the little kid from hell. While everyone else received their two children, somehow I had been the chosen "lucky one" to take care of just one child; an eight-year-old girl with "special needs." It took me about five minutes to figure out this kid was an absolute terror.

She didn't understand that she was there to have fun and to talk about her life and her problems in a safe, Christian environment; no, all this kid realized was that she was away from home where she could run wild and do whatever she wanted.

Slightly mentally challenged and wearing hearing aids in both ears, she had been the victim of severe physical abuse as a baby – and as a result, she had been completely catered to and spoiled beyond belief by her foster parents. This little girl wasn't about to let rules apply to her, and so she did her level best to make my life miserable. After two days of wearing myself out trying to "reach her" through kindness, understanding and compassion while running non-stop after her to keep her out of trouble, I finally gave up and told the hierarchy that either she goes, or I go. So, lo and behold, it suddenly dawned on the organizers of the camp that this special needs child hadn't really been qualified to attend Royal Family Kids Camp, anyway….

By that time, of course, I was ready to quit altogether. The only thing that kept me there was the knowledge that another one of Pastor John's prophecies had unfolded and I knew deep in my gut that God wanted me to be there. This actually happened at breakfast on the very first morning after the arrival of the children, when a group of volunteers presented a children's puppet show, using the Muppets….

And as for those kids, you'll know you're on God's path when you're around a whole bunch of kids and you see hand puppets – something like the Muppets or whatever. It's gonna come to pass, I promise you that....

As it turned out, the Muppet Show was a regular morning treat for the children, a constant reminder that I was here for a reason yet to be experienced.

And so I stuck around, which was a good thing because, after "my little girl" left, I was allowed to share in the care of the kids given to the other female counselors – and the results were awesome!

To my total surprise, these "normal" kids absolutely **loved** me! In fact, at one point, several of them argued over who was going to get me as a counselor next year. "I want Carmen next year!" "No, I'm gonna get her!" "Miss Carmen, is there a sign-up sheet for who gets to be your child next year?"....

Before I knew it, I was in love with **all** of the children – to the point where, if I could have adopted them and taken them home, I would have. As a matter of fact, I grew so close with some of them, I felt as if they were my own. Never before in my life – except, of course, with my own two brothers, Teddy and Lonnie – had I felt so bonded with little children.

There were a couple of events during the final three days of camp that I hold especially near and dear. One was when a little girl named Justine and another child bumped heads while jumping around in an inflatable "moon bouncer." When Justine began to cry, my "new" mother instincts caused me to instantly reach out to her as she flew, screaming, into my arms, tightly wrapping her arms and legs around me like a little monkey and clinging to me for all she was worth. Out of the corner of my eye, I noticed one of the Child Services people watching the scenario, because we had been specifically instructed not to allow this kind of contact, but at this moment, I didn't care. This little girl was in pain, and nobody in their right mind could have misconstrued what was going on. All I knew was that "my" little girl was hurt and I needed to take her pain away.

The other incident – and no one could ever convince me otherwise - was the reason God had caused me to be at this camp.

It happened while I was counseling a withdrawn little seven-year old named Kendra who had been sexually abused by both, her father and grandfather. When I heard one of the Child Services counselors discussing the girl's history, I knew I had to reach out to her – as a matter of fact, I felt the Holy Spirit telling me that I had been *chosen* to sow some healing seeds in this hurting child's mind….

Kendra was extremely shy and introverted, and consequently, she had refused to "open up" to anyone until the day I was allowed to take her aside to sit on the front steps of the women's cabin (in full view of the Children's Services counselors who kept a respectful distance) to have "a little talk" with her.

"Honey," I said gently, "Would you like to talk to me about what your father and grandfather did to you?"

Just as expected, she lowered her gaze in shame and shook her head.

"Would it help if I told you that I know exactly how you feel, because my Daddy did the same thing to me?"

Her eyes were wide as she looked up at me. "Really?" she asked in a tiny voice that made me want to cry.

"Yes, my father did bad things to me. Just like what happened to you. So, I understand what you're going through."

I could tell by the way she looked at me that she realized we were kindred spirits, instantly bonded through our shared experiences.

"It was awful, wasn't it, getting touched in private places?" I asked after a short silence.

She nodded. "...Do you think they did it because they were mad at me?" said in tones so low I could hardly hear her.

"No, sweetie," I replied. "They were being bad. People sometimes do bad things."

Kendra's eyes filled with tears as she nervously fidgeted with a pigtail. "Then I guess God's mad at me."

"Oh no, sweetie," I cried as my heart went out to her. "God loves little children! As a matter of fact, Jesus even said in Matthew 18:6 that anyone who harms one of the little ones who believe in Him, it would be better for him that a millstone of a donkey would be hung on his neck and he be drowned."

"But then why did He let that happen to me?" she cried in a tiny, heart-wrenching voice that was filled with pain and anguish.

I didn't try to stop my own tears as I attempted to formulate an answer. This poor little child was asking the same questions I had asked so many years ago. Unfortunately for me, I had no one to talk to back then. "Because," I replied tenderly, "He allows us all free choices. He allows us the choice to do things *His* way, or Satan's. Unfortunately, many people choose to follow Satan, that evil entity who constantly whispers bad things into our ears. Most don't even realize it and so they do whatever he suggests, and that's when others end up getting hurt sometimes. God doesn't want it to happen to us – *they* do! Do you understand what I'm saying?"

She nodded as her eyes took on a far-away look. "Uh-huh," she answered. "It's like when I want to hit my baby sister sometimes when she makes me mad, but I don't because she's just a baby."

"That's right!" I cried happily. "Other little girls and boys might go ahead and hit their baby sisters because they don't stop to think that what they're doing is a bad thing. But, you did it God's way, see? That's a good thing! God wants us to be good and kind."

"I don't hit my baby sister because I love her."

"Right! And we don't purposely want to hurt those we love. Or anyone else, for that matter. God wants us to treat everyone the same way we want to be treated."

Squirming where she sat, Kendra's eyes wandered across the horizon and I could tell she was deeply in thought – wanting to talk, but yet not quite trusting me enough to open up. "So, what Daddy and Grandpa did wasn't really their fault?" she said after some moments.

"Yes, it *was* their fault, honey," I replied a little harsher than intended. "It was their fault for listening to that desire that told them to do those awful things to you. They both knew better. Every grown-up knows they're not supposed to do forbidden things with little girls, especially things that are reserved only for grown-up married people. They **chose** to allow that nudging from Satan to overtake their better judgment. Do you know what I mean by that?"

"Uh-huh." She fidgeted with her shoelace for some moments, then quietly muttered something that totally caught me off guard. "Am I going to have a baby now?"

A fresh round of tears welled in my eyes. A question like that should never have to come from the lips of an innocent seven-year-old! I found myself wishing I knew the identities of her father and grandfather so I could find them and break their necks – or, at the very least, castrate them with a rusty carving knife…

"No, sweetie," I said as I remembered how I feared pregnancy every time Bill raped me, especially during my teenage years. "You're too young to have babies.

You'll be okay....But from now on, if anyone ever tries to touch you in a wrong way again, you yell at them as loud as you can! Don't be afraid to tell them ***NO!*** in the biggest voice you can possibly find! You tell them that God is watching them, and that you intend to tell someone if they touch you, okay?"

As if by magic, a huge, relieved smile appeared on her face.

"You're living with your grandmother now, and don't have to be afraid anymore, right?" I asked hesitantly.

"Yes," she replied. "She loves me. My Daddy and Grandpa are in jail now."

"Okay, good. See? Things are looking up for you!" Her eyes were twinkling and I loved the brilliant smile my words had helped to provoke.

"Okay, then," I went on. "There's one more thing I need you to know. No matter how badly someone has hurt us, God wants us to forgive them. Now, that doesn't mean we have to allow them to continue hurting us, or that we have to love them or even live with them. It just means we're not going to allow the memory of what they did to control us in the future. Satan loves to keep us in a rut, constantly bringing into our lives the same kinds of people who will hurt us with their willful sinning, over and over again, and often in the same ways."

Kendra's innocent little girl eyes were wide as saucers as she earnestly took in my every word.

"We have the power to break that cycle, sweetie, I continued. "And the way to do that is to give your life to God and constantly ask for His protection. Even though I hadn't given my life to Him back when my father was doing bad things to me, God protected me by keeping me sane. He hated what was happening to me, but like I said, God doesn't interfere with anyone's choices. He didn't even interfere when bad people were crucifying His Son! But we all will be standing before Him some time after we die, to give an account of our lives. Those who deliberately chose to ignore God and do Satan's will, will not end up in Heaven."

I was delighted with the comprehension reflected in Kendra's face. Little children simply understand; they grasp things that many adults with their stubborn "educated" mindsets, miss.

"What happened to you was done out of ignorance and deliberate sinning on the part of your father and grandfather," I assured her. "They *will* stand before the Lord one day to give an account of what they did. But in the meantime, you need to forgive them so that the memory of what they did won't follow you around anymore and make you miserable. Do you know what I mean?"

"Yes, I do," she said with surprising conviction.

Sergeant Lassiter's face came to mind, and for the first time since he had uttered those same basic words so long ago, I realized he had been right! The problem was, his "witnessing technique," like that of so many other well-meaning Christians, had been all wrong.

You can't *force* someone to believe you; all you can do is to do as Yeshua did: proclaim the Truth and then leave it up to the person to accept or reject it. God knows who is and who isn't going to accept Him, and He works in the lives of those who will ultimately come to Him. The rest, he turns over to their own desires....

As I beheld Kendra's tiny face, which was now no longer drawn and brooding, I realized what God had meant during my Schweitzer Methodist vision about using my pain for **His** glory, and I silently thanked Him while asking His protection over this innocent little child.

"Do you feel a little better now, Kendra?" I asked.

She nodded, looking up at me with a huge smile on her face that told me our counseling session had succeeded.

"May I have a little hug?"

I cannot express the feelings I experienced when this poor, abused little child pressed against me. It was almost as if I was hugging little Carmen, and it was all I could do to keep from breaking down into a puddle of tears.

As I watched Kendra being reunited with her regular camp counselor, I couldn't help but wonder who had been healed the most; that little girl or me....

Rags to Rabbi

Chapter 26

I actually hated to see Royal Family Kids Camp come to an end. Never before in my life had I felt more alive and "worthy" than during that week. Never before had children and I bonded with such intensity. While I realized this bonding was due mostly to our respective abusive pasts, it had been an extraordinary healing experience; one that I would certainly never forget.

For some reason, after that experience I felt as if another chapter of my life had been put to rest and that soon, something new and wonderful was about to take place.

And once again, I was right....

* * * *

The first time I met Bill Welker was in July 1998 when he, as a new systems engineer at System Technology Associates, processed through the office in which I worked.

Although I had basically quit dating after I "gave my heart to Jesus," I found myself slightly disappointed to see that Bill was wearing a wedding ring. He wasn't really my "type," but he was very good looking and there was "something about him" that made me wish I could get to know him better. But that wedding ring let me know, in no uncertain terms that he was not for me, and so I figured any kind of relationship – other than a professional one – was a moot point.

Bill, a retired Air Force officer, was a shy, quiet and apparently reclusive man who seemed to keep mostly to himself. As time marched on, I happened to notice the photos of his three children – two boys and one girl – on his desk; and so that, coupled with the fact that I ultimately saw him as an excruciatingly boring person, made me feel relieved to know he wasn't "on the dating circuit" after all.

For months, our relationship consisted of the sporadic "hello" in the hallways and, on very rare occasions, we engaged in meaningless small talk in the break room while milling around the microwave.

This all changed, however, on the day he came to ask me to notarize his divorce papers in early 1999. Until then, I had no clue that he had, in all these months, been in the process of a divorce.

"My wife had me served on the afternoon of my oldest son's high school graduation," he told me. "After twenty-two years of marriage, she decided I wasn't 'meeting her needs' and, on the advice of her counselor, she filed for divorce last year."

Although he tried to come across as someone who was able to handle whatever life threw at him, I could sense the underlying pain and anguish in his voice, and my heart went out to him. He seemed like such a nice and kind-hearted man, someone who was stable and reliable – a true family man – and I couldn't fathom why any woman would want to throw him away.

I was filled with a mixture of sorrow and gladness when he left a few minutes later because, after knowing him for about eight months, this was probably the longest conversation we had ever had. I was a little sad that our first real conversation had consisted of his crumbling marital status, but on the other hand, I hoped he realized that he had found a new friend in me, should he ever need someone to talk to. Obviously, "friends" is all we could ever be, thanks to the fact that he had a daughter....

After that, communication with Bill was less difficult, and we began to be more at ease with each other. There were times I thought maybe he was interested in me, but thankfully, he never said anything...at least not until that following September of 1999 – and only then, after his divorce was final and he discovered I was leaving the company to take a position with MCI WorldCom.

My initial reaction on that day in the break room when he finally got up the nerve to ask me out, was to find an excuse to turn him down. Not only did I feel he was a total bore with whom I probably had nothing in common, but he had that ***darn daughter***....

While Bill certainly didn't strike me as a pedophile or any other kind of pervert, I knew I could never handle being married to a man who had a daughter because, down deep, I couldn't help but feel there might be sexual tension at some level, however small it might be – and the very thought sent my blood pressure through the roof.

But as I watched Bill standing there, looking lost and forlorn, next to the microwave, struggling to figure out a way to make a date with me, I found it impossible to say "no." I simply couldn't risk further damaging his already bruised ego by turning him down, and figured it wouldn't kill me to go on one little date with him.

And so, in the days before our first date, we ended up talking for hours on the phone every evening. The more we talked, the more I realized Bill was quite a different person away from the workplace. He was chatty and funny – and in all honesty, one of the most intelligent people I had ever met. By the time we went out to the movies on our first date that following weekend, I was totally smitten.

Granted, he still wasn't my "type," but at this point in my life, I realized that my type had always been patterned after my adoptive father – ironically, the "other Bill" who had ruined the first half of my life. God had healed me from the inside out since I "got saved," and so Bill Forrester no longer had that certain hold on me that made me yearn for the tough, abusive "macho men" – although, down deep, I must still have had the remnants of those desires, or else I wouldn't have found "good guys" like Bill Welker "boring."

Regardless, this "new" Bill was the complete opposite of the old one. The only problem I had with him when we first started dating was that I thought he wasn't a Christian, as he never mentioned God. And so, one afternoon, I sent him an email, telling him that it probably wasn't a good idea for us to take our relationship any further because I didn't want to – as the Bible termed it – be "unequally yoked" with an unbeliever. God was the center of my life now, and I was not about to allow anyone to take that away from me.

Bill replied with an email asking if he could come to my condo that evening to prove that he indeed was a believer. "I want to tell you my testimony, "he wrote. "Have a bottle of aspirin and a glass of water and some Kleenex handy."

By the end of that evening, I knew beyond a shadow of a doubt that God had sent me Bill.

Quite embarrassed because he wasn't used to talking openly about God, he forced himself to relate a tearful testimony about how he had felt Jesus' hand on his shoulder in the early Spring of 1986 while he, with his pregnant wife and two sons were being pushed down a slippery mountainside as their camper jack-knifed behind them. Watching Bill agonizing over the memory revealed exactly what kind of a man was sitting in my living room; and, after that, there was no doubt that I needed to hang onto him with all my might because a man like Bill didn't come along every day....

And that's when I realized that yet another of Pastor John's prophecies had just been fulfilled.

That following Saturday, I invited him to attend my synagogue, with the provision that, if he didn't like it, I wouldn't force him to return. But, as it turned out, he was "sold" after just one visit because – as he told me – for the first time in his life he finally heard what his gut told him was actual Biblical Truth!

And the rest, as they say, is history. Bill and I were married under the *Hupa* at our synagogue seven months later, in April 2000. His children, the two boys and yes, that "darn daughter" too (who was actually a sweetheart who was totally comfortable around her father) – each received a ring from me as a token of my acceptance of them as a family unit.

I wasn't about to let Satan ruin my one chance at happiness by giving in to my fears about possible pedophilic tendencies on Bill's behalf. By that time I knew him well enough to know he would have cut off his arm first....

Chapter 27

Before we were married, Bill and I prayed that God would put all kinds of "roadblocks" in place if our plans didn't exactly line up with his.

But in the end nothing, absolutely *nothing* stood in our way. He sold his place, I sold mine, and we bought a nice house together and began to live like a real family, with absolutely no glitches or hassles. For the first time in my life since I had been stolen from my foster parents in Germany, I finally felt like a "real" family, even though Bill's children didn't live with us. The two younger children, Jeremy and Christine came for a visit every other weekend, and the oldest son, Jay, was a student at the Air Force Academy; and so we hardly ever saw him.

But everything "felt" right to me; life was good for once.

One of the first things I did after our wedding was get on the internet and look up old friends and acquaintances to let everyone know that I had remarried and was living "happily ever after" in Colorado Springs. Although I hadn't heard from Mama and Jürgen for years, I decided they needed to know, too. Unfortunately, the old phone number I had for them was no longer valid, and there was no information to be found on either her or Jürgen. It was Ulla Mertens, the lady who years ago had found my long-lost brothers, who later informed me that my precious Mama had died in the early Nineties. Although devastated over the news, I had felt for years that Elfriede Neumann wouldn't last much longer. And so I spent some time silently thanking God for the opportunity and privilege of having had a relationship with the one person who was solely responsible for me having turned out "normal."

Grieving for Mama reminded me of my first love, David, whose mother had been so much like my precious Mama, and so I decided to contact her after nearly thirty-five years, just to "catch up." And, in all honesty, I was a little curious to find out how David was doing and whether he had found the kind of happiness I was finally blessed with.

David's mother, now in her eighties, was thrilled to hear from me, and I have to admit, I was just as excited to hear her voice. When the conversation eventually got around to "how David is doing these days," I got the shock of my life when his Mom told me he was in prison.

"Prison?" I asked. "What on Earth for?"

There was silence on the line, then: "He got his twelve-year-old daughter pregnant."

"*My* David?" I said incredulously. I was stunned at the news. She might as well have punched me in the gut.

"He got twenty years, honey. He won't get out until 2010."

"But why? I mean, how could he do such a thing?...My God, David was the love of my life! He was the first one in whom I ever confided about what Bill Forrester had done to me, and he wanted to *kill* him for it because he *knew* what a broken person I had become because of the sexual abuse....Didn't he remember that?"

"I guess not, honey," David's Mom said. "It was a very stupid and unforgivable thing...I don't know why his wife didn't kill him on the spot."

"Well, he'd better be glad he wasn't married to me!" I half-shouted as memories of David, my knight in shining armor, came crashing down in one fell swoop. I obviously had no clue back then as to who he really was.

Anger rose and then quickly ebbed as I realized why David and I hadn't ended up married! God, who knows the beginning from the end and everything in between, knew that David had the heart of a pedophile, and He had prevented our love from culminating in marriage. *Oh, thank God!* I mouthed in silent prayer. *Thank You, Lord, thank You....*

Chapter 28

In May 2001, a year after we were married, Bill and I decided to honeymoon in Europe, centering, of course, on Germany. I was thrilled because Bill was the first husband I'd ever had who was actually interested in discovering who I was, and in seeing my hometown and finding out where I had grown up. He was ecstatic about our trip because he had never been to Europe before, and suggested, since I was from there and had been stationed in Germany three times, I would be the perfect tour guide.

Little did either of us know that this upcoming trip was to be the adventure of a lifetime which was to ultimately spill over into the latter part of 2004, nearly three years away, and bring the kind of closure that only happens in fairy tales....

* * * *

The first stop in Germany after our landing at Frankfurt was a brief visit with my brother Ingo, whom I hadn't seen in eleven years. Of course, both of us had gotten a little older. I was now fifty and Ingo was forty-eight. Years of smoking had carved a network of wrinkles into his face, but he had the same twinkle in his eyes and a smile that lit up the entire airport when he first caught sight of us.

Ingo, as we soon discovered, had broken up with his long-time girlfriend, which meant we had him completely to ourselves over that particular weekend. He seemed genuinely happy for me when I mentioned that I had "found God" and we even had a chance to discuss the Books of Daniel and Revelation and how things were unfolding in the world exactly as the Bible foretold. Unfortunately, after that, there were no other opportunities for further discussions because the next time we saw him in Neckargemünd on our final two days in Germany, he brought along a new girlfriend, Barbara, whose presence completely dominated Ingo's concentration.

On Monday morning, we began our European tour by taking off for my hometown of Wietze, which was to be our first stop. My heart pounded like a jackhammer as we drove through Wietze – not only because of the familiar sights and the memories they evoked, but also in anticipation of finally getting to meet Ulla Mertens, the lady who had been responsible for helping to find some of the missing pieces of my life's puzzle.

Although we had never met, I felt obligated to stay in contact with her over the years, hoping that one day we could finally meet. And today was the day!

Ulla, with a cute blond bob and brilliant blue eyes twinkling behind large glasses, had retired from the courthouse several years earlier. She and her husband turned out to be wonderful hosts – people we were pleased to add to our small circle of friends, and we talked (while I translated for Bill) into the evening about me, the Neumanns who had raised me, and how much Wietze had changed over the years.

When it was time to leave, we asked Ulla for suggestions about local hotel accommodations and, without hesitation, she picked up the phone and called the Hotel Steinförde to reserve a room.

"Surely you know where it is, Carmen," she said, "because it used to be known as Rauschenbach."

My mouth dropped in disbelief. "…That's where my foster father used to spend our entire welfare check on beer!"

"Oh, don't worry," Ulla replied. "It's been renovated since then. The new owners, Günther and Irene Buske, took over about twenty-five years ago." Her face lit up as she seemed to remember something, and then she snapped her fingers and said, "I just thought of something. You probably know the owner's wife, Irene. You two are the same age, so you must have gone to school together."

I blinked stupidly before deciding I didn't know any Irene.

"Sure you do!" Ulla insisted. "You'll remember her when you see her."

"No, I don't think so. I don't know any Irene."

But the truth was, I did. On the way to the hotel, I remembered that parents often called little girls named Irene "Reni," bringing to mind the face of my long-lost friend.

The last time I saw Reni was in 1959, at school, just before my mother and Bill Forrester took me away from the Neumanns. It had happened so quickly, that I was never afforded the opportunity to say "goodbye" to my friends and, as far as I knew, they never discovered what had really happened to me.

* * * *

Jetlag was taking its toll as we pulled onto the curb beside the Hotel Steinförde. After two and a half days in Germany, we were still trying to get used to the time difference, which seemed to be a nearly impossible task.

Memories flooded my mind when the hotel marquis came into view. It had played a major role in my early years, as Mama had sent me there on countless occasions to fetch Papa home for supper. Oftentimes, instead of allowing us to leave right away, one of Papa's friends would hike me up onto a barstool and buy me a Coca Cola. Even now, I could still remember every detail of the dark wood interior - the tall bar, the noisy people, and the smell of beer, stale cigarettes, and Bratwurst.

Although it was fairly dark when we entered, I could tell the place had been completely renovated. The former dirty white exterior was now a dark beige with white trim; the pinnacled brown beams that once graced the old Tudor style facade were gone; even the sidewalk in front of the building was different; smoother, more modern.

Suddenly it struck me as odd that, although I had visited Wietze a couple times while stationed in Germany, I had never bothered to stop at the Steinförde Hotel. It simply didn't seem that important to me back then. This time, however, I couldn't shake the feeling that something was special; something I couldn't quite put my finger on. Perhaps it was because, this time, I was a middle-aged retiree and things just "looked different" from the way they had ten or twenty years ago. Or, perhaps it was because this time I had someone with me who was interested in sharing my precious memories and in helping me re-live whatever was left of my past. I glanced at my husband and smiled.

The man behind the bar greeted us with a *"Guten Abend!"* as we approached, and pulled his lips into a tired smile when we told him we were the people for whom Ulla Mertens had made a reservation.

"Sorry about the late hour," I said in my native German, "but we couldn't find anything open earlier this afternoon upon arrival in Wietze. We had such a good visit with Ulla, we forgot about the time...."

Herr Buske waved his hand in dismissal and continued checking us in. When finally I could stand the suspense no longer, I asked to see his wife. "Ulla said I might know Irene," I blurted in response to the questioning look on his face. He shrugged, and then disappeared into kitchen.

While we waited, my bloodshot eyes darted around the once familiar room. Like the outside, it too, had been totally renovated. New corner benches, chairs, and tables had replaced the old, drab, cheap, dark, wooden ones. The entire bar area had been replaced with one that surprisingly resembled an early-American style. Pretty blue and white curtains had replaced the old yellowed, stained ones. Although things were newer and different, ghosts of the *Gasthaus*-past consumed me with a melancholy that made me want to cry over my lost childhood.

Although I was tired to the point of numb, my whole body began to tremble with excitement as I waited for Reni to appear – if, indeed it was *my* Reni. And if it was, would she even remember me after all this time? Had thoughts of me ever crossed her mind, I wondered, or had she simply forgotten about me? I distinctly remembered that my reason for not keeping in touch with her was because I knew my mother would read my mail….

My heart skipped when Irene emerged from the kitchen. **It *was* her!** It was my Reni, the same Reni who helped me to endure mean ol' *Fraulein* Reckel in first grade; the same one I used to play with at my house, at her house, and down by the Wietze River….It *was* Reni, now middle-aged and looking worn and haggard after a hard day's work in the hotel. I recognized the round shape of her face, the dark ash blonde hair, the brown eyes, the shape of her lips; everything. It was definitely my Reni....

With adrenaline crashing through my system I asked, as calmly as possible, in formal German, "Were you, by any chance, known as Reni when you were a child?"

Perplexed, she said, "*Ja*," and gazed at me with questioning and almost suspicious eyes.

"Well," I said, barely able to contain my excitement, "I used to be known as Carmen Neumann!"

Obviously stunned, Reni inhaled sharply. Her hands flew first to her breast, then to her face, then back to her breast as she seemed to search for something to say. "*Nein!*" she finally exclaimed with a look of disbelief. "*Ach mein Gott!* Whatever happened to you?"

It was an extremely awkward moment. Although I wanted to reach out and hug my old friend, I realized the person standing before me was a complete stranger. It had, after all, been forty-two years. Reni, too, seemed somewhat hesitant, but the small talk suddenly caught fire and we soon found ourselves immersed in the past while our husbands stood silently by.

At one point Reni stopped speaking, took a step backward, and with hands on hips, began to survey me from head to foot. "I remember you as being very dark. Whatever happened to that skinny little, dark, kinky-haired girl I used to know? I can't see anything of the old Carmen now!"

Emitting a silly giggle, I admitted that I used to appear dark in color because I was dirty. "The Neumanns didn't have water or electricity, and so we hardly ever bathed," I told her.

"Yes, but they adored you, Carmen," Reni said. "You might not have had anything back then, but you had their undying love. I was sorry to hear that *Frau* Neumann had died."

"Yes, me too...."

In order to change the subject, Reni formally introduced her husband, Günther, who, like Bill, had been quietly and patiently standing on the sidelines, listening. My husband, whose knowledge of German consisted only of the few phrases he had learned in the months before we embarked on our honeymoon, merely smiled as he took it all in, and though he understood some of the goings-on, I promised I would translate it all later.

The whole scenario seemed quite surrealistic. There are simply no words to describe the feeling of seeing a long-lost childhood friend who had literally been out of your life for almost half a century.

Later, in bed, as tired as I was, I could not get to sleep. I lay awake for hours, my mind whirring like a jet engine. I wasn't sure whether to be happy or sad about this reunion. On one hand, being taken from the Neumanns had been a good thing because Papa was an alcoholic and Mama was slightly retarded and God only knows how my life might have turned out back then. A perpetual welfare couple, I remember they had been considered the dregs of Wietze, with some people openly making fun of them. But they loved me and did the best they could and, as dysfunctional as they might have been, I credited them – specifically my Mama – for helping me on the road to becoming the person I was today.

My one regret had always been that my childhood had been literally yanked out from under me, and I always wished things could have been different. Until that May evening in 2001 when I laid eyes on Reni, I never realized exactly how cheated I had actually been.

* * * *

In a typical, family-owned *Gasthaus*, it is not unusual to see the owners cooking, serving the drinks or food, washing the dishes, or cleaning the rooms. Although Tuesday was their *Ruhetag* (rest day) Irene and Günther prepared and served our breakfast before leaving for Hannover to attend to some business. Realizing that Bill and I would have to leave that afternoon for Paris, Reni insisted on putting on a quick *Kaffee Klatsch* before our departure, planning to invite my other two "best friends" from my childhood, Annette and Wera.

After breakfast, just as we were about to leave, Reni, quite out of the blue, said, "Carmen, does the name Franz Klekawka mean anything to you?"

I balked. "Well, yes, he's...my father," I said. "I mean, I guess he is; I don't really know him. I met him only once, when I was about six. He never claimed me, but his name is on my birth certificate. Why do you ask?"

Irene bit her lower lip. "He's my brother-in-law," she replied as if the words would be painful for me to hear. "He's married to my husband's sister. They were married back in the Fifties, right after he divorced your mother....I've been having a hard time convincing Günther it's really you; he doesn't quite believe you are the person we've been discussing over the years; quarreling over, actually, whenever your father and his wife, Elfi, became upset at the mere mention of your name."

I tossed a quick glance at Reni's husband whose incredulous look matched my own. "It's really me," I assured him with a forced giggle.

"You have two half-brothers, Carmen," Reni went on. "Their names are Thomas and Arnold."

"Wow!" I said, not bothering to contain my excitement. Turning to Bill, I quickly translated this new revelation.

When Reni continued, her expression was somber. "....Carmen, I hate to tell you this," she said, "but your father is very sick now. He's not expected to live much longer…."

While the news saddened me, it didn't bother me all that much, especially since I remembered how adamant he had been about not wanting me after I initiated contact with him back in 1975. After all, he was a stranger who had left no doubt as to how he felt about me, and any hopes for a relationship had been pretty much dashed when he sent that awful six-page letter outlining his stormy marriage to my mother and demanding that I leave him alone forever.

I shrugged and translated this amazing development for my husband who seemed more upset about it than I was. Again, I wasn't sure how to feel, but I do remember my heart fluttering at the sound of Franz's name. As far as I was concerned, whether he claimed me or not, his name was on my birth certificate, which made him my father.

A week or so later, as our trip through Europe was coming to an end, I called Reni from the Garmisch-Partenkirchen area to tell her goodbye.

"I'm afraid I have some bad news, Carmen," she told me. "Your father died yesterday. I'm sorry…"

Oddly, this information hit me harder than I thought – mostly because I realized that now there would never be an opportunity for us to get to know each other. It was sad, really, especially if it turned out that he really had been my biological father.

Still, even though I had never been a part of his life, I had been afforded the opportunity to at least have had *thoughts* of him in the week before his death. Somehow, I felt that was no accident. There was no doubt in my mind that God had brought us to Germany at this particular point in time, setting events in motion that would cause Bill and me to end up at Reni's hotel so I could have some type of closure. My father, the man whose name was on my birth certificate, was dead; an era had come to an end.

* * * *

In the meantime, in Wietze with a few hours to spare before Reni's *Kaffee Klatsch*, I decided to show my husband what we had come here for, in the first place: my old home site.

Having visited the site twice before, I knew the old hovel had been torn down shortly after I left the Neumanns. This time, though, I hardly recognized the area, because the surrounding woods had been cut down and a new housing development had sprung up all around. The only remnants were two ancient, gray apartment dwellings that had been built back in the Fifties while I still lived there.

The place where my old home had once stood was still vacant only because of the *Salzberg*, "Salt Hill." Since the *Salzberg* had severely weathered away over the years, it was now only three or four yards high and maybe twenty or thirty yards long.

With tears freely flowing, mostly because I was walking straight into the bulls eye where all my childhood memories were centered, I led my husband to the spot where I thought my beloved home once stood, the home where I had felt so safe in my Mama's arms; my beloved Mama who was now dead and buried in an anonymous grave....

Feeling weighed down by melancholy for a life that was forever gone, I busied myself showing Bill the things that stuck out in my memory. Over there, one could still see part of the narrow dirt lane that I had walked so often; and right over here were the remnants of the wall that had separated us from the *Kurhaus*, which used to be a hospital for tuberculosis patients....In my mind's eye, I could still hear Mama warning me to stay away from those sick people "in that place," lest I catch a disease and die.

We were standing on a dirt and weed-covered knoll, surveying the area and reminiscing about my past, when my husband suddenly asked if my old home had been made from red bricks.

"Yes," I replied. "How did you know that?"

"Well, see, here? This mound is full of them. I think we're standing on your old house!"

Stunned, I crouched to retrieve and examine one of the protruding pieces. "Oh!" I exclaimed with joy and tears as I lovingly fingered a piece of history that had, in its inanimate way, witnessed the worst day of my life. "*Omigosh, it is*! It's definitely my old house!"

Who knew that I would one day stand here on the very spot where my Mama had stood and screamed my name on that horrible day when I was ripped from her life, to ultimately be comforted by another pair of loving arms – arms that belonged to the first person in forty-two years that I trusted as much as I had my Mama….

Bill held me as I wept and we both thanked God for the closure He was bringing into my life. It was no wonder that my previous husbands had never accompanied me here; this privilege had, no doubt, been reserved only for Bill.

Realizing we were pressed for time, he gently urged me toward the car. As we turned to leave, I reached down and tucked one of the bricks safely under my arm to take back home to the USA.

* * * *

A few minutes later we were headed toward the *Waldfriedhof* - the cemetery where my foster parents were buried. While I didn't care so much that Papa had been tossed into the anonymous gravesite reserved for those who couldn't afford to buy their own plots, I hated the fact that Mama was buried there, too. Had I known that that chattering cheapskate Jürgen wasn't going to buy her a plot, I would have gladly paid for one….

The small cemetery, located in a quiet, wooded area, was still as beautiful as I remembered from childhood. As Bill and I walked the dirt paths between the mounds of graves, I felt the lump in my throat rapidly swelling.

My knees crumpled when we finally located the site reserved for the *Anonymen Toten*, "the anonymous dead." Sandwiched between the forest on one side and myriad graves on the other, the huge, grassy plot resembled a soccer field. Kitty-cornered at one edge was a small flowered memorial containing a single stone marker. I felt numb as I bent over to touch the grass, wondering if I was touching the exact spot where Mama lay. Suddenly the dam broke and tears began to flow in hot, rushing rivulets of anguish. Mama had deserved better than this. I found myself regretting that I had not done more for her while she was alive....

I flinched as my husband's warm hand touched my shoulder. "Honey," he said, "if we're going to take a walk through the Bergen-Belsen Concentration Camp yet, we need to get going because two o'clock will get here before we know it, and we don't want to be late for Reni's Coffee *Klatsch*."

* * * *

A couple hours later, with an emotionally exhausting trip to Bergen-Belsen behind us, we returned to the Hotel Steinförde, heels clanking dejectedly on the pavement as we headed inside. The very idea that millions of innocent people had been abused and killed inside Hitler's hideous death camps had left us with a feeling of hopelessness for humanity. It so happened, on the day we visited Bergen-Belsen, some

German group had stretched scrolls more than a kilometer long across the entire expanse of the camp containing signatures of thousands of people wishing to say, *"We're sorry!"* With tears clouding our vision, Bill and I found an empty space on the scroll near the site of the *"Krematorium"* and added our own signatures. It was gut wrenching to realize that more than fifty thousand people had died on those very grounds and that, unlike those who had been imprisoned there, we would be free to leave at will....

To our amazement, we discovered that the camp had been liberated on April 15th, 1945, which happened to be around the same time as the Biblical Feast of Passover, the time when Yeshua was crucified and thus released the world from bondage to Satan. Most concentration camps in Europe were liberated around the Passover timeframe, and so it seemed like no coincidence that God's "Chosen People" were released on or around that same High Holy Day from their bondage to the demonic antics of a brutal madman – all of which served to set the stage for Israel's becoming a nation once more in 1948, just as the Prophet Isaiah had foretold...

The aroma of coffee and freshly baked cake tickled our nostrils as Reni welcomed us with a big smile. Before her on the bar, lay an open photo album containing pictures of various stages of her life, and she quickly beckoned us over for a walk down Memory Lane.

There was Reni as a small child, just as I remembered her; Reni in her teenaged years; Reni as a grown woman with a husband and children; and Reni at her fiftieth birthday party. I frowned as she called out the names of some of our classmates, because after all these years, I hardly recognized anybody.

When the phone rang, Reni excused herself and went to answer it, only to discover it was for me. "Carmen, it's Wera for you!" she said. "She can't get away from work, but she wants to at least talk to you." Handing me the phone, she winked and said, "Annette will be here shortly, though!" And she then crossed the room to start cutting the cakes.

I was astounded to discover that, after all these years, I was able to recognize Wera's voice when she said, "*Hallo*, Carmen, is this really you?"

As with Reni the night before, Wera and I talked over each other, trying to catch up on forty-two years worth of events in our respective lives. By the time we were finished, we had promised to keep in touch and to get together as soon as possible.

My jaw dropped when Annette walked in a few minutes later, as she looked nothing like the tall, skinny bean pole I remembered. This woman who threw her arms around me was big and matronly, and grinning from ear to ear.

"I've changed a little, haven't I?" she said with a loud laugh. "That's what a life of raising kids and grandkids, and being a housewife can do to you."

"Yes, you've changed," I replied happily, "but, that blonde hair and those twinkling eyes are unmistakably you!"

Within minutes, we were seated at the table Reni had prepared, partaking in an animated conversation. Irene's husband, Günther, popped in and out of the room, playing host while at the same time trying to stay out of the way. At first I tried to translate most of what was being said for my husband's sake, but eventually, it became too much of a chore. Bill, always patient and understanding, simply smiled and told me to enjoy and not worry about it.

As if this visit to my hometown hadn't already turned into enough of a miracle, Annette, at one point, related a story that nearly knocked me from my chair. It was about Mama's partner, Jürgen, whose bout with a severe case of Emphysema kept him wheelchair-bound and living with some family who was being paid to take care of him.

"So, who lives in their old shack now?" I asked nonchalantly. "Or has it been torn down?"

"Oh," Annette said excitedly, "I guess you didn't know. Your Mama's house burned down after she died...And Carmen," she went on animatedly, as though she couldn't wait to tell what happened next. "I ran into Jürgen at a grocery store several years ago, and he told me that he managed to run into the house to save just a couple of things...and among them was a photo album containing **all your original old childhood photos!** And he told me several years ago when I happened to see him in a grocery store, that if you ever returned to Germany, he wanted to give them to you."

I was thrilled! "Omigosh!" I cried, translating this latest bit of information for Bill. "I can't believe this!"

"I know you're on a strict travel schedule," Annette went on, "so, I would be happy to find out where Jürgen lives and then go get those photos to send to your home in America, if you want me to...."

The afternoon was nearly gone when we finally managed to wind down; and with tear-filled eyes, the girls and I promised to keep in touch and never lose sight of each other again. Bill and I managed to leave Wietze just before sunset, which was hours later than we had originally planned, but this wonderful diversion was worth every second of the delay.

When we returned to the U.S. two weeks later, we agreed that, although our whirlwind European honeymoon was one huge adventure that had taken us through Germany, France, England, Switzerland, and the two concentration camps of Bergen-Belsen and Dachau, *nothing* came close to our experiences in Wietze.

While we were sure that God's hand had been guiding the miracles in Wietze, we had no clue that we would be returning three years later to watch "the rest of the story" unfold....

Chapter 29

After a year or two, I stopped waiting to hear from my half-brothers, Arnold and Thomas. Apparently, I would simply have to come to grips with the fact that my natural father's side of the family was to forever remain a mystery. If they didn't want a relationship with me, there was nothing I could do. And so, eventually, I forgot about them and continued to concentrate on my own life.

* * * *

Working in MCI WorldCom's "cubicle city" was like swimming in a river of perfume every day. There was no way to get away from the various scents, many of which made me physically ill. And so, every night for the next two and a half years, I came home with a sore throat and a headache, basically feeling as though I had the flu. That, coupled with the fact that my ever-worsening neck and low back problems from years-old injuries and stress (which ultimately led to – among other things – neck, shoulder, elbow and hand surgery over the course of the next few years) were causing constant pain and preventing me from performing my job properly. In short, I was miserable.

Finally, in mid-2002, Bill suggested I quit work altogether and stay home.

"But what am I going to do at home," I whined. "I'm not used to being a plain ol' housewife...."

"Well, maybe, for some reason, it's what God wants you to do."

While it sounded like a good idea, I continued to agonize for several months at work before finally giving in. "Father," I begged of God one evening, "I believe Bill was right and You want me to stay at home. As you know, I love my job and my boss, and I really don't want to quit, but I will if You want me to. So, if this is really of You, could you please give me some kind of a sign?"

The answer came within the next few days in the form of an old friend with whom I had worked in Heidelberg in the late Eighties. Marilee, after marrying a traditional Jewish man, a lawyer, had converted from Christianity to Judaism. I remembered that in Germany she had often told me that Judaism made more sense to her than any other religion, and she occasionally tried to nudge me into checking it out. Back then, however, I wasn't interested in Judaism or anything else that even smacked remotely of religion.

And so, one day, after thoughts of Marilee kept coming to mind, I decided to give her a call and catch up on the events of our lives since we had last seen each other back in 1989.

Her life was going well, I was told, and she was happy to know that I had finally found my true "knight in shining armor," and our conversation was filled with animation and joy – until I mentioned that

I had become "saved" in a Baptist church, but God had led me to find my way to Messianic Judaism. The moment that little tidbit left my lips, the conversation with Marilee became noticeably strained and we decided, very diplomatically, to hang up and continue our "catching up" via email.

Her first email arrived the very next day, and in it, after reiterating how glad she was to have heard from me, she suggested I contact a Rabbi Tovia Singer, who would "set me straight" concerning my Jewish heritage. "Carmen, you cannot mix Christianity with Judaism," she wrote. "It's a dangerous theology, one you truly need to steer clear of."

Realizing that Marilee only had my best interests at heart, I checked out this Rabbi Singer – and after less than fifteen minutes on one of his websites, I found myself fuming over some of the arrogant, ignorant and unfair comments against believers in Yeshua, especially towards "missionaries" – Messianic Jews/believers who were verbal about their belief in Yeshua *and* Torah.

To my horror, after doing an internet search, I found several other Jewish rabbis who came across as even more hateful and misguided than Singer, along with several downright disgusting "anti-missionary" websites and blogs aimed at countering the "missionaries," in the most foul language imaginable. While Singer and his ilk certainly had some valid "beefs" against Christians and Messianic believers – including the fact that the Christian faith was directly responsible for the death and misery of millions of innocent Jews over the millennia – I came to the conclusion that they were teaching their own form of bigotry through the use of misquoted, misunderstood and even transparent attempts to deliberately twist Scriptures to push their propaganda against "missionaries."

Although I was a believer now, I certainly hadn't forgotten how much some Christians had pushed *me* to the limits of insanity during my lifetime, and so I could certainly understand why traditional Jews got irritated at the very mention of "Jesus." Most Christians with their "New Testament only" mentality, have no clue who the God of Abraham, Isaac and Jacob really is or that their theology, based mainly on the misunderstood writings of the Apostle Paul, has turned Him into someone unrecognizable. While Jews have never, ever pushed their religion on anyone, Christians continue to be relentless in their "witnessing" and their often holier-than-thou insistence that "You're gonna go to hell unless you believe in Jesus" – never even realizing that they have no clue who He is!

So, yes, Jews had a right to be angry. But by the same token, they – like the Christians – were coming from an uninformed viewpoint, as well, and were therefore just as guilty of "using God's Name in vain." While Christians were forever busy perpetrating their "New Testament concussions on the world," traditional Jews were pushing the "Tanach-only" (Old Testament) idea that the "suffering servant" mentioned in Isaiah 53 referred to Israel, along with some other major misconceptions. They had no clue that the Jewish Messiah – the One for whom they are still waiting – has already come once and is about to return....

And worst of all, rather than to discuss their respective beliefs rationally in order to try to Biblically show each other where both sides were right or wrong, they had resorted instead to fighting and hate-mongering – just like in the world of politics where men who can't come to a mutual agreement resort to war and terror and building better bombs so they can kill each other more effectively....

While reading the traditional Jewish website articles, I came to the conclusion that hardly anyone ever stops to think to don "the mind of Christ" and do what Yeshua did: Talk it, teach it, live it, share it – and if someone is too uncaring, too stupid or too hard-headed to grasp it, let them be because, one day, they *will all* stand before YHWH/Yahweh on Judgment Day to explain why they chose to ignore it!

Anyway, it soon became clear as to what God was wanting me to do: Create a website designed to tell **Biblical Truth** without any man-made opinions, and to lead traditional Jews to Yeshua and Christians to Torah!

Bill was as excited as I when I presented the idea to him that evening. He immediately got to work building a "skeleton" website for me to populate, and afterwards when we prayed about what to name it, the song "Refiner's Fire" kept coming to mind.

Little did I know then that my website, "The Refiner's Fire," would ultimately become a teaching website, and that it would evolve into taking on anyone who is against Yeshua and Torah, reach millions around the world, and become instrumental in leading many to the Truth of the Bible, including some Muslims, atheists and Satanists – and even a "White Supremacist Skinhead," who admitted to "ending up in an all Black Baptist church and being a completely changed person" after finding his way to God, "thanks to The Refiner's Fire"….

It didn't really dawn on me until one day in 2003 that none of this would have happened had I chosen to disobey God's will for me to take that plunge and quit work. Pastor John in Missouri, through his Spiritual gift of prophecy, had been adamant about the fact that God was planning on using me for His glory; even God Himself had told me that back at Schweitzer Methodist! And so here was another of John's prophecies come true – and it had come true only because I had chosen to obey, even when God's will didn't make any sense to me at the time.

I was absolutely stunned to realize that John, the simple country bumpkin pastor who had never seen a computer before, thought he was "seeing" a television while he was prophesying about seeing me "in Israel, on television doing something creative." That "something creative" was the website I had created, which was constantly being updated with new articles designed to show the world that God was real. And, "in Israel" hadn't necessarily meant physically, but spiritually….

As a Messianic Jew, I was considered to be spiritually "in Israel"….

Chapter 30

I could have very well ended my story here, or even after my experiences in Germany, but the miracles just kept coming in spades!

One of them happened in a most unusual place; a place I never expected to see again: The quarters at Fort Carson.

It happened in late 2002, after another doctor's appointment at the Evans Army Community Hospital. Rather than to head out the back gate and go home as I had originally planned, something told me to drive by our old quarters again, "just to see" if they still had an effect on me. I had purposely, over the years, passed by occasionally to try to anesthetize myself against the memories.

As it turned out, on this particular day, the couple who lived there was in the process of moving out. Without giving it a second thought – and before I had a chance to change my mind – I parked the car, walked up to the open door, and asked the woman standing in the living room if she would mind if I had a quick look inside. "I lived in these very quarters in 1960," I said pasting a huge, fake grin on my face and hoping I didn't sound as nervous as I felt. "Just happened to see you were busy moving out, and figured you wouldn't mind my popping in for a minute...."

To my great relief, the lady just smiled, waved me in and continued talking to some woman who was helping her pack.

From the moment I entered, I felt as if I had stepped backwards in time. The first thing that caught my attention was that the hardwood floor was the very same floor my feet had walked on so long ago. It was so old now that much of it appeared gray and weathered, even slightly buckled and cracked in places. I couldn't believe it hadn't been replaced yet.

And there, straight ahead of me, was the attached dark room divider that separated the staircase from the living room. It was the typical Sixties design, a network of large, wooden squares that reached all the way to the ceiling. My mother had an endless array of "knick-knacks" lining dozens of those squares, which were a major pain to dust and clean.

My knees were weak as I began my elective walk down Memory Lane. The place looked so much smaller than I had remembered it. The living room was a tiny box, appearing even more cramped because of the addition of a small half-bath between the entrance and the dining area. But there, in the corner opposite the window, was where our sofa had stood – the place where Bill Forrester had raped me for the very first time. My heart beat wildly at the memory because it felt as though this all had happened just yesterday....

Wishing to put some distance between myself and the tenant who had stopped talking to her friend in order to stare at me, I quickly stepped into the kitchen area and pretended to have a look around. All I really noticed, however, was the broom closet where I used to hide from Bill; a dark and dusty place that was barely wide enough to hold a broom, a mop and a skinny little ten-year-old....

Without further ado, I headed down the steep stairway into the cool, gray basement where Teddy and I used to roller skate in the wintertime. No bad memories there....

Realizing I had subconsciously saved the worst for last, I slowly trudged up the stairs, to the second floor where the bedrooms were. My old room which, through my adult eyes, now seemed no bigger than a large walk-in closet, was off to the right, situated directly above the living room. In my mind's eye, I could still see the twin bed, and feel Bill crawling under the covers with me, time and time again, while my mother was away at work at the Broadmoor Hotel.

Straight ahead on the left was the miniscule walk-in closet where I had tried so often to hide from Bill. Of course, he always found me. There was no place to hide in that house.

The other two bedrooms held no special memories and so I basically skipped them and headed for the bathroom where some truly evil memories resided.

Feeling a little light-headed, I took a deep breath and stuck my head through the door. Nothing much had changed there, either. From what I remember, the walls used to be pale yellow, whereas they were an ugly off-white now. The tub was straight ahead, with the sink and mirror on the left – the very mirror in which I had been admiring myself when my mother walked in to tell me I shouldn't bother because I would never be Miss America, anyway....

The toilet was immediately to the right of the entrance. Tears of anger welled as I stood there glaring down at it, as if it had been to blame for the things that happened. I'll never forget how I was sitting on that very toilet one evening when Daddy walked in on me without knocking, pants unzipped – and without a word, forced me to perform oral sex, only to berate the act, afterwards. The embarrassment of it all still had such a profound effect, it made me blush as I stood there feeling the awful memories unfold. I even remembered how badly I had wanted to throw up; but being too afraid of what he might do, I didn't dare....

It was on that toilet when, at the tender age of eleven, I first discovered that women had monthly menstrual cycles. Until then, I never had a clue because, back in those days, these things weren't discussed, much less, seen in television ads. But the memory of finding blood in the toilet one morning will haunt me forever, because I thought it was because of what Daddy had been doing to me. The fear of bleeding to death, however, outweighed the fear of "outing" my father, and so, panic-stricken, I called for my mother – who, instead of explaining what was happening, began to guffaw at my stupidity before telling me it was just something that happens to girls. And then she called in my father to say, "Hey Bill, look, Carmen's started her period," whereupon he too, laughed and they both began engaging in a series of jokes about how their little girl had been "whacked between the legs with a hatchet"....

Oh, this bathroom, and that toilet....if I had had access to a sledge hammer right then, I would have smashed that thing into a million pieces. In the back of my mind, I couldn't help but wonder how many other children had been sexually abused in this devilish place.

Suddenly, I could take no more; it was getting difficult to breathe in that house of horrors. Seconds later I was dashing through the living room, thanking the tenant over my shoulder as I headed out the door.

Not caring if anyone was around, I threw myself into the driver's seat of my car; and, with hands tightly clutching the steering wheel, I began to sob as years of pain and anguish were being released from my soul. "Oh God, oh God, oh God," I cried, over and over again, while "Don't use the Lord's Name in vain" echoed hollowly through my mind.

"Satan!" I yelled, angrily, staring at nothing particular through a veil of hot, streaming tears, "you didn't win, you bastard! You didn't succeed in killing me off. **GOD** won! I'm here and I'm alive, and guess what – I intend to do whatever I can to thwart your dumb butt for the rest of my life!"

Afterwards, feeling numb and exhausted, I sat there in my car, glaring at our old quarters.

Somewhere in the back of my mind I realized the pain was gone. I felt nothing when I looked at those quarters now; nothing at all. It was just a building where a crime had been committed years ago; and there was nothing I could do about it now except to put it all behind me. There was no reason to allow this place to haunt me anymore. Forrester was dead and buried, and I was still here – alive and happy with a husband who loved me with all his heart.

God had, in His grace and mercy, given me a "new Bill" and a new life, and that's all that mattered now. The old Bill didn't deserve the waste of time and energy it took to remember him....

Chapter 31

Over the years, I have made it a habit of asking God as to whether or not I'm still on His path. Having been without God for the first forty-four years of my life, I am not about to veer away from His will, but being "only human," I know that can be a very real possibility.

About a year after Bill and I had moved into our "dream house" near Black Forest, "out in the country," God's response to my question was a resounding "*YES!*" as I was to discover in late 2003 when He saw fit to provide me with yet another miracle…

It happened in September 2003 when I received an unexpected call from a German woman who claimed to be my cousin. Her name was Uschi from Dortmund, Germany, and her mother was my deceased father's sister. She told me that I had a half-brother and several aunts, uncles, and cousins who wanted to meet me.

Bill and I were literally floored as, once again, something had just "dropped into our laps" – and we weren't even looking for it!

The interesting part was *how* Uschi had found me: It seems that my father was a rather famous German amateur artist who has had various articles written about him, along with a German television documentary highlighting his accomplishments. One day, Uschi told us, her cousin Peter typed my father's name into a search engine, just to see what he might find. To his surprise, among the various German articles was an article from my website, which I had entitled "Hometown Miracles" which outlined the many wonders we encountered in my hometown during our honeymoon trip to Europe – including Reni's crucial phrase: "Carmen, does the name Franz Klekawka mean anything to you?"

Peter, not wanting to trust his limited English, forwarded my article to Cousin Uschi, a schoolteacher who happens to speak fluent English – and together they discovered that they had located a long-lost family member who lived in the USA. Uschi told me later that, when she contacted her other cousin, Arnold – my half brother – to tell him the news, he informed her, much to her surprise, that he already knew about me through Reni and Günther who had given him my phone number and address back in 2001! Arnold said he never bothered contacting me because he had doubts that his father might have been married before, or that I could possibly be his sister. And he didn't bother mentioning it to his younger brother, Thomas, he said, because Thomas was estranged from the family and no one knew his whereabouts.

But Uschi had no doubts because, as a child, she had often heard the grown-ups discussing a "baby Carmen" in hushed and secretive tones, and so she decided, she told us, to set the wheels in motion by telling the family – specifically, her husband, her parents and her Uncle Heinz, my father's only remaining living brother.

And so, in May 2004, after numerous "getting to know each other" emails, my husband and I returned to Germany to meet the family my natural father had insisted I wasn't a part of, because I "couldn't possibly be his daughter."

* * * *

It was truly a fairy tale "magic moment" when Bill and I came off the train in Dortmund to meet for the first time my cousin Uschi and her husband, Wilfried! With a bouquet of flowers in hand, they immediately made us welcome and treated us like "part of the family."

Although in those days my hair was "streaked and highlighted" which basically matched Uschi's long, dark blond hair, the resemblance ended there. Uschi, who was six months older than I, was stocky, extremely personable and a lot more outgoing. A schoolteacher by trade, she came across as extremely intelligent and sophisticated. As we were soon to discover, she and Wilfried, a retired school teacher, historian and philosopher who had been raised in an orphanage during the Second World War, were both well-rounded, educated people who had friends and acquaintances around the world. In short, they were an absolutely delightful and interesting couple with whom we had many intriguing late-night discussions.

I got the shock of my life when I met Uschi's parents, Änne and Horst, later at the house because, as it turned out Änne, at seventy-four, was an older version of me! We had the same basic build, bone structure, height, facial features, coloring – everything. Änne could just as well have been my mother or older sister, the resemblance was that great.

Bill was the first one to notice the old black and white photo of Änne as a child, on the wall in the foyer. "Carmen," he said with a tinge of excitement in his voice, "if they didn't know about you, how come they have a picture of you on their wall?"

Baffled, I examined the photo and broke into a grin because the resemblance was absolutely remarkable. "This isn't a picture of me; that's Änne as a kid!" Shock and surprise played across everyone's faces when we later pulled out some childhood photos of me that we had brought along, because – except for the fact that I was a lot thinner than Änne when we were children, it was difficult to tell us apart.

So much for my natural father's assertion....

It's hard to put in words the seesawing emotions as we examined and compared photos and got to know each other over the course of the next two weeks. I trembled with a mixture of excitement and sadness amidst an incredible new sense of "belonging" after meeting my "new" relatives. It was good to find out, after fifty-three years, that I really was my father's daughter!

Aunt Änne, Uncle Heinz, and Aunt Mia, my father's remaining living siblings, were overflowing wells of historical information concerning my family – filling me with tidbits about Grandfather Klekawka who hailed from Poland near the Russian border and found the love of his life after immigrating into Germany in 1918. And they told me of my Aunt Änne who, in her youth at age fourteen during the Hitler years, was forced to undergo an embarrassing physical examination because of her Polish father, to determine if she "looked Aryan enough."

The stories about my father and his ancestors kept unfolding at Aunt Mia's apartment one afternoon. While Mia and her son, Peter – the one who discovered my article on the internet – engaged me in lively conversation on one hand, Mia's husband, Dieter, was busy teaching my husband the delights of Pear *Schnapps*. After awhile, although neither man spoke the other's language, the *Schnapps* apparently served as a translator of sorts because they somehow became best buddies before we left late that evening, and out in the parking lot Bill, slurring in broken German, told me he felt he had found a new father.

Over the course of the two and a half weeks in Dortmund, I heard endless, wonderful stories about my "new" family. It was an amazing reunion, and I will forever be grateful to my Cousin Uschi, who made it all possible!

A plethora of emotions – quite as I had expected – gripped my soul when Uschi took us to see my father's grave. On one hand, I felt tremendous love for this man that I never knew, yet on the other, I wanted to kick his stone over and smash it to bits.

It was a strange feeling to realize that, lying there in the earth beneath my feet, in all his cremated glory, was the man who basically had sex with my mother and then tossed both her and me – the product of that sexual union – aside like garbage. Part of the reason I felt anger towards him was because I now knew that my father had *two women* pregnant at once back in the 1950/1951 timeframe – his wife and his new love, Elfi – and that he had chosen Elfi and her unborn child over my mother and me, which ultimately caused me to be given away. One "gives away" a dog, not a child….

Yet, on the other hand, I knew that he, my mother and Elfi were all very young at the time, and it's no secret that young people often do stupid things. God only knows that *I* had! So, in all honesty, how could I hold their actions against them?

What I did hold against him, and I guess I always will, is that he turned down my request for a relationship back in 1975. I felt that, even if I wasn't his daughter, *he* was the one who was married to my mother at the time; *he* was the one who chose to just toss me aside over the *mere opinion* that I wasn't his biological child. Granted, being married to my mother was surely no picnic, but committing adultery with another woman and then choosing her child over the one that he was legally obligated to at the time, well, that was a hard pill to swallow. Even if it turned out I wasn't his child, I felt he could have at least reached out to me and my desire to find my "roots."

While staring down at his grave, I realized for the hundredth time, that God commanded us to honor our parents. He said nothing about loving them or living with them, or even having a relationship with them.

And so, in the end, I placed two stones from our garden – one, lay on his headstone (as is the Jewish custom), and one with my name written on it in indelible ink, to plant deep inside his grave where his widow, Elfi, couldn't discover it, since we had promised Uschi to keep our visit a secret from my father's widow. Uschi had mentioned that, by suddenly springing the long-lost Carmen on Elfi, she might think Uschi was going behind her back to "dig up skeletons" and so we made a pact to leave Elfi completely out of the picture.

* * * *

Not surprisingly, all the Klekawkas had stories to tell about my mother whom they briefly knew – and the stories weren't very pretty. (It's amazing how long a bad reputation will follow you around!) My mother died at age 45 in 1977, yet everybody who knew her in my hometown of Wietze and also in my father's hometown of Dortmund remembers, in detail, "what she did" and how she acted way back when. During our second week in Germany, after I finally met my brother Arnold – who, it turns out, is exactly six months younger than me – I was able to remind everyone that Arnold was living proof that my father wasn't exactly a paragon of virtue, either, since he had had two women pregnant at once....

Meeting my brother, Arnold – whom I in no way resembled – was somewhat awkward at first, especially in view of the fact that he had problems believing that he had a half-sister. Although Reni had told him about me after our first visit to Germany in 2001, Arnold said he had been skeptical all along. As a matter of fact, he found it very hard to believe that his parents would have kept this kind of a secret from him. He said, until Reni gave him my phone number back in 2001, he never knew that his father had been married before.

In talking at length with Arnold over the next couple of days, we both discovered just how much we had been cheated out of a brother-sister relationship. The biggest irony was, the more we talked the more we realized that we had actually known each other as young children, and possibly even attended the same school before I was removed from my foster home - we just didn't know we were brother and sister!

"Carmen," he told me on the night he and his wife, Dimitra, had us over for dinner. "I just can't believe, and I honestly don't think my father was married to your mother."

Empathizing with his pain and sense of betrayal, I gave him a kind smile and said, "I have their divorce papers to prove it, Arnold. I also still have that old six-page letter he sent me while I was stationed in Heidelberg back in 1975, in which he outlined their stormy marriage.

"He even sent me copies of witness testimonies, a couple of men who swore they had witnessed my mother's 'slutty behavior' while she was pregnant with me! His letter truly hurt me, and it revealed what a very self-centered man he was; someone who clearly cared only about himself…I'll send you copies of both that letter and the divorce certificate when I get back to the U.S."

The look on Arnold's face exuded confusion along with pain and bewilderment, but any doubts he may have had were completely doused when I presented him with my childhood photos.

"Can you tell me who this is, Arnold?" I asked pointing to a specific black and white photo of me at age six.

"That's *Tante* Änne," he replied without hesitation.

I shook my head. "Guess again…."

Taking a second, closer look at the photo, he shook his head and finally shrugged his shoulders. "It's *Tante* Änne."

"No, it's me. That picture was taken by the *Salzberg*, where I lived."

The look on Arnold's face was priceless as he lifted the photo from the coffee table to examine it more closely. "This is you?" he asked incredulously? "You lived at the *Salzberg*?"

"Yes. For almost nine years."

There was a slight pause before he said, "Then I guess we definitely did now each other as children, because my mother used to take me to the *Salzberg* sometimes. I distinctly remember playing with some little dark-haired girl who lived there…."

I nodded as the memory of a little boy emerged whose name I couldn't remember, and deep in my gut, I felt a twinge of anger against both my foster mother and Elfi for not bothering to tell us we were siblings. Granted, Elfi didn't believe I was Franz's daughter, either, but the fact remained, Franz's name was on my birth certificate.

There was melancholy in Arnold's voice when he confided that he had been estranged from our father when he was a young teenager because Franz was an extremely strong and overbearing disciplinarian. This confession confirmed in my mind that it was probably a good thing I hadn't been raised by Franz Klekawka, after all - and that, even though his actions had initiated a series of tragic events in my life – perhaps everything had unfolded *just exactly* as it was supposed to, in the grand scheme of things.

"Carmen," Arnold said at one point. "Would you like to meet my mother? She lives across the hall from us."

I balked and quickly informed him that we had promised Uschi to keep Elfi "in the dark," so to speak.

His wife Dimitra, however, suggested we simply tell Elfi that I was "an old friend of hers," and minutes later, I had the dubious privilege of shaking hands with the woman who, in my eyes, had been partly responsible for my having been thrown away like a piece of trash....

Elfi was clearly taken aback when I introduced myself; and I could tell the name Carmen clearly signified turmoil in her mind. Since I've never been good at lying, I felt myself blushing when I told her I was an old friend of Dimitra's, but quickly covered it with a fake cough and prayed she wasn't planning on staying very long.

Once settled across from us, Elfi turned out to be quite a talker, and most of her conversation, thankfully, centered on her deceased husband – my father – which released me from the burden of telling any further lies. Bill and I were both extremely relieved when, after just fifteen minutes or so, she rose to leave.

* * * *

Our decision to break up our two and a half week stay in Dortmund by hanging out in Wietze for a few days resulted in another strange twist in this story – Truth be told, it actually resulted in a couple more miracles, and here is how the events unfolded:

Ulla Mertens who was leaving for vacation the day after we arrived, graciously allowed us to stay in her home while she was away. It was great using her place as a base while visiting old friends and my brother Ingo and his wife, Barbara, who were now living near my hometown. Since Ingo's birthday happened to fall in the same timeframe, we used the opportunity to celebrate at a local restaurant one evening, and to just enjoy each other's company.

On the spur of the moment, we also paid an obligatory visit to Mama's partner Jürgen who, it was clear, was near the end of his life in his battle with emphysema. After nearly an hour of listening to him nattering on and on about nothing, Bill and I left, using the excuse that we had yet to visit Mama's grave and several other people in town before sunset.

In other words, we made the most of the four days in Wietze, not knowing when or if we would ever see any of our friends or family again. Oddly, Günther and Reni were last on our agenda, as they "were busy" for most of the week, and so we finally managed to get together on our last day in Wietze, when they had us over for brunch.

It was that particular get-together which set some things in motion that would turn out to be life-changing events for some people back in Dortmund.

Unbeknownst to Bill and me at the time, Günther's and Elfi's sister happened to be living with Günther and Reni, and, after our visit – although Reni knew that Elfi was never to discover that Uschi had found me – she told the sister that "Franz's daughter, Carmen, was in Germany, looking for her brothers."

Naturally, the sister, believing she had the gossip story of the century, called Elfi to warn her....

Elfi, literally "freaking out" over the news, and obviously backed into a corner, immediately dashed across the hall to inform her son of the dark secret that had been kept from him for fifty-some years, which basically consisted of: "Your father was married before and he had a daughter named Carmen who is here in Germany, looking for you."

Arnold, in his quiet, gentle and patient way, beckoned his mother inside and told her to take a seat in the living room, where he promptly informed her that he had already met Carmen – "And, by the way," he said, "so have you. That was her, last night."

Although I felt sorry for Uschi who was now in the middle and having to explain herself to Elfi, I personally found these events to be hilarious; it was poetic justice for Elfi, as far as I was concerned. To me, it was God's way of bringing closure to not only myself, but to the entire family who had harbored this secret for half a century.

With this saga finally behind us, the Holy Spirit nudged me to let go of the terrible animosity I felt towards Elfi. I knew it wouldn't be easy because, it seemed, most of my anger was simply displaced aggression directed at Elfi because she was my father's widow – Franz was dead, but his wife was still here….

My cousin Uschi, however – my new best friend and sounding board – reminded me that nobody is perfect and that we all have done "stupid things" in our lives. With this in mind, I tried my best to "give it to God," but it wasn't until we returned to the U.S. that I was able to process this problem properly.

And so, shortly after we returned to the U.S., I decided to write Elfi a long letter outlining my life, because I thought she deserved to know all that had happened to me as a result of her involvement in my father's life; and assuring her that, while I wasn't happy about their choices, I totally understood they, as young kids, had made a mistake, and that I didn't want us harboring ill feelings towards each other. Afterwards, I even called her on the telephone to try and mend the fences that had been broken by the awful tragedy that had occurred in 1950. Elfi, like me, seemed audibly relieved and the exchange actually turned out to be a healing event for both of us.

Ironically, my decision to forgive resulted in **yet another unexpected miracle** which involved my brother, Ingo, when – during the course of my conversation with Elfi who was a native of Wietze – I was able to learn the name of the man who was my mother's boyfriend while she was pregnant with Ingo! Astonishingly, it happened to be Gerhard Pieper, one of the guys listed as a witness *against* my mother during her divorce! I couldn't believe it! My mother was a despicable and immoral person, according to his written statement – but that apparently wasn't enough to stop this hypocrite from having sex with her later on....

Anyway, I immediately called my brother Ingo to share this great news. At first, he laughed and told me he didn't care whether he ever discovered the name of his father, but then said, "So, okay, who is it?"

"Well," I said, hardly able to contain myself, "according to my father's widow, our mother was dating a guy named Gerhard Pieper when she was pregnant with you!"

After a lengthy silence in which I started to think we'd been disconnected, Ingo finally said in a voice that sounded as though he had just been punched in the gut: "Carmen, my middle name is Gerhard...."

Chapter 32

There were so many healing miracles in just this last story alone, I cannot help but believe they were all from **Adonai Rapha** - "God who heals." He used the decisions made by many people along the way to choreograph His desired outcome for my life, which was to be a rabbi – teacher of His Word. As He showed me in one of my visions, I was to ultimately become an Eliezer, an obedient servant who would be willing to go out and "fetch His Son a bride."

Whether one believes in God or not, the fact remains that everyone, at one time or another, experiences occasional events and inexplicable twists and turns in their lives that simply cannot be explained away as mere "coincidence." My own experiences, as you have just read, are proof of that. My life was a series of unfortunate events, one after the other, which ended only after I "found" God and began to pattern my actions after Yeshua, the Torah observant, seventh day Sabbath and Biblical Feast keeping Jewish Messiah who personally taught us how to properly worship and obey His Father, YHWH.

If I hadn't obeyed God's nudging to sell my house and move to Colorado Springs – a place I hated worse than any other on Earth – I would never have received that total healing from my childhood pain; a healing that came from the inside-out, when God literally sent me back into the "fire" of my past and forced me to face it, head-on.

If I had chosen to remain in Seymour, I would never have found my way to Torah, God's divine teaching and instruction, which has led to an intensely deeper relationship, knowledge and understanding of Him. I would never have met my wonderful husband, Bill, who was the reason I returned to Germany where we were *lived* the events that ultimately kicked off the discovery of my father's side of the family.

Without Bill to build that website "skeleton" for me, "The Refiner's Fire" would never have been born, which means I would never have reached millions for God over the years; nor would there have been that fateful article for my cousin Peter to discover while Googling "Franz Klekawka."

Plus, if I had not been keenly aware of that "nudging" to keep in touch with Ulla over the years which resulted in our meeting face-to-face while Bill and I were on our European honeymoon, Ulla would never have had the chance to send us to Hotel Steinförde on that fateful evening....

What's more, if Ulla had chosen to ignore that "nudging" which she told me she had felt back in 1984 after receiving my request for help in locating my long-lost brothers, she could never have been used as a conduit to ultimately help me find the missing pieces of the peculiar puzzle that I call "family." Ulla's willingness to obey that "nudging" – whether or not she realized it was from God – allowed her to be a key player in my life!

These types of events happen in *all* our lives, and I cannot and will not pretend that they can always be chalked up as mere "coincidence."

There is a "ripple effect" in our every decision. As a matter of fact – truth be told – the "ripple effect" that caused me to be where I am today, **can be traced all the way back to the decisions made by my natural parents** who, for whatever reason, came to the conclusion that I couldn't be a part of their lives. If not for their decision to give me away, I would never have ended up with Elfriede Neumann whom I credit with my becoming a "normal person" who would ultimately be able to make positive contributions to the world.

I whole-heartedly believe that, because of my personal unwavering willingness to obey God, I knowingly and/or often unknowingly helped others to gain closure in their own lives. This was evident, not only in Ingo's case, but also when my seventy-six year old Uncle Heinz came for a three-week visit in October of 2004.

Heinz, who had been an American Prisoner of War during World War II, had a "bad taste in his mouth" when it came to the United States and Americans, in general. However, after meeting many of our friends and relatives during a whirlwind tour of the Western United States, he made a sobering announcement one evening after coming to the conclusion that he had harbored resentment against a people he had known only through the painful filter of war.

"Americans are so nice," he said with the conviction of someone who had just had an epiphany. "They're very warm and hospitable people! I never knew that before."

These occurrences were all inextricably linked to form a chain of events that ultimately brought closure to several people and proved that God was, in fact, working "behind the scenes."

Looking back from my present perspective, I can see clearly that God **had** been with me throughout my life, even when I didn't realize it. But, my life changed only after I sought a true **relationship** with Him. He cannot, I learned over the years, work with someone who is "straddling the fence" between the carnal and the spiritual.

God gives us all the choice to do things His way, or Satan's. Every choice impacts our life in some way, and if we find that "nothing ever seems to go right," it could very well be because *we* have strayed from His Path. YHWH gave us His Torah as a blueprint for holy living. Once we decide to step out of the bounds of Torah, we are on our own.

An example is our dog, Dallas, who has five fenced-in acres in which to romp around. He is safe as long as he remains on our property, which is his "Torah." But, every once in awhile, he likes to go through the fence to cross the road and visit the neighbors, and so occasionally, he comes home with knots on his head because someone threw rocks at him. He could just as well have been hit by a car or trampled to death by a neighbor's horse....The thing is, we can't keep an eye on him or protect him once he has left the property. He risks his life every time he leaves the safety of his parents' house.

I learned these things a long time ago, right after moving to Colorado Springs. With the help of the Holy Spirit, as the years passed, I dove into the Word, studying – often under the direct tutelage of Messianic rabbis – everything I could get my hands on, and weeding out anything that didn't perfectly "line up" with the Bible. It was through the Bible that I learned how to forgive Bill Forrester for the things he had done so the awful memories would no longer have power over me, and healing could finally begin.

One of the things I learned, as well, was something that almost knocked me off my chair one day when I "happened upon it"....

Isaiah 53: 2 *For before him he grew up like a young plant, like a root out of dry ground. He was not well-formed or especially handsome; we saw him, but his appearance did not attract us.*

This was a description of Yeshua – the One I had seen while in the coma back in 1972! Whenever I related my coma story over the years, people often "went ballistic" whenever I told them the Jesus I saw wasn't very good-looking. "No, that can't be!" they would angrily retort. "Jesus is *beautiful*!"

But, here was proof positive that I **had** seen Him because, until I "got saved" in Seymour in 1995, I had **never even read the Bible** and had no way of knowing that I had been right all along!

In early 2007, the rabbi of our synagogue approached me with the revelation that the Holy Spirit had told him to ordain me. "Carmen," he said, "you know more about God and the Bible than anyone I've ever met, and I believe you should have some kind of a title." This couldn't have come at a better time because I was becoming weary of pastors and rabbis and other men attacking me on my website for being "just a housewife" who was "arrogant enough to think" I had the authority or knowledge to teach others about the Bible....

A couple months later, after I begged God once again to let me know whether I was still on His Path, His answer came in the form of the most incredible opportunity that has ever been afford me: The editorship of a wonderful project that was to be ultimately titled the "Aramaic English New Testament," by Andrew Gabriel Roth and Baruch ben Daniel!

It happened quite unexpectedly when I "was nudged" to contact Canadian businessman Baruch ben Daniel about one of the articles on his website, "Mashiyach." This was an unusual move for me as I rarely write to anyone's website. But, during the course of our correspondence, Baruch recognized my writing talents and asked me to become a part of the Aramaic English New Testament, which is a translation of the oldest New Testament ever discovered, the Khabouris Codex, which was written in Aramaic, and translated directly into English by author and Aramaic scholar Andrew Gabriel Roth. (Please see the website: www.aent.org.)

During the course of my proofreading/editing, Yahweh "nudged" me to write three books, including "Should Christians be Torah Observant?"; "Surely You Know!" designed to reveal the truth of Yeshua to traditional Jews; and the one you are reading now, "Rags to Rabbi" whose purpose was to show that God is real....

Although I had been compelled to "tell my story" for many years, it had to wait on God's timing. My story was to reveal the many ways He healed me and steered me exactly where He needed me to go. In the end, He gave me the closure and healing I needed – not only for my own benefit, but to reveal to the world **His** Hand in it.

And so, I give YHWH all the glory. Without Him this story would not have been possible. Although this book was about "me" and "my life," the bottom line is that it ***is ultimately all about God and what He does with those who choose to obey Him.***

What happened to me was in no way a series of random "coincidences" but, rather, a well-choreographed true story perfectly depicting the struggle between God and Satan for my soul.

And guess who won!

* * * *

Proverbs 3: 5 Trust in Yahweh with all your heart and lean not on your own understanding....

Epilogue

Update on yet another unexpected miracle!

Remember Goldie, the woman I called "Mom" throughout most of my adult life? Well, while in Springfield, Missouri in July 2009 to attend my 40th high school reunion, I felt an urgent need to drive out to see her. After 15 years, she would either accept or reject me; but I needed some closure because I never got over the pain of losing her.

I had to suppress my surprise at the gaunt, ailing old lady who came to the door. At 85, Goldie was a mere shadow of her former self, appearing very pale and sickly despite a backyard tan. She was obviously taken aback to see me standing on her porch, but when the shock wore off she simply smiled and croaked in a weakened voice, "Well, hello honey! How are you doing?"

Minutes later, as we were seated at the old familiar kitchen table, she related that she was suffering from congestive heart failure and was "having problems remembering things," but that her neighbor, Mary Fritz, was taking "very good care" of her. She had changed in many ways, but I was happy to hear I had often crossed her mind over the years. My eyes welled with tears when she told me she couldn't remember why she had kicked me out of her life, and that she was overjoyed to have me back now!

At that point something wonderful occurred to me: Everything, including this, had been part of God's plan! Had Goldie NOT kicked me out of her life when she did, I would never have moved to Seymour to get my "spiritual grounding" at First Baptist Church – and I would certainly *never* have considered moving to Colorado! Part of the reason I had decided to settle in Missouri back in the Nineties was because I planned to take care of Goldie in her old age.

Had Goldie not kicked me out of her life, I would never have found my way to my present faith and ended up being a Messianic rabbi, teaching the world about YHWH and Yeshua. And I would never have met my wonderful husband, Bill, who has given me that unconditional love I've always craved and who made my life on Earth worth living....With Goldie now back in my life, I am complete!

YHWH truly DOES work in mysterious ways!

Some final thoughts:

A note to victims of physical or mental abuse: As you have just read, there *is* healing from an abusive past – but it doesn't come from human sources. Yes, psychiatrists are able to help you clear up some issues; there's no doubt about that. But, in today's world, where most counselors provide human solutions instead of referring to God-given Scriptures, their guidance tends to offer only short-lived, "band-aid" remedies.

If you want to be healed from the inside out, the *only* solution is to turn to the Bible to discover who our Creator is and how you can become one of His Children. HE will guide and help you, but you must first make the effort, and then grab onto Him with all your might and become willing to obey. In the meantime, by all means, seek out a good Christian counselor to help you on your road to healing ***through the use of the Scriptures***, not by some secular counselor's false ideology that suggests you have "all the power and the control," etc. We humans are no match for Satan when he's got his mind made up to ruin our lives, and those secular "band-aids" only serve to humor him and strengthen his resolve. True healing can only come from the One who created us; the One who knit us together in the womb (Psalm 139:13). He loves you and is waiting patiently for you to make the first move....

A note for sexual offenders: Whether you've sexually abused just one time, or have been doing it all your life, you need to seek God and repent immediately. What you've done (or are currently doing) is **not** "normal" and will ultimately separate you from God throughout eternity (Revelation 20:14-15). You don't want to stand before your Maker on Judgment Day and make excuses for your behavior, because on that day, it will be too late! Yeshua said: *And anyone who causes one of these little ones who believe in me to stumble, it would be better for him if the millstone of a donkey were* *placed on his neck and he were cast into the sea.* (Mark 9:42)

Know also that, as a sexual offender (especially of children), you are not "teaching" them about sex; you are merely making them aware of their sexuality far too early, way before they are able to handle the feelings and emotions. Plus, the most likely outcome is that they will hate you for your inappropriate touching – not to mention, they will always loathe you for taking away their choice of when, where and with whom to experience love at the proper time in their lives.

Chances are, down deep, you *know* you are sinning, and you hate yourself for your actions but can't seem to stop yourself. If so, please email me and let me try to help you: Carmen@betorahobservant.com ....

For those wondering why I don't use the title of "rabbi" in front of my name, it is because we really only have one Rabbi, and He is Messiah Yeshua who came to teach us about YHWH, to show us first-hand how to worship and please Him; and then to martyr Himself as our Final Sin Sacrifice.

The word "rabbi" in Hebrew means "teacher," and that is what I am; nothing more, nothing less. Those of us who teach the Word of God must remember that it is a privilege, not something to boast about, or to use as a stepping stone to fame, or as a "get rich quick" scheme. In biblical times, the *cohens* (Levitical priests) received no monetary compensation; they were supported solely by their respective communities (see Numbers 19). They received only what they needed to survive – unlike many pastors today whose constant demands for money have helped build "mega churches" with enough left over to foot the bill for the pastors' personal jets and yachts....

For those who insist there are no female rabbis or attempt to use 1 Corinthians 14:34-35 and 1 Timothy 2:11-12 as evidence that "women cannot teach men," or should hold subservient roles in the church, I would ask this:

If a woman can be an apostle like Junia (Romans 16:7), a disciple like Tabitha (Acts 9:36-43), a deacon like Phoebe (Romans 16:1), evangelists like Euodia and Syntyche (Philippians 4:2-3), or a *judge like Deborah* (Judges, Chapters 4 and 5) who headed the army of ancient Israel, why can't she be a pastor or a rabbi?

Chosen by YHWH, Deborah – prophetess, wife and mother – became a Judge, which was the highest public office in Israel, at a time when Israel was experiencing spiritual and moral decline, partly due to the loss of their national leaders, Moses and Joshua.

"In those days there was no king in Israel; every man did what was proper in his own eyes." (Judges 17:6; 21:25)

"A prophetess, the wife of Lapidot; she sat under the date palm of Deborah, between Ramah and Bethel on Mount Ephraim, and the children of Israel went up to her for judgment." (Judges 4:5)

Without getting into deep theological debates over this issue, please consider this: The Bible reveals that God sometimes did, and still does, allow women to fill in a gap whenever men aren't fulfilling His purpose. Paul, in his letter to the Galatians, proclaimed that in Messiah, "There is no longer Jew or Greek, there is no longer slave or free, there is no longer male and female; for all of you are one." (Galatians 3:28)

I believe YHWH has chosen me to teach and reveal the need for both, Yeshua and Torah – not necessarily because I'm smarter or holier than anyone else, but because, like the Apostle Paul who was a *murderer* before he became a disciple of Messiah Yeshua, I made the decision to repent and ***obey***.

If anyone wishes to learn more about God and the Bible, I invite you to send an email to:

Carmen@BeTorahObservant.com

Shalom and may YHWH be with you all!

Carmen Welker

Blessed be Elohim, the Father of our Master Y'shua the Mashiyach, the Father of mercies, and the Elohim of all consolation; Who comforts us in all our sufferings that we might be able to comfort those who are in all their sufferings, with the consolation where we are comforted by Elohim. For as the sufferings of the Mashiyach multiply in us, so also our consolation multiplies by the Mashiyach. (1 Corinthians 1:3-5, AENT)